# VICKSBURG IS THE KEY

GREAT CAMPAIGNS OF THE CIVIL WAR

SERIES EDITORS

Anne J. Bailey
*Georgia College &*
*State University*

Brooks D. Simpson
*Arizona State University*

WILLIAM L. SHEA AND
TERRENCE J. WINSCHEL

# Vicksburg Is the Key

*The Struggle for the Mississippi River*

University of Nebraska Press
Lincoln and London

© 2003 by the University of Nebraska Press

Manufactured in the United States of America

∞

Library of Congress Cataloging-in-Publication Data
Shea, William L. Vicksburg is the key: the struggle for the
Mississippi River / William L. Shea and Terrence J. Winschel.
p. cm. (Great campaigns of the Civil War)
Includes bibliographical references and index.
ISBN 0-8032-4254-9 (cloth: alk. paper)
1. Vicksburg (Miss.)—History—Siege, 1863.
I. Winschel, Terrence J.  II. Title.
E475.27.S54  2003
973.7'344—dc21
2003042652

See what a lot of land these fellows hold, of which Vicksburg is the key. . . . Let us get Vicksburg and all that country is ours. The war can never be brought to a close until that key is in our pocket.—*Abraham Lincoln*

# Contents

List of Illustrations   viii

List of Maps   ix

Series Editors' Introduction   xi

1. The River and the War   1

2. Gibraltar on the Mississippi   17

3. On to Vicksburg   33

4. The First Onslaught   46

5. Dark Winter   60

6. Detour in Louisiana   76

7. River of No Return   90

8. The Odds Are Overpowering   106

9. The Shriek of an Eagle   117

10. Indecision, Indecision, Indecision   127

11. A Grand and Appalling Sight   140

12. Outcamp the Enemy   153

13. Too Weak to Save Vicksburg   161

14. The Glorious Fourth   170

15. No Longer a Point of Danger   179

16. The Mississippi Is Opened   187

Epilogue   205

Notes   213

Bibliographical Essay   221

Index   223

# Illustrations

*Following page 100*
David D. Porter
USS *Cairo*
Ulysses S. Grant
John C. Pemberton
John A. McClernand
CSS *Arkansas*
Nathaniel P. Banks
Franklin Gardner
Orion P. Howe
Shirley house
Mine explosion
Coonskin's Tower
Grant and Pemberton

# Maps

The Mississippi Valley   3

Vicksburg and vicinity   19

Union operations: November 1862–January 1863   40

Chickasaw Bayou   49

Union operations: February–March 1863   66

Union forces sever the Vicksburg–Port Hudson corridor   86

Grant moves south through Louisiana   97

Grant moves on Vicksburg   107

Port Gibson: Afternoon   113

Raymond   122

Champion Hill: Afternoon   134

Vicksburg: May 19 attack   144

Vicksburg: May 22 attack   148

Banks concentrates against Port Hudson   191

Port Hudson: May 27 attack   196

Port Hudson: June 14 attack   200

# Series Editors' Introduction

Americans remain fascinated by the Civil War. Movies, television, and video—even computer software—have augmented the ever-expanding list of books on the war. Although it stands to reason that a large portion of recent work concentrates on military aspects of the conflict, historians have expanded our scope of inquiry to include civilians, especially women; the destruction of slavery and the evolving understanding of what freedom meant to millions of former slaves; and an even greater emphasis on the experiences of the common soldier on both sides. Other studies have demonstrated the interrelationships of war, politics, and policy and how civilians' concerns back home influenced both soldiers and politicians. Although one cannot fully comprehend this central event in American history without understanding that military operations were fundamental in determining the course and outcome of the war, it is time for students of battles and campaigns to incorporate nonmilitary themes in their accounts. The most pressing challenge facing Civil War scholarship today is the integration of various perspectives and emphases into a new narrative that explains not only what happened, why, and how but also why it mattered.

The series Great Campaigns of the Civil War offers readers concise syntheses of the major campaigns of the war, reflecting the findings of recent scholarship. The series points to new ways of viewing military campaigns by looking beyond the battlefield and the headquarters tent to the wider political and social context within which these campaigns unfolded; it also shows how campaigns and battles left their imprint on many Americans, from presidents and generals down to privates and civilians. The ends and means of waging war reflect larger political objectives and priorities as well as social values. Historians may continue to debate among themselves as to which of these campaigns constituted true turning points, but each of the campaigns treated in this series contributed to shaping the course of the conflict, opening opportunities, and eliminating alternatives.

As William L. Shea and Terrence J. Winschel skillfully demonstrate, the Vicksburg campaign, which was really a series of separate operations, was the longest and most complex of any during the Civil War. The Confederacy began fortifying the "Gibraltar of the Mississippi" early in the war and eventually encircled the river port with earthworks that transformed it into an enormous fortress. By the summer of 1862 the Confederate defensive position at Vicksburg had become a focus of Union operations; Northern political and military leaders understood the significance of cutting the Confederacy in half.

The Vicksburg campaign was a critical stage in Ulysses S. Grant's development as a military leader. As he evolved from soldier to general, he learned to anticipate difficulties and adjust his plans as situations developed. It was not always an easy road, for Grant had to deal with powerful political generals appointed by Abraham Lincoln. The president, unhappy with progress along the river, had hoped men such as Nathaniel P. Banks and John A. McClernand would energize the army. What they did was provide an added political element to military planning.

This campaign was also one of the few operations that successfully combined army and navy resources. Perhaps one of the most dramatic events was Adm. David D. Porter's run past the Vicksburg batteries in order to ferry Union infantrymen across the river below the city. Grant's bold decision to move inland remains one of the great feats of the war—in seventeen days the army marched two hundred miles, fought five battles, and pushed the Confederates into their defensive works. The hardships suffered within the Vicksburg fortifications by civilians and soldiers alike were some of the most extreme during the entire four years of fighting. Moreover the Confederate surrender on Independence Day, 1863, was a crushing setback for Southerners. After the fall of Port Hudson five days later, Grant informed the president that the river was once more open to Northern shipping; Midwesterners again had access to the outside world. Strategically Union control of the Mississippi separated Arkansas, Louisiana, and Texas from the other eight Confederate states; an accomplishment of immeasurable consequences. Coupled with Robert E. Lee's defeat at Gettysburg the previous day, Vicksburg was a devastating loss for the Confederacy.

# VICKSBURG IS THE KEY

CHAPTER ONE

# The River and the War

Long before cannon thundered at Fort Sumter, Americans North and South recognized the economic importance of the Mississippi River and its tributaries in the sprawling region west of the Appalachian Mountains. The vast river system provided farmers and merchants in more than a dozen states with an easy and inexpensive means of transportation. It was a vital outlet to the Gulf of Mexico and the world beyond, not only for Southern cotton and sugar cane but also for the bountiful produce of the Midwest.

When the Civil War erupted in the spring of 1861, the Mississippi acquired additional importance. In military terms the river was both an asset and a liability to the nascent Confederacy. The Mississippi's silt-laden waters connected many of the western secessionist states, but its broad surface also served as a natural avenue of invasion.

Bvt. Lt. Gen. Winfield Scott, the aged commanding officer of the U.S. Army at the outset of the war, recognized the strategic importance of the Mississippi River. He suggested to Pres. Abraham Lincoln that Union military forces carry out a two-pronged offensive against the Confederacy by blockading its seaports and gaining control of the Mississippi. The Confederacy would slowly collapse of economic strangulation. Critics derisively dubbed Scott's proposal the "Anaconda Plan," after its pythonlike approach to squeezing the rebellious states into submission. Scott's proposal was, in truth, too passive and too limited and would not have suppressed the rebellion by itself, but the old warrior had grasped the Confederacy's crucial geographic weaknesses. Lincoln shared Scott's strategic vision. "The Mississippi is the backbone of the Rebellion," he observed; "it is the key to the whole situation."[1]

Scott soon retired, but his ideas were incorporated into Union military strategy. Blockading forces began to seal off Southern seaports from Chesapeake Bay to the Rio Grande, and plans were laid to move down the Mississippi River from Cairo, Illinois, and up the river from the Gulf of Mexico. In mid-1861, contracts were let to boatyards in the Midwest to build seven partially iron-clad, shallow-draft gunboats. In addition, nearly seventy existing steamboats were purchased and fitted with various combinations of timber and iron armor. This innovative riverine force was intended to demolish Confederate fortifications along the Mississippi and its tributaries, defeat any Confederate vessels that might appear, and escort troop convoys downstream. Meanwhile, in the Gulf of Mexico, a fleet of powerful oceangoing naval vessels slowly gathered off the Louisiana coast. One by one these deep-draft warships worked their way over mudflats and sandbars and entered the mouths of the Mississippi.

The Confederates were far from idle during the first year of the war. Soldiers and civilians alike could see the threat posed by growing Union naval strength in the West, but the very size of the Mississippi River made its defense problematical. Below Cairo the river is so wide and its current so strong that chains, pilings, sunken hulks, and other barriers could not be relied upon to prevent vessels from passing. In addition its channel is so deep that for much of the year oceangoing ships could enter the river's mouths below New Orleans and venture upstream for nearly a thousand miles.

The topography of the lower Mississippi Valley complicated matters for both attackers and defenders. The east bank of the Mississippi is bordered for much of its length by an impressive line of bluffs. Atop the northern third of this escarpment lie Columbus, Kentucky, and Memphis. South of Memphis, the river bends westward away from the middle third of the escarpment, but it returns to it at Vicksburg, where the bluffs reach their greatest height, towering over two hundred feet above the water. From Vicksburg the bluffs crowd the east bank of the Mississippi down to Baton Rouge. Perched atop or nestled along the base of this southern third of the escarpment are Grand Gulf, Natchez, Port Hudson, and Baton Rouge. Below the Louisiana capital the river loops across a swampy plain of recently deposited alluvium. Located precariously amid this sea of mud, ninety miles from the Gulf of Mexico, is New Orleans. The intermittent highlands along the Mississippi presented numerous

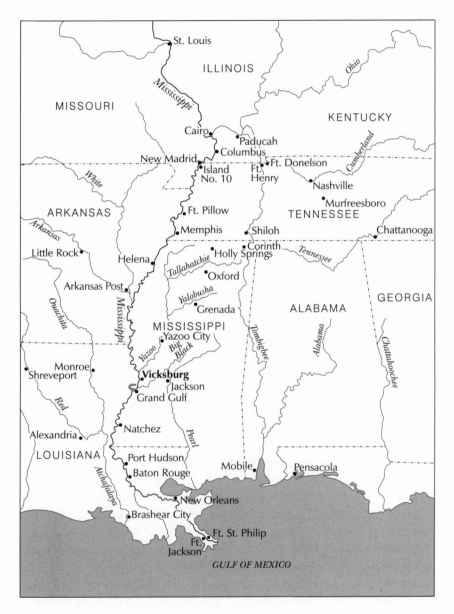

The Mississippi Valley

locations for defensive positions, but the extensive lowlands permitted unfettered movement of ships and boats.

If Union strategy regarding the lower Mississippi Valley was offensive in nature, Confederate strategy was defensive and relied primarily on fortifications. Thus the struggle for control of the Mississippi River featured a textbook example of strategic opposites: an active approach based on maneuver versus a passive resistance dependent on fixed positions. With the benefit of hindsight it is apparent that the Confederacy's static defense, like all static defenses from the Great Wall to the Maginot Line, was doomed to fail when tested by an aggressive and resourceful enemy. Fortifications along waterways have several inherent weaknesses. When improperly sited or weakly constructed, or when manned by dispirited garrisons, they generally can be pounded into submission by naval forces. Fortifications that prove resistant to bombardment often can be bypassed by naval commanders willing to take risks. A bypassed stronghold generally becomes irrelevant. Its garrison might escape to fight again elsewhere, but its weapons and stores, transported and emplaced at great cost in both time and money, are usually lost. Fortifications also are vulnerable to overland encircling movements. Troops disembarked from transports can threaten them from the rear and compel their garrisons to evacuate or surrender.

Whenever a fixed position is captured, bypassed, or otherwise neutralized, the river is opened to the next stronghold, if any exists. The process is inexorable. No fortification, no matter how strongly built or ably manned, can halt a determined advance; it can only delay the inevitable. This was not at all clear in the middle of the nineteenth century, however, because the implications of industrial military technologies such as steam engines, iron armor, rifled artillery, and explosive shells were imperfectly understood. For the first time in centuries, new weapons and methods of warfare were emerging, and no one knew just what to expect when the shooting started.

Despite the Confederacy's belief that batteries of heavy guns behind brick or earthen walls would keep Union forces out of the lower Mississippi Valley, construction of fortifications during the first year of the war was delayed by woeful mismanagement, chronic shortages of money and material, and a strange lack of urgency. By the beginning of 1862 an embryonic defense in depth, that is, a series of fortifications one behind the other, existed only along the Mississippi above Memphis. With the crisis approaching, Confederate defenses in the West resembled a perilously thin, hollow shell.

The principal reason for the Confederate reliance on fortifications was the lack of a navy. Nearly all of the steamboats plying the Mississippi and its tributaries before the war were Northern owned and operated. When fighting broke out, these vessels and their crews, which included many valuable pilots and mechanics, returned home. Some were purchased by U.S. authorities and converted into gunboats; many others were purchased or leased as transports. The Confederates had to make do with what remained. They converted fourteen ships and boats at New Orleans into the rather grandly named River Defense Fleet and began work on five ironclads: two at Memphis, two at New Orleans, and one on the Tennessee River. Unfortunately the skills and machinery needed to create such behemoths were hard to come by in the agricultural South. While boatyards in the Midwest cranked out vessels of every size and description, progress on the Confederate ironclads lagged.

Such was the situation in the West at the beginning of 1862. Both sides recognized the economic, political, and military importance of the Mississippi Valley. With superior resources and industrial capacity, the Union was determined to gain control of the western rivers. The Confederacy, short of resources, was equally determined to dig in and hold on.

Confederate forces west of the Appalachian Mountains were commanded by Gen. Albert S. Johnston, a professional soldier and a friend of Pres. Jefferson Davis. Johnston faced an impossible task. His defensive perimeter ran along the northern boundary of Tennessee, Arkansas, and the Indian Territory, eight hundred miles of rugged country divided into segments by several major rivers and served by a poorly developed transportation system. Johnston recognized that no commander could hope to exercise effective control over such an immense area. Consequently he allowed his subordinates a great deal of leeway.

One such subordinate was Maj. Gen. Leonidas Polk, West Point graduate, Episcopal bishop, and military incompetent. Polk commanded in western Tennessee and was responsible for the defense of the Mississippi River. He believed that the village of Columbus, located twenty miles north of the Kentucky-Tennessee state line atop a line of towering bluffs, was the perfect place to stop a Union thrust downstream. Polk ignored the inconvenient fact that Kentucky was not a part of the Confederacy.

In early September 1861 he occupied Columbus. Confederate engineers threw up immense earthworks along the heights, brought in 150 guns, and attempted to block the Mississippi River with a mile-long chain.

The Confederate occupation of Columbus did not go unchallenged. The Union commander at Cairo, Brig. Gen. Ulysses S. Grant, led a small waterborne force down the Mississippi to Belmont, a landing on the Missouri shore opposite Columbus. Though Grant was compelled to withdraw in the face of superior numbers, his aggressive response was a harbinger of things to come. The Confederate victory could not disguise the fact that Polk had stirred up a hornet's nest.

Instead of ordering Polk to return to Tennessee, Johnston gambled that a bold show of strength would confound Union commanders and mask Confederate weaknesses in the West. He led most of his troops into Kentucky and established a strong position at Bowling Green in the south-central part of the state. The only Confederate contingents to remain behind in Tennessee were the garrisons at Fort Henry on the Tennessee River and Fort Donelson on the Cumberland.

The Confederate incursion into Kentucky had serious consequences. Having maintained a precarious "neutrality" since the outbreak of hostilities, most Kentuckians were outraged at the presence of Confederate troops on their soil. Kentucky declared its allegiance to the United States and permitted Union land and naval forces to enter the state without hindrance. Polk got Columbus, but the Union gained both banks of the Ohio River and direct access to Tennessee across a four-hundred-mile front. The Columbus affair was a blunder, but it remained to be seen how the Federals would take advantage of the altered strategic situation in the West.

The Union commander in St. Louis at the beginning of 1862 was Maj. Gen. Henry W. Halleck, known rather derisively in the prewar army as "Old Brains." Halleck did not cut a dashing figure, but he was a first-rate administrator and strategist. He also was more offensive minded than any other Union commander at that stage of the war, and he was determined to move against Johnston.

Halleck recognized that victory in the West depended on control of the rivers. With the Ohio and upper Mississippi in Union hands, he turned his attention to the Tennessee, Cumberland, and lower Mississippi, all of which flowed through Johnston's line. In the first half of the new year, Halleck launched three loosely coordinated offensives that wrenched over a thousand miles of navigable waterways out of Confederate hands and punched three gaping holes in Johnston's defensive perimeter.

West of the Mississippi, a small army under Brig. Gen. Samuel R. Curtis swept Confederate forces out of Missouri and into Arkansas. This operation secured the Union supply depot at St. Louis and allowed Halleck greater freedom of action elsewhere. Beginning in February 1862, Curtis's army struggled across the Ozark Plateau into Arkansas, routed a Confederate army at Pea Ridge on March 7–8, and then turned east toward Helena at the Mississippi River.

East of the Mississippi, Grant pondered the lessons learned at Belmont and tried again. He assembled a powerful waterborne force and steamed up the Tennessee River. Naval support was provided by Flag Officer Andrew H. Foote's revolutionary Western Flotilla, an assortment of ironclad and timberclad gunboats. On February 6, 1862, Foote's gunboats attacked Fort Henry, just inside Tennessee, with spectacular results. The fort surrendered after a brief pounding, though most of the garrison escaped to nearby Fort Donelson along the Cumberland River. The Confederates capitulated so quickly that Grant's soldiers did not have a chance to participate in the battle. With Fort Henry neutralized, Foote launched a raid up the Tennessee. His gunboats penetrated all the way to Muscle Shoals in the northwest corner of Alabama, captured the unfinished ironclad *Eastport,* destroyed railroad bridges and other military stores, and created havoc generally in the Southern heartland.

The capture of Fort Henry and all that followed was a model of interservice cooperation and demonstrated the tremendous advantage that command of the rivers conferred on Union forces in the West. It was a terrific blow to the Confederates, who saw for the first time what could result from the failure of a fortified position. Worse was to come.

A few days after the fall of Fort Henry, Grant marched his army eastward across the narrow neck of land that separates the Tennessee and Cumberland Rivers. He partially surrounded Fort Donelson and waited for Foote to arrive and pound the Rebels into submission. Following the raid up the Tennessee, the gunboats of the Western Flotilla returned to the Ohio River, then moved up the Cumberland toward Donelson. Foote also hoped for a repeat of the success he had enjoyed against Fort Henry, but he was in for a rude awakening. Donelson was better sited then Henry, and its battery of heavy guns was larger.

On February 14 the ironclads of the Western Flotilla approached Fort Donelson and opened fire. After several hours of furious combat at close range, Foote was forced to withdraw. All of his gunboats were damaged, some seriously, and casualties were many, including Foote himself. The next day the Confederates attempted to break through the encircling Union forces and escape. The effort failed by the narrowest of margins, and Fort Donelson surrendered to Grant on February 16. It was the first great Union victory of the war.

It also was the first great Confederate disaster. Johnston lost sixteen thousand men—about one-fourth of the troops under his command— along with irreplaceable guns, munitions, and stores. Even worse, the Cumberland River was now open to Nashville, due south of Bowling Green. In danger of being cut off, Johnston abandoned Kentucky and fell back through Tennessee all the way to northern Alabama. On February 25, Federal troops raised the Stars and Stripes over the Tennessee State Capitol in Nashville. Kentucky and much of central Tennessee were in Union hands.

The success of the Union offensive up the Tennessee and Cumberland Rivers had strategic repercussions far beyond the states of Kentucky and Tennessee. When Grant and Foote broke through the center of Johnston's defensive perimeter, they also dealt a severe blow to the Confederate defense of the Mississippi River. The lower Tennessee River flows roughly parallel to the Mississippi for two hundred miles and lies only about one hundred miles to the east. The Union forces that surged up the Tennessee past Fort Henry spilled around and behind Polk's impressive fortifications at Columbus. In military parlance Polk's position had been "turned," and he was in danger of being cut off.

There was nothing for Polk to do but abandon Columbus, which he did on March 4. He sent his men and over one hundred guns to a secondary position thirty miles southeast at Island No. 10, a large mudflat on the Tennessee side of the Mississippi River roughly opposite New Madrid, Missouri. Despite the earlier setback at Belmont, Grant now succeeded in evicting the Rebels from Columbus. Following the hard-won victory at Fort Donelson, Grant led his army back to the Tennessee River and moved upstream to a place called Pittsburg Landing, only a few miles north of the Mississippi state line. There the Federals awaited the arrival of Maj. Gen. Don Carlos Buell's army, which was approaching slowly from Nashville. When the two Union forces were united, Halleck intended to push into northeast Mississippi and capture the vital railroad junction at Corinth.

While these developments were unfolding in Tennessee, the third and last of Halleck's operations got underway in the Mississippi Valley. Foote's

Western Flotilla returned to the Mississippi River to deal with the new Confederate position at Island No. 10. He joined forces with Brig. Gen. John Pope, whose Union army was moving down the west side of the river toward New Madrid. After being handled so roughly at Fort Donelson, Foote was reluctant to make another head-on attack against fortifications. He relied instead on a flotilla of recently constructed mortar boats to bombard the Confederates from a safe distance.

On March 14, Federal troops occupied New Madrid after a brief fight. Pope now controlled the west bank of the Mississippi below Island No. 10. If he could get his men safely across the river to the Tennessee shore, the Confederates on the island would be cut off and captured. Up to this point Foote had been a model of vigor and cooperation, but now, ill and exhausted, he hesitated. Pope and his men chafed at the delay. When asked what the navy was doing at Island No. 10, a frustrated army officer replied: "It is still bombarding the State of Tennessee at long range."[2]

Under pressure from his subordinates, Foote finally authorized an attempt to run the Confederate batteries. On the night of April 4, illuminated by flashes of lightning and rocked by crashes of thunder louder than any artillery fire, an ironclad successfully passed Island No. 10 and reached New Madrid. A second ironclad did the same a few nights later, covered by a similarly ferocious thunderstorm. Meanwhile, several light-draft transports arrived at New Madrid after a circuitous voyage along winding bayous and across flooded lowlands. The two gunboats escorted the transports downriver, and Pope's troops crossed to the Tennessee shore a few miles below the Confederate position. It was the end for Island No. 10 and its immense collection of arms and ammunition. The garrison of forty-five hundred men surrendered on April 8. The only remaining obstacle between the advancing Union forces and Memphis was Fort Pillow, another bluff-top earthen fortification located forty miles north of the city and sixty miles south of Island No. 10. Foote and Pope planned to repeat the successful flanking tactics they had employed. Thousands of Federals disembarked on the Arkansas shore near Osceola, about eight miles above Fort Pillow. Pope planned to lead his troops downstream while Foote sent some of his ironclads and transports past the fort. The vessels would rendezvous with the army downriver and ferry the troops across to the Tennessee side. The plan had every prospect of success, but it had to be abandoned in mid-April when Halleck summoned Pope and most of his command to reinforce Grant at Pittsburg Landing following the battle of Shiloh. Pope's army steamed up the Mississippi on an armada of transports, leaving Foote with only fifteen hundred soldiers.

The rapid movement of so many men and so much equipment from one front to another in the vast western theater was an impressive demonstration of the great strategic mobility command of the rivers conferred upon Union military leaders. But while Halleck's decision to rush reinforcements to Grant in the aftermath of Shiloh seemed sensible at the time, it was a serious error. For the rest of 1862 only a relative handful of Union troops were available to support naval operations on the Mississippi River. The Western Flotilla was effectively on its own.

Shortly after Pope's departure Foote was reassigned to a less taxing position and replaced by Flag Officer Charles H. Davis, an accomplished oceanographer but not a particularly aggressive officer. While Davis familiarized himself with his new command and considered his options, Union ironclads and mortar boats began a long-range bombardment of Fort Pillow.

On May 10 the officers and men of the Western Flotilla got the shock of their lives when eight vessels of the Confederate River Defense Fleet put in a wholly unexpected appearance. The flotilla had arrived from New Orleans a few weeks earlier but had played no meaningful role in the struggle for Island No. 10. Now led by Capt. James E. Montgomery, the hodgepodge of lightly armed ships and boats boldly fell upon the unprepared Union gunboats at a bend in the river named Plum Point. In the melee that followed, the Rebels rammed and sank two ironclads in shallow water, then escaped downriver to the protection of Fort Pillow.

Casualties on both sides were light despite the furious expenditure of powder. The two waterlogged ironclads were raised and towed upriver for repairs; they would be back in service within six weeks. The affair at Plum Point (sometimes called Plum Run) demonstrated the vulnerability of the isolated Union flotilla, now well inside the rebellious South. Davis's natural caution was reinforced by these events, and the Union drive down the Mississippi stalled for the second time in two months.

Once again a standoff on the Mississippi River was dramatically affected by events one hundred miles to the east. Three days before Plum Point, on April 6–7, the dreadful battle of Shiloh was fought along the banks of the Tennessee River. Shiloh was the result of General Johnston's extraordinary effort to reverse the course of events in the West. Johnston ordered troops from nearly every point in the western Confederacy to join him at Corinth, Mississippi. He intended to concentrate an enor-

mous force, defeat Grant at Pittsburg Landing before Buell arrived from
Nashville, and then recover the huge expanse of territory lost in the
aftermath of the disaster at Forts Henry and Donelson.

The Confederates caught Grant by surprise at Shiloh and dealt him
a heavy blow, but Johnston was killed during the intense fighting, and
Buell's column arrived midway through the battle. It was the Confederate
army that staggered away from the battlefield after two days of appalling
slaughter. Seven weeks later, on May 30, the combined forces of Grant,
Buell, and Pope, with Halleck in personal command, captured Corinth
without a serious fight. The Confederate army, now commanded by Gen.
Pierre G. T. Beauregard, withdrew deeper into Mississippi.

The loss of Corinth was a crippling blow to the Confederacy because
the only direct east-west railroad connection to Memphis passed through
the town. Like Columbus several weeks earlier, Fort Pillow and Memphis
had been turned. Confederate troops abandoned both places in early June
in order to avoid being cut off. After taking possession of Fort Pillow, Flag
Officer Davis proceeded downstream to Memphis. There his Western
Flotilla again encountered Captain Montgomery's River Defense Fleet,
which made a valiant but foolish attempt to defend the indefensible city
in one of the few fleet engagements of the Civil War.

Davis's powerful but clumsy ironclads had been roughly handled at
Plum Point, but now they were accompanied by several specially prepared
boats designed to beat the Confederates at their own game. These vessels
were the brainchild of Col. Charles Ellet Jr., who had convinced the army
to convert seven fast steamboats into rams. When the River Defense Fleet
deployed for battle in front of Memphis on June 6, the Confederates
were thrown into confusion by the rapid approach of two Ellet rams. The
vessels sped past the plodding Union ironclads and headed directly for
Montgomery's gunboats.

Thousands of Memphis citizens watched in dismay from the bluffs as
the Union rams sank or disabled one Confederate gunboat after another.
Then the ironclads came up and finished the job with their guns. One
Rebel boat escaped downstream; the rest were destroyed or captured.
Montgomery ran his own disabled vessel ashore and got away, but losses
among his crews were heavy. The only Union fatality was Ellet, whose
minor wound became infected. His place as commander of the ram fleet
was taken by his brother, Lt. Col. Alfred W. Ellet. The spoils along the
Memphis waterfront included six steamboats, a huge quantity of naval
stores, and thousands of bales of cotton.

The loss of this bustling commercial center was yet another serious blow to the Confederacy, but even more serious in immediate military terms was the loss of one of the two ironclad rams under construction there. The *Tennessee* could not be moved and was burned on the stocks, though her engines were taken to Mobile and incorporated into a later ironclad of the same name. The *Arkansas,* considerably further along, was towed downstream to Yazoo City, Mississippi, where workers labored to complete the vessel. The *Arkansas* would be heard from later in spectacular fashion.

In less than five months of active campaigning, Union naval and land forces had seized the navigable portions of the Tennessee and the Cumberland and were in control of the Mississippi all the way down to Memphis. The Confederates were reeling, but Flag Officer Davis was not the sort of man to deliver a knockout blow. Seeing no particular reason to continue the offensive, he decided to stop at Memphis and allow his men and boats to rest and refit. The Union advance down the Mississippi once again sputtered to a halt.

The Union offensive south from February to June 1862 riveted Confederate attention on the threat to the Mississippi Valley from the north. President Davis and Secretary of the Navy Stephen R. Mallory were so mesmerized by the progress of the Western Flotilla downstream that they feared New Orleans would be captured from above. Their concern for the safety of New Orleans is understandable; no place in the Confederacy was more important. The Crescent City is fabled today for its architecture, entertainment, and cuisine, but in 1862 it was far more than that. With nearly 170,000 people, annual trade in excess of $185,000,000, dozens of banks and insurance firms, and a myriad of boatyards, foundries, and machine shops, New Orleans was the South's largest, wealthiest, and most industrialized city. The loss of such a vital place would be a calamity of immeasurable proportions to the Confederacy.

President Davis and Secretary Mallory were aware of New Orleans's primacy, but they misread the strategic situation in the Mississippi Valley. Throughout this critical period they drained men and material away from New Orleans to strengthen sagging defenses in other parts of the Confederacy. In so doing they unaccountably ignored the buildup of Union warships in the Gulf of Mexico.

Maj. Gen. Mansfield Lovell, the Confederate commander in New Orleans, reported steady increases in Union naval activity near the mouths of the Mississippi and pled for reinforcements. Davis and Mallory not only refused to send reinforcements but also crippled Lovell's efforts to organize a coordinated defense. They refused to give him command of Confederate naval forces at New Orleans, such as they were, and sent half of the River Defense Fleet to assist in the defense of Island No. 10, Fort Pillow, and, fatally, Memphis. To make matters worse they did little to speed construction of two large ironclad rams, *Louisiana* and *Mississippi*, being built side by side in New Orleans by two different contractors. The contractors competed for scarce funds, workers, and supplies, thereby delaying completion of both vessels for months.

The defense of the most important city in the Confederacy rested primarily on two isolated forts located between New Orleans and the mouths of the Mississippi. Fort Jackson and Fort St. Philip were substantial brick structures flanked by earthworks. They mounted about three hundred guns, two-thirds of which faced the river. Supporting them were a half dozen lightly armed vessels of the River Defense Fleet along with the tiny *Manassas*, the first ironclad vessel built in the Civil War. Strung between the forts was a floating barrier of hulks, logs, and chains to obstruct the channel.

The Union naval force below New Orleans was commanded by Flag Officer David G. Farragut. His West Gulf Blockading Squadron consisted of a dozen warships augmented by a flotilla of mortar schooners commanded by Cmdr. David D. Porter, his foster brother. Both men were courageous, tireless, determined, and daring. There were no officers in the U.S. Navy better suited to take on the challenging task of wresting control of the lower Mississippi away from the Confederates.

In mid-April Farragut led his command to within range of Fort Jackson, which is a short distance downstream from Fort St. Philip, and directed Porter to open fire. For a week the huge mortars blasted away at Jackson. The rain of explosive shells inflicted considerable superficial damage but did not significantly impair the fort's fighting ability. Farragut did not have much faith that the mortars could pound the forts into submission, and he decided to try a different tactic. Shortly after midnight on April 24, Farragut led his warships upriver toward Jackson and St. Philip. An advance party of Union sailors opened a gap at the eastern end of the floating barrier, which had been weakened by the river's powerful current. When Confederate gunners in the forts discovered ships slipping through the barrier, they opened fire. The ships responded, and a thunderous artillery duel ensued. Thousands of muzzle flashes lit up the billows of smoke blanketing the river. The scene was illuminated by the hellish glow of blazing fire rafts that drifted through the melee. The *Manassas* and the other Confederate vessels entered the fray, but they were no match for the Union men-of-war. The one-sided battle was over well before dawn. One Union ship went down but thirteen others fought their way past the forts. Thirty-seven Union sailors were killed and four times that number were wounded. All of the Confederate vessels were sunk, scuttled, or captured. Confederate losses amounted to at least eighty-four sailors and soldiers killed and over one hundred wounded.

Farragut did not tarry to coerce the forts into surrender but boldly pressed on toward his objective. All morning the Union warships steamed up the broad river, propellers and paddlewheels churning against the current. As they approached New Orleans the Federals were treated to the spectacle of thousands of smoldering bales of cotton along the banks and at least a dozen burning vessels drifting downriver. Hardly had the ships finished weaving through that set of obstacles when they were fired upon by batteries in earthen fortifications constructed near the old Chalmette battlefield, where Andrew Jackson and his hodgepodge army had defeated a British invasion force in 1815. A few broadsides convinced the Confederate gunners to abandon their pieces.

At noon Farragut's warships, their gunports open and their rails and rigging crowded with sailors, dropped anchor along the New Orleans waterfront. More bales of cotton along with large quantities of molasses, sugar, corn, rice, hams, and bacon were ablaze atop the levees, and a pall of aromatic smoke hung over the scene. Lovell ordered the destruction of the two unfinished ironclads and marched his small force out of the city. No shots were fired on either side.

Farragut was alone, cut off from Porter, low on ammunition and coal, and without military support, but he demanded and received the capitulation of New Orleans on April 29. A few days later a fleet of transports steamed past Forts Jackson and St. Philip, which had surrendered to Porter shortly after Farragut's passage, and reached New Orleans. These vessels carried Maj. Gen. Benjamin F. Butler and an occupation force of fifteen thousand soldiers. The First City of the Confederacy was firmly in Federal hands only a year after Fort Sumter.

The Union triumph seemed almost ridiculously easy, but in fact it had been a near thing. Had Farragut delayed his attack by only a few days, as Porter had urged in order to allow the mortar schooners more time to reduce Fort Jackson, one of the Confederate ironclads would have been marginally operational. Had Davis and Mallory not sent half of the River Defense Fleet upriver to Island No. 10, the engagement above Forts Jackson and St. Philip would have been more of an even fight. And had Lovell been allowed to keep even half of the men and guns raised in and around New Orleans, Farragut would not have been able to anchor so boldly in front of the city and demand its surrender.

Admirable audacity on one side and bewildering ineptness on the other had produced a stunning Union victory with enormous military, economic, and diplomatic consequences. The Confederacy never recovered from the loss of New Orleans and its inestimable resources. The effect was felt even in faraway Europe, where governments considering recognition of the Confederacy were compelled to view the matter in a new light. Historian Charles L. Dufour described Farragut's passage of Forts Jackson and St. Philip as "the night the war was lost." If that is an exaggeration, it is a very slight one.[3]

Farragut's instructions from Secretary of the Navy Gideon Welles called for him to ascend the Mississippi River to meet the Western Flotilla. In early May, however, Flag Officer Davis was stalled at Fort Pillow, hundreds of miles to the north. After making such repairs as were possible without a dry dock or navy yard and taking onboard as much food, ammunition, and coal as could be found, Farragut rounded up a handful of pilots and proceeded upriver. He was determined to maintain the initiative. "Depend upon it," Farragut informed the Navy Department, "we will keep the stampede up on them." A small convoy of transports carrying a brigade of soldiers under Brig. Gen. Thomas Williams followed the warships up the river.[4]

The Confederates had not constructed any fortifications above New Orleans, and the Union fleet made steady progress upriver, steaming through a landscape of willful destruction. "The most of the planters between here and New Orleans have obeyed Jeff Davis' instructions in regard to destroying their cotton," observed a bemused William H. Smith aboard the *Winona*. "They seem to think they are doing us a great injury by destroying their own property. As we came up the river it was for two hundred miles covered with cotton which had been thrown into it. Along the banks was one continuous bonfire."[5]

The leading vessels reached Baton Rouge on May 9 and Natchez on May 12. The two defenseless cities capitulated and Farragut pushed on. He was undaunted by the smoke that hung over the river, but he grew

increasingly uneasy over the bluffs that crowded in from the east and
loomed ever higher as his ships moved upstream.

Lovell followed the progress of the Union warships up the Mississippi
with mounting alarm. Weeks earlier he had suggested that Vicksburg be
fortified, but at that time he was concerned about stopping the Western
Flotilla from sweeping down the river from the north. He now believed
that Vicksburg was the only place where a two-way defense might succeed
in keeping Farragut and Davis apart. Lovell sent Brig. Gen. Martin L.
Smith to Vicksburg to do what he could to hold off the converging Union
forces. Smith was an accomplished military engineer and an officer of
uncommon good sense. When he arrived on May 12 he found slaves constructing a handful of artillery emplacements in a lackadaisical manner.
Smith immediately increased the pace and scope of the work.

On May 18, Confederate soldiers and citizens of Vicksburg gathered
on the bluffs and watched as columns of smoke appeared on the southern
horizon. A few hours later a line of dark ships came into view and anchored
below the town. A boat came ashore with a message from Farragut
demanding the surrender of the city. Smith answered politely but firmly:
"I have to reply that, having been ordered here to hold these defenses,
my intention is to do so as long as it is in my power." The local military
commander, Lt. Col. James L. Autrey, was considerably more defiant.
"Mississippians don't know, and refuse to learn, how to surrender to an
enemy," he responded. "If Commodore Farragut or Brigadier General
Butler can teach them, let them come and try." With these bold words
the struggle for Vicksburg began.[6]

# CHAPTER TWO

# Gibraltar on the Mississippi

Vicksburg, aptly nicknamed the Hill City, sprawls up a series of terraces from the river's edge to the top of a line of bluffs over two hundred feet high. In 1862 at least forty-six hundred people, of whom perhaps fourteen hundred were slaves, lived in Vicksburg-on-the-hill. A substantial but uncertain number of other residents—riverboatmen, gamblers, and progressively more shady characters—lived and plied their trades in Vicksburg-under-the-hill, a rowdy red-light district along the waterfront.

Like other bustling towns on the Mississippi River, Vicksburg was surprisingly cosmopolitan. Only about one-third of its adult population were Southern-born; the rest had made their way to the Hill City from Europe (primarily Ireland, Germany, and Britain) and from practically every state in the Union. Citizens could choose from six daily and weekly newspapers, a variety of churches and synagogues, and an impressive array of mercantile establishments along Washington Street, the principal thoroughfare. Dominating the town's modest skyline was the recently completed Warren County Courthouse, the tallest structure between Memphis and Baton Rouge.

But Vicksburg was more than just a prosperous and impressively situated little metropolis. Railroads and riverboats made it the principal transfer point across the Mississippi River south of Memphis. The trans-Mississippi states of Louisiana, Texas, and Arkansas provided the rest of the Confederacy with substantial amounts of manpower and food—including irreplaceable quantities of flour, cornmeal, beef, sugar, and salt—and with vital stocks of weapons, munitions, uniforms, and medical supplies. Most of the manufactured material was of European origin and reached the Confederacy via Matamoras, Mexico.

People, produce, and products from the trans-Mississippi moved toward Shreveport and Alexandria on the Red River in Louisiana. The principal all-water route wound down the Red River and up the Mississippi to the wharves at Vicksburg. An alternate route followed the Ouachita River to Monroe, Louisiana. From there the Vicksburg, Shreveport, and Texas Railroad ran to De Soto Point, directly opposite Vicksburg. Every half hour ferries shuttled back and forth across the Mississippi between the railroad terminus and the Hill City's crowded waterfront. In 1862 no other riverport in the Confederacy was the scene of so much activity.

But it was the Southern Railroad of Mississippi on the east side of the Mississippi River that was Vicksburg's economic and military lifeline. Its iron rails linked Vicksburg to Jackson and other points north, east, and south. During the first year of the war, those rails carried tens of thousands of men and immeasurable quantities of food and military stores to Confederate armies operating in Tennessee and even in distant Virginia. Now the traffic was reversed as those same rails hurried men and material to defend the Hill City and its vital link with the trans-Mississippi.

When Flag Officer Farragut's ships anchored below Vicksburg on May 18, General Smith had only thirty-six hundred Confederate soldiers and eighteen guns at his disposal, but even then reinforcements were rattling along the tracks toward the threatened city. After months of ineffectual dithering punctuated by occasional acts of blinding stupidity, Confederate authorities had finally awakened to the threat posed by Farragut's ships moving upstream and to Vicksburg's sudden strategic importance as the only remaining Confederate lodgment on the Mississippi south of Memphis, which was at that moment threatened by the Western Flotilla pressing downstream.

Smith chose to disperse his guns rather than concentrate them in a single large fortification such as Fort Donelson or Fort Pillow. Parties of slaves and soldiers constructed battery positions on mudflats, terraces, and irregular headlands along four miles of waterfront and bluff top. (Contrary to legend most of the guns were located close to the river; only a relative handful were perched atop the bluffs.) Thus began the process that eventually encircled Vicksburg with earthworks and transformed the town into an enormous fortress, a Confederate Gibraltar on the Mississippi.

Geography was the Confederacy's strongest ally from the very beginning of the campaign. Farragut was four hundred miles above New Orleans (hardly a friendly port of call) and thousands of miles from his supply centers on the Northeast coast. He realized that he did not have

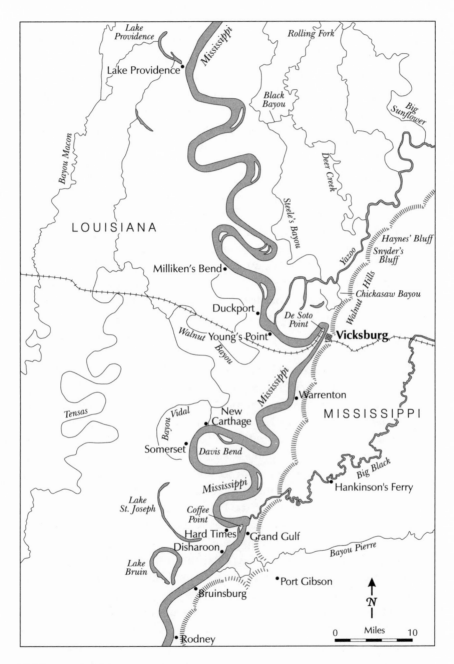

Vicksburg and vicinity

the means to take and hold Vicksburg. He also realized that it would serve no purpose to run past the town in order to reach the gunboats of the Western Flotilla somewhere upstream. Farragut did not know where Flag Officer Davis was, and he did not think his warships should be wandering around the interior of North America in search of him. Having done as much as he could—and having shown more boldness than any other ranking officer on either side thus far in the war—on May 26 Farragut retired downstream to New Orleans. He intended to return to Vicksburg as soon as possible, though he already suspected that nothing less than a major land campaign would succeed in capturing the city.

The lull in Union operations on the lower Mississippi River lasted less than a month. In June Farragut again moved on Vicksburg, his original naval force now augmented by Commander Porter's mortar schooners. General Williams returned as well, his command doubled in size to about thirty-three hundred troops. By this time, however, the Confederates had assembled a substantial force in and around Vicksburg under the overall command of Maj. Gen. Earl Van Dorn, who had succeeded Lovell as commander of the Department of Southern Mississippi and East Louisiana.

Van Dorn was a native of Port Gibson, Mississippi, a small town located thirty miles south of Vicksburg. He was a professional soldier who had spent much of his army career on horseback fighting Indians on the Great Plains. Van Dorn lacked administrative skills, had no engineering experience, and had recently suffered a resounding defeat at Pea Ridge, but his West Point education, his friendship with Jefferson Davis, and his strong ties to the Vicksburg area probably explained his selection for such a crucial position. (A poor judge of character and ability who showered choice assignments on his friends, President Davis was one reason why the upper ranks of the Confederate army were filled with so many long-serving mediocrities and incompetents.)

Farragut's ships arrived below Vicksburg on June 18. The next day Porter's mortar schooners began a sustained but ineffective bombardment of the Hill City. The dispersed Confederate artillery emplacements were almost impossible to hit with the inaccurate siege mortars of the day. Unnerved at first by the earthshaking impact of the huge shells, the Confederates gradually realized that the Union attack was mostly sound and fury; it was Island No. 10 and Fort Jackson all over again. One Confederate officer dismissed the bombardment as "the grand but nearly harmless sport of pitching big shells into Vicksburg." Confederate morale steadied, then rose at the end of June when Maj. Gen. John C. Breckinridge arrived with a veteran division, increasing Van Dorn's strength to about fifteen thousand men.[1]

While Farragut and Van Dorn confronted each other at Vicksburg, Union land and naval forces captured Corinth, Fort Pillow, and Memphis in rapid succession. Although Flag Officer Davis remained at Memphis, he sent a force of gunboats and transports up the White River in Arkansas. The object of the mission was to establish a waterborne supply line to General Curtis, who was heading toward the Mississippi River after his earlier victory over Van Dorn at Pea Ridge. The Union vessels encountered a small Confederate fort at St. Charles on June 17. During the brief engagement a shot struck the ironclad *Mound City* in the steam drum with appalling results. The vessel was only slightly damaged, but the blast of steam killed or severely wounded most of her crew. It was all for naught, however, as the convoy failed to make contact with Curtis.

Unaware of what was happening on the White River, Colonel Ellet left Memphis with five rams and steamed down the winding Mississippi in search of Farragut. On June 24 Ellet approached the west side of De Soto Point, the neck of land where the Mississippi made a hairpin turn immediately above Vicksburg. The masts of Farragut's ships were visible on the east side of the narrow peninsula, so Ellet sent a courier across the swampy terrain with an account of Union successes upstream.

Farragut was pleased at having made contact with a portion of the Western Flotilla, but he was puzzled by Davis's inclination to linger at Memphis. Ellet dispatched a ram with a request from Farragut for Davis to proceed to Vicksburg as quickly as possible. A week later, masthead lookouts on Farragut's ships spied plumes of smoke moving downstream in their direction. The gunboats and support vessels of the Western Flotilla eventually came into sight and reunited with the rams above Vicksburg. Union saltwater warships and freshwater gunboats now were only five or six miles apart by water and less than two miles by land.

Emboldened by the arrival of his riverine cohorts, Farragut decided to take his warships past Vicksburg after all. Porter and his mortar schooners, along with Williams's transports, remained behind to continue hammering the enemy positions, much as they had done a few weeks earlier below New Orleans. It is unclear what tactical advantage Farragut hoped to gain by this maneuver. Perhaps he wanted to demonstrate his disdain for Confederate attempts to control even a small stretch of the Mississippi, or perhaps he simply could not stand to be idle.

Before sunrise on the morning of June 28, the Union warships formed into line and steamed past Vicksburg through a barrage of shot and shell. The Confederate artillery along the river—now increased to twenty-nine guns of varying size and type—roared into action. Within minutes the river was blanketed by a cloud of smoke lit up by muzzle flashes, exploding shells, and bonfires intended to provide illumination for Confederate gunners. No ships were sunk or seriously damaged, but the passage was not without cost, for the navy lost eight killed and thirty-six wounded.

For the first time the Union naval forces that had gained control over so much of the Mississippi Valley saw each other. There could hardly have been a more vivid contrast between two groups of fighting vessels. Officers and men on the ships of the West Gulf Blockading Squadron—still majestic even though their upper masts, spars, and rigging had been removed—crowded the rails and looked down through ventilation gratings into the partially armored casemates of the ironclads. Farragut thought the stumpy, stubby gunboats were appropriately nicknamed "turtles." Most of the men of the Western Flotilla were Midwesterners "borrowed" from the army who had never seen an oceangoing vessel before, and they gawked at the huge sloops of war and their crews of saltwater tars.

While Union sailors traded stories and friendly insults above Vicksburg, General Williams disembarked his troops from the transports below the city and set about digging a ditch across the base of De Soto Point. The idea was to create a canal that would allow vessels to bypass the heavy guns at Vicksburg. Farragut, Davis, and Williams also hoped the canal might divert the Mississippi into a new course and leave Vicksburg high and dry, thus rendering the town and its defenses militarily useless.

A canal across level terrain seemed a fairly rudimentary engineering exercise, but the dense clay subsoil of the peninsula resisted shovels and picks, and the river dropped faster than the men could dig. Malaria, dysentery, and other diseases decimated the troops. Williams rounded up a thousand slaves from plantations in the neighborhood and put them to work alongside his soldiers, but the additional manpower still proved inadequate and the effort finally foundered. The one important result of this fiasco was the destruction of the eastern terminus of the Vicksburg, Shreveport, and Texas Railroad, which ran between De Soto Point and Monroe. Henceforth the economic lifeline of the Confederacy was reduced to the all-water route between Shreveport and Vicksburg, a route that could only be used when the Red and Mississippi Rivers were free of Union vessels.

Farragut was convinced that the navy had done all that ships and boats could do. He believed that the Confederates could not be pried out of Vicksburg "so long as they have the military force to hold the back country," meaning the railroad connection to Jackson. Wresting control of the "back country" away from the Rebels clearly was a job for the army. Unfortunately Union military forces in the West were stretched dangerously thin. In a sense the Federals were hamstrung by their own success. The enormous swath of Confederate territory conquered during the spring and early summer required an immense occupation force. Neither Halleck nor Butler had any men to spare.[2]

Secretary of the Navy Gideon Welles ordered Farragut to withdraw to New Orleans. Welles reasoned that the West Gulf Blockading Squadron had accomplished much despite being out of its element. He would not continue to expose the ships and men to danger unless there was something concrete to be gained. Even before he received the order, Farragut decided on his own that it was time for him to go. Sickness among both sailors and soldiers had risen to alarming proportions, and the level of the Mississippi was dropping. This was a normal occurrence in late summer and fall that posed a particularly serious danger to Farragut's deep-draft warships.

On the eve of Farragut's departure, the Union navy was involved in one of the most memorable episodes of the struggle for control of the Mississippi River. For weeks the Federals had picked up rumors that the Confederates were building an ironclad gunboat somewhere up the Yazoo River. The vessel in question was the *Arkansas,* which had been towed to safety before the capture of Memphis. Farragut was particularly anxious about this matter, for his ships had survived a brush with the *Manassas* and the unfinished ironclads at New Orleans, and he had a fair idea of just how formidable such vessels could be. But the shallow, winding Yazoo flowed into the Mississippi several miles above Vicksburg. The *Arkansas,* therefore, was the Western Flotilla's responsibility.

During the last week of June, while waiting for Davis to arrive from the north, the energetic Colonel Ellet took two rams a short distance up the Yazoo. The Confederates panicked and burned three boats, including the only survivor of the fight at Memphis. Ellet did not encounter the *Arkansas,* which was still being fitted out at Yazoo City above a protective floating barrier, but his probe spurred the Confederates to bring the ironclad out as quickly as possible, lest she be trapped and destroyed by a more powerful Union expedition.

Two weeks later, on July 15, Davis did exactly the sort of thing the Confederates were worried about. He sent a tiny flotilla of three mismatched boats—the ironclad *Carondelet*, timberclad *Tyler*, and ram *Queen of the West*—on another probe up the Yazoo under the command of Capt. Henry Walke. If Davis hoped to obtain information about the elusive Confederate ironclad, then the expedition was a complete success. A short distance above Old River, sailors on the leading Union boat saw a low-lying vessel steaming toward them. Walke had found the *Arkansas*.

After leaving Memphis and experiencing various misadventures, the *Arkansas* had been completed at Yazoo City under the direction of its commander, Lt. Isaac N. Brown, one of the most effective officers in the Confederate navy. Like all Confederate ironclads the *Arkansas* reflected the weak industrial base of the Southern economy. Boatrights in Memphis had produced a strong wooden hull and superstructure, but the engines and drive train within were weak and unreliable. Iron plating was unavailable, so the boat was covered with rails taken up from abandoned railroads. Even paint was lacking in the backwoods of Mississippi, and the rust-colored armor, stack, anchors, and other iron components gave the vessel a distinctive mottled reddish-brown appearance. Despite her flaws, which were considerable, the *Arkansas* was a formidable craft, and Farragut was right to be wary of her.

Back in Vicksburg Van Dorn was beside himself with frustration at being forced to maintain a passive defensive posture. He was desperate to strike a blow at the dozens of Union vessels lying above and below the town. On June 24, the day Farragut and Ellet made contact, he urged Brown to bring the *Arkansas* to Vicksburg to smite the Yankees. A master of the melodramatic phrase, Van Dorn appealed to valor and referred to the ignoble fate of the Confederate ironclads at Memphis and New Orleans in a single sentence. "It is better to die game and do some execution than to lie by and be burned up in the Yazoo." Three weeks passed before Brown felt his vessel was ready to "do some execution." On July 14 the Confederate ironclad got up steam and proceeded downstream. Neither captain nor crew knew what to expect from their untried craft.[3]

The next day, July 15, the *Arkansas* resumed its progress down the Yazoo. About ten miles from the Mississippi River, the ironclad encountered Walke's three boats probing upstream. Brown did not hesitate but proceeded directly toward the enemy. Walke panicked and lost control of his flotilla. The Union boats turned around and fled in disorder. The *Arkansas* caught up with the *Carondelet* and drove the slow-moving ironclad into the bank, then hurried after the other two vessels, firing shot after shot through their wooden superstructures. The timberclad *Tyler* put up a remarkable fight with her single stern gun. She wrecked the *Arkansas*'s pilothouse and tore the stack away from the boilers. The interior of the ironclad filled with smoke, and she lost most of her speed. Pursued and pursuer entered the Mississippi and churned downriver toward the Union anchorage on the west side of De Soto Point.

The *Arkansas* rounded a bend and found itself among the Union warships and gunboats lining both banks of the Mississippi. Most of the vessels did not have steam up because of a shortage of coal and were unable to move. The *Arkansas* plowed slowly through the anchorage, firing left and right, while Union gunners tried to hit the low-lying ironclad without striking their comrades. It was all over within thirty minutes. Several Union vessels suffered hits, including one ram that was struck in the steam drum and suffered numerous casualties. Although the *Arkansas* did not emerge unscathed, her armor plating was buckled and dislodged by the hail of shot, she did make it around De Soto Point and reached the safety of Vicksburg.

Van Dorn watched the latter stages of the running fight from the tower of the Warren County Courthouse. Thousands of less privileged spectators lined the bluffs and climbed atop other buildings. Van Dorn was so excited he rushed down to the river and rowed out to congratulate Brown before the ironclad tied up along the wharves. The *Arkansas* had made its long-awaited appearance and had done so in the most dramatic manner possible. In a single stroke Union naval superiority on the Mississippi had been neutralized, or so it seemed. The affair was the talk of the town. "Every one is elated and astonished at the daring achievement," noted a Mississippi artilleryman.[4]

Davis was philosophical about the episode, but Farragut was embarrassed and infuriated. He feared that the *Arkansas* would attack the mortar schooners and transports anchored below Vicksburg, which were protected by only a handful of warships. Farragut was no less a man of action than Van Dorn or Brown, and he decided to return past Vicksburg that very evening and sink or seriously damage the ironclad while she lay immobile. At the very least the presence of his warships below Vicksburg would prevent the *Arkansas* from rampaging downstream.

Shortly after sunset on July 15, the Union ships and the ram *Sumter* rounded De Soto Point and steamed past Vicksburg. Farragut had planned to make his move when the setting sun would be in the eyes of the defenders, but delays prevented his fleet from going into action until twilight, when the rusty *Arkansas* was almost invisible against the east bank. "I looked with all the eyes in my head to no purpose," reported Farragut. "We could see nothing but the flash of the enemy's guns to fire at."Van Dorn had guessed that Farragut might attempt such a maneuver and had every cannoneer at his station as the sun sank. A tremendous exchange of fire erupted between ships and shore batteries. Farragut passed the town safely, but darkness and smoke prevented his vessels from striking the *Arkansas* a fatal blow.[5]

Davis declined to join in the attack. "I think patience as great a virtue as boldness," he wrote Farragut. Davis believed that tackling the *Arkansas* while she lay protected under the batteries of Vicksburg was a poor tactical decision. He thought it better to wait for the ironclad to emerge and then engage her with the combined guns and prows of the entire Western Flotilla or West Gulf Blockading Squadron. Nevertheless, after some prodding from Farragut, Davis agreed to a limited follow-up action.[6]

On July 22 Ellet, in the ram *Queen of the West,* and Cmdr. William D. Porter (brother of David Porter and foster brother of Farragut), in the ironclad *Essex,* set out in an attempt to ram the stationary Rebel boat. As they rounded De Soto Point and approached the Vicksburg wharves, the Union vessels were buffeted by powerful eddies and pounded by Confederate guns, but both managed to strike glancing blows against the *Arkansas.* Firing at pointblank range the *Essex* also sent several solid shot smashing through the ironclad's armor. The agile *Queen of the West* returned upstream to the Western Flotilla, but the ponderous *Essex* joined Farragut below town. Like all of the underpowered Union ironclads, the *Essex* could barely stem the current of the Mississippi. If she had tried to inch her way back upstream, she would have been a nearly stationary target for Confederate gunners.

"The whole thing was a fizzle," exclaimed a disappointed Union officer. But while Farragut and Davis failed to sink the Confederate ironclad, the repeated hammering took a toll on her crew, hull, armor, and machinery. After the *Essex* disappeared downstream amid a torrent of shell splashes, Lieutenant Brown had only twenty officers and men left on their feet, barely enough to serve two of the *Arkansas*'s guns. The hull was holed, planks were sprung, and many of the railroad tracks bolted to the casemate were broken, buckled, or knocked loose. Even more alarming was the condition of the ironclad's rickety propulsion system. The engines had never worked properly; now after the stresses and shocks of the past few days, they hardly worked at all. Two weeks passed before the battered Confederate ironclad was back in anything resembling fighting shape, and she never again had more than a skeleton crew.[7]

Both the excitable Farragut and the cerebral Davis were correct in their analyses of the situation. The mere existence of the *Arkansas* had a strong psychological effect on all concerned. Both sides imbued the rattletrap ironclad with an importance wildly out of proportion to its actual capabilities. In this sense Farragut was correct in attempting to destroy the *Arkansas* at the earliest possible moment, or at the very least demonstrate the Union navy's willingness to engage her under even the most unfavorable circumstances, lest she become a war vessel of mythical power. Certainly Van Dorn viewed the ironclad as a gift of the gods and did all he could to use her as a rallying point for the defense of Vicksburg and a means of reasserting control of the Mississippi. Davis's cooler appraisal was based on a reasonably accurate assessment of the *Arkansas*'s capabilities. His view that the ironclad would prove to be vulnerable as soon as she ventured away from Vicksburg turned out to be correct.

With nothing more to do, Farragut picked up General Williams's sadly depleted infantry brigade and withdrew once again to New Orleans. There he learned that he had been promoted to rear admiral for his passage of Forts Jackson and St. Philip and capture of the Crescent City. It was a singular honor: Farragut was the first admiral in the history of the U.S. Navy. He received the news with mixed feelings after what he considered to be his failures at Vicksburg.

While proceeding downstream, Farragut landed Williams and his soldiers at Baton Rouge. To support Williams he detached William Porter with the ironclad *Essex,* the ram *Sumter,* and three warships. Porter's primary responsibility was to cover the Union garrison and keep an eye out for the *Arkansas.* He also was encouraged to patrol the miles of winding river between Baton Rouge and Vicksburg in order to disrupt the flow of men and supplies between the two halves of the Confederacy. It was a very large assignment for a handful of ships and boats, one of which (*Essex*) was of limited mobility. It turned out that Farragut had gained the services of a second foster-brother only to lose the services of the first. David Porter and his mortar schooners were called to the James River in Virginia to take part in Maj. Gen. George B. McClellan's ill-fated attempt to capture Richmond, temporarily removing that industrious officer from the Mississippi River.

Shortly after Farragut's departure from Vicksburg, Davis pulled the

Western Flotilla back to the mouth of the Yazoo River. While sweltering on the Yazoo and accomplishing nothing of significance, he learned that Curtis and his army had emerged from the wilds of Arkansas and on July 12 occupied Helena, located on the only high ground along the west bank of the Mississippi between Missouri and the Gulf of Mexico. In late July Davis withdrew upriver to refit. He stationed some of his gunboats at Helena to provide support for its isolated Union garrison. For the next twelve months Helena would be the southernmost permanent Union enclave on the Mississippi above Vicksburg.

After a series of stunning successes, the overextended Union forces on the Mississippi River had failed by a slim margin to cut the Confederacy in half. Combat casualties at Vicksburg were modest, but losses due to illness in the subtropical climate were staggering. Indeed the real enemy for soldiers and sailors on both sides in the Mississippi Valley throughout the war was disease, primarily malaria but also a host of "camp diseases" such as dysentery and typhoid. The Union troops mired in the swamps of De Soto Point suffered the most, but the Confederate soldiers on the bluffs across the river were in miserable straits themselves. Forty percent of Van Dorn's men were ill by the time Farragut and Davis withdrew. "The condition of our men is truly deplorable—all sick and I am pretty bad," observed a disheartened member of the Nineteenth Tennessee.[8]

Despite this somber state of affairs, Van Dorn seized the initiative. He recognized that Vicksburg was of limited strategic importance. Confederate possession of the town denied Union warships free use of the Mississippi but did little else. Vicksburg was a strongpoint, and that was the problem: Confederate control of the Mississippi was limited to the stretch of water within range of the town's batteries. Supplies from the trans-Mississippi flowed down the Red River then up the Mississippi to the wharves at Vicksburg, where the tracks of the Southern Railroad began their journey eastward. Recent events had demonstrated that this traffic could be interdicted whenever Union ships at New Orleans or Baton Rouge ventured above the confluence of the Red and the Mississippi. Van Dorn felt it was a "matter of great necessity to us" that the tenuous all-water link between Vicksburg and Shreveport be kept open and free from interruption.[9]

To accomplish this the general believed that the Confederacy had to maintain *two* strongpoints along the Mississippi, one above and one below the mouth of the Red. Vicksburg was the northern anchor, and it seemed to Van Dorn that Baton Rouge was the obvious place to establish the southern anchor. The mouth of the Red lay about halfway between the two cities. Even more important, Baton Rouge was located atop the southernmost section of the long line of bluffs extending south along the river from Vicksburg. Finally, Baton Rouge was the capital of Louisiana, and its recovery would boost Southern morale. If strong Confederate fortifications could keep Farragut's ships below Baton Rouge and prevent any interruption of supplies flowing down the Red, the vital connection with the trans-Mississippi could be maintained and the damage of losing much of the Mississippi Valley would be substantially reduced. Van Dorn also believed that Baton Rouge would serve as a jumping-off point for a bid to liberate New Orleans.

Some of this was wishful thinking, to put it mildly. The bluffs at Baton Rouge are low and the river is wide, straight, and deep. Farragut's ships had twice run the batteries at Vicksburg under far more trying circumstances, and they probably could have steamed past any guns at Baton Rouge with impunity. Nevertheless, Van Dorn was right to attempt to roll back Union gains along the lower Mississippi before they could be consolidated. Butler's small military force in and around New Orleans was stretched thin to begin with, and disease was felling hundreds of Union soldiers every week.

President Davis approved of Van Dorn's assessment of the strategic situation and his proposed solution. "The importance of the object at which you aim cannot be overestimated," Davis wrote. On July 26 Van Dorn directed Maj. Gen. John C. Breckinridge to "dislodge" the sickly Union garrison at Baton Rouge, which was composed largely of General Williams's worn-out, ditch-digging infantry.[10]

Breckinridge and four thousand troops rattled down the railroad from Jackson to Camp Moore, Louisiana, about sixty miles northeast of Baton Rouge. The Confederate cantonment was flooded by torrential rains, and the Rebels fell ill in droves. When the water receded enough to allow Breckinridge to slog toward Baton Rouge through a miasma of heat and humidity, he had only about twenty-five hundred men able to shoulder a musket and totter forward into battle. The coming fight would be a struggle between two contingents of invalids.

Breckinridge watched with dismay as his command melted away, then he learned that the Union garrison in Baton Rouge was supported by five naval vessels. Casting about for some way to improve the odds, he hit upon the idea of launching a simultaneous attack on Baton Rouge by land and by river, telegraphing Van Dorn and asking him to send the *Arkansas* at once. If all went as planned, the rusty ironclad would scatter Porter's ships and boats while Breckinridge's troops overwhelmed Williams's soldiers and captured the capital. This was just the sort of high-risk, all-or-nothing gamble that Van Dorn found irresistible. He assured Breckinridge that the *Arkansas* would make an appearance on the appointed day.

Williams detected the Confederates' approach to Baton Rouge. He deployed his twenty-five hundred men on the east side of the city to await the onslaught. If pressed, Williams planned to fall back to a fortified position overlooking the Mississippi River, where he could be supported by Porter's flotilla. The general also picked up rumors that the *Arkansas* might participate in the attack and so informed Porter. Upon learning of this alarming possibility, Porter appealed to Farragut for help, then prepared to engage the Confederates on land, on water, or both as circumstances dictated.

On the foggy morning of August 5, Breckinridge struck the center of the Union position. For a time the Confederates gained ground, pressing the Federals back into the eastern suburbs of Baton Rouge, but mounting casualties slowed their advance. Williams was killed midway through the battle, but his troops continued to resist stubbornly. As the day wore on, Breckinridge awaited some sign that the *Arkansas* had arrived. He finally gave up and withdrew. Like so many Civil War engagements, the clash at Baton Rouge was a bloody tactical draw. The Union defenders suffered 383 casualties; the Confederates, 467.

The next day Breckinridge learned why the *Arkansas* had failed to support his assault. Van Dorn tended to ignore inconvenient facts and rush ahead, but on this occasion he outdid himself. As soon as he received Breckinridge's request for the *Arkansas*, Van Dorn directed the vessel to depart at once for Baton Rouge. The battered ironclad was in the midst of repairs, without her captain and chief engineer, manned by a skeleton crew, and would have to travel 270 miles in only thirty hours. Nevertheless, orders were orders, and the *Arkansas* steamed away from Vicksburg early on August 3 under the command of her first officer, Lt. Henry K. Stevens.

The rickety vessel experienced a host of mechanical problems during the voyage but still managed to reach the vicinity of Baton Rouge on the appointed day. Unfortunately this maritime miracle was achieved by racing the engines at top speed between breakdowns. Just north of Baton Rouge the propulsion system disintegrated and the pilot nosed the

*Arkansas* into the west bank of the river. The crew worked through the night to repair the engines and drive train but to no avail. As soon as one part was repaired or replaced, another failed. The next day, August 6, William Porter inched upstream in the *Essex*, drawing ever closer to the strangely inert Confederate warship. The two ironclads exchanged several shots at long range, but neither scored any hits. Seeing that the situation was hopeless, Stevens ordered the crew ashore and set the *Arkansas* afire. Thus ended the career of the only operational Confederate ironclad in the West. She was in active service twenty-three days.

Disappointed by the dismal turn of events, Van Dorn remained determined to secure the mouth of the Red River. If Baton Rouge could not be made the southern anchor of a defensive corridor, then another place would have to do. On August 13, a week after the battle, Van Dorn settled on the village of Port Hudson, sixteen miles north of Baton Rouge, and directed Breckinridge to march his depleted command to that point. It turned out that Breckinridge had come to the same conclusion a day earlier. "Port Hudson is one of the strongest points on the Mississippi (which Baton Rouge is not)," he informed Van Dorn, "and batteries there will command the river more completely than at Vicksburg." Confederate soldiers occupied Port Hudson in mid-August and began constructing artillery positions on the bluffs overlooking the Mississippi.[11]

When Farragut learned of the Confederate attack on Baton Rouge and the expected appearance of the *Arkansas,* he immediately steamed north from New Orleans with every available warship, determined to catch the ironclad in the broad river and destroy her. It is easy to imagine his relief and satisfaction—and perhaps even his disappointment—when he reached Baton Rouge and learned that the ironclad was no more.

Ironically Van Dorn's unsuccessful lunge at Baton Rouge and his subsequent occupation of Port Hudson caused Benjamin Butler to consolidate his forces around New Orleans. The Federals evacuated Baton Rouge on August 21. The garrison thoughtfully boxed up the books of the Louisiana State Library and carried them to New Orleans for safekeeping. They also removed a statue of George Washington from the statehouse and sent it to New York, with instructions that it should be "held in trust for the people of Louisiana until they shall have returned to their senses." The West Gulf Blockading Squadron, accompanied by the *Essex* and *Sumter,* escorted the Union transports downstream to New Orleans.[12]

By the summer of 1862 Union political and military leaders were gaining a better idea of what would be required to achieve their goals in the West. Confederate authorities also were able to see where their energy and resources should be directed in the future. Despite experiencing a string of defeats and disasters across the vast region, the Confederates had established a broad corridor across the Mississippi anchored by two formidable defensive positions at Vicksburg and Port Hudson. For the next ten months Vicksburg and Port Hudson would be the focus of an intensifying struggle for the Mississippi Valley.

# CHAPTER THREE

# On to Vicksburg

In the North events were gathering speed. President Lincoln appointed Henry Halleck general in chief of the Union army in July 1862. Before leaving for the East Halleck divided his department, placing Maj. Gen. Ulysses Grant in command of the District of West Tennessee on the east side of the Mississippi River and Samuel Curtis in charge of the Department of the Missouri on the west side.

Grant was a West Point graduate and Mexican War veteran who had resigned from the army in 1854 because he disliked being separated from his family. He had not prospered in civilian life and was working as a clerk in his father's store in Galena, Illinois, when the Civil War broke out. The Union needed men with military experience, and Grant soon found himself back in a blue uniform. He demonstrated a strong aggressive streak that resulted in the capture of Forts Henry and Donelson, the first great Union triumph of the war. Grant was surprised and nearly defeated at Shiloh, which temporarily left him under a cloud, but his accomplishments brought him to the attention of the Lincoln administration.

The District of West Tennessee encompassed the southern tip of Illinois, all of Kentucky and Tennessee between the Mississippi and Tennessee Rivers, and a swath of northern Mississippi; it included over fifty thousand troops, most of whom were stationed between Memphis and Corinth along the Tennessee-Mississippi line. Grant's primary mission was to keep the Confederates away from the network of railroads that linked Memphis, Corinth, Columbus, Paducah, and other key points in western Kentucky and Tennessee. This was a defensive assignment, and Grant hated it, for he was by nature one of the most offensive-minded commanders on either side in the Civil War.

His Confederate counterpart was the equally offensive-minded Earl Van Dorn, who commanded the Department of Southern Mississippi and East Louisiana from Vicksburg. In September Gen. Braxton Bragg launched a major Confederate counteroffensive into central Tennessee and Kentucky, the region occupied by Maj. Gen. Don Carlos Buell. Bragg asked Van Dorn to keep Grant busy and prevent him from sending reinforcements north. The Mississippian was only too happy to oblige. He hoped not merely to distract Grant but also to recover Corinth and drive the Federals out of Mississippi altogether. Van Dorn led about six thousand men north from Vicksburg to rendezvous with Maj. Gen. Sterling Price's seventeen thousand troops in the northeast corner of the state.

Sensing an opportunity Grant struck before the Confederates could join forces. He attempted to trap Price with a two-pronged attack. On September 19 Maj. Gen. William S. Rosecrans and nine thousand men hit Price near Iuka, twenty-five miles east of Corinth. Maj. Gen. Edward O. C. Ord and eight thousand additional Union soldiers were poised to march into Price's rear while he was engaged with Rosecrans, but because of a phenomenon called "acoustic shadow," they failed to hear the roar of battle only a few miles away and remained idle. Price withdrew after several hours of hard fighting and eventually joined Van Dorn near Tupelo. Losses at Iuka were about 1,560 men killed, wounded, and missing on the Confederate side and 825 casualties on the Union side.

Grant was certain the Confederates would make another attempt to dislodge his forces from Mississippi. Van Dorn did not disappoint. The Rebel commander moved north from Tupelo toward the railroad junction at Corinth with twenty-two thousand men. Grant rushed Rosecrans back from Iuka and poured in reinforcements until the Union garrison totaled twenty-three thousand men. Rosecrans strengthened the extensive earthworks thrown up by the Confederates earlier in the year and constructed a second ring of fortifications near the center of town. Unaware of these defensive preparations, Van Dorn swung around to the northwest side of town, hoping that an attack from that direction would take the Federals by surprise.

On October 3 the Confederates assaulted the outer line of earthworks. After hours of intense fighting they drove the Union defenders back to the inner line of fortifications, which they did not know existed. The next day they resumed the attack but were repulsed with horrendous losses. Corinth was one of the most severe battles of the war. Van Dorn's army lost more than 4,800 men killed, wounded, and missing, a casualty rate of over 20 percent. Rosecrans's force fought from behind earthworks much of the time but still suffered 2,350 casualties.

The mangled Confederate army staggered away toward the Hatchie River, its morale shattered and many of its finest men left behind in front of the fatal fortifications. Coming so soon after the bloodletting at Baton Rouge and Iuka, the dreadful affair at Corinth was the last hurrah for Confederate forces holding the Vicksburg–Port Hudson corridor; never again would they muster the strength to take the offensive.

Van Dorn's defeat in northern Mississippi was overshadowed by the even greater Confederate failure in Kentucky, where Bragg's offensive came to naught after a dramatic push northward to within a day's march of the Ohio River. Following a confused and costly battle at Perryville, Kentucky, on October 8, Bragg abandoned Kentucky and withdrew into south-central Tennessee. The Rebels regrouped at Murfreesboro while Union forces returned to Nashville. After six weeks of immense effort on the part of the Confederates, the strategic situation in the West was essentially unchanged. The only high-ranking officers on either side who emerged from these affairs with their reputations enhanced, or at least intact, were Grant and Rosecrans.

In late October Halleck removed the inept Buell and placed Rosecrans in charge of the Department of the Cumberland. Halleck rewarded Grant by transforming the District of West Tennessee into the Department of the Tennessee. Grant's new command extended as far south as he could push his army and potentially included all of the Mississippi Valley north of the Union enclave around New Orleans, which was rather grandly termed the Department of the Gulf. He was authorized to draw upon troops and supplies in Curtis's Department of the Missouri as needed. After several months of holding his ground and responding to Confederate moves, Grant was free to resume offensive operations. Once again in his element, he organized an overland campaign against Vicksburg.

Grant's plan was simplicity itself. The Army of the Tennessee would advance south along the route of the Mississippi Central Railroad toward Jackson, forty miles east of Vicksburg. The Southern Railroad of Mississippi, the vital east-west line that linked Vicksburg with the rest of the Confederacy, passed through the Mississippi capital. Grant believed that its capture would compel the Confederates to evacuate Vicksburg, just as the Union advance earlier in the year up the Tennessee River to Corinth had caused the progressive abandonment of Columbus, Fort Pillow, and

Memphis. With Jackson in Union hands, Vicksburg would be cut off from supplies and reinforcements. If the Confederates failed to abandon their position, Grant would swing west and approach the Hill City from the rear.

There were some unsettling aspects to Grant's plan. An overland route required the Army of the Tennessee to cross several substantial rivers flowing west to the Mississippi, notably the Tallahatchie and Yalobusha. Each was a natural obstacle and a potential moat. Perhaps even more daunting was the certainty that the Confederates would destroy the Mississippi Central Railroad as they fell back, forcing the Union army to rebuild the tracks every step of the way. If the Confederates were thorough and tenacious, the campaign would be slow and costly.

By advancing on a narrow front—a single railroad—with two vulnerable flanks, Grant departed dramatically from his previous experience in the war, wherein he had quickly transported his troops by water to Belmont, Forts Henry and Donelson, and Pittsburg Landing. If he underestimated the hazards of a sustained offensive dependent entirely on a railroad for logistical support, it was because he was the first commander in history to attempt such a thing. Grant had no precedent to rely on, for it was still relatively early in the war, and no one knew what could or could not be accomplished with railroads. He apparently felt that the Confederates were so demoralized by their recent losses that his forces could push forward along the Mississippi Central Railroad without much resistance. Hoping for the best but preparing for the worst, Grant established working parties to repair the tracks and rebuild bridges and culverts and prepared to detach troops to guard every water tank, wood yard, and supply depot.

The Confederates, meanwhile, were making changes of their own. Van Dorn's costly blunders at Pea Ridge and Corinth, coupled with political missteps and a scandalous personal life, finally proved too much even for his old friend in the Confederate White House. In October President Davis removed Van Dorn and replaced him with John C. Pemberton, commander of the Charleston coastal defenses. A Pennsylvania native who had married a Virginia woman, Pemberton was a West Point graduate and professional soldier who preferred staff work to duty in the field. His only apparent qualification for such a critical post was his friendship with Davis. Newly promoted to lieutenant general, Pemberton hurried west and assumed command of the expanded Department of Mississippi and East Louisiana.

Pemberton discovered that he was blessed with several able subordinates. Foremost among them was Martin Smith, the military engineer
whom Lovell had sent to Vicksburg the previous May. Smith continued
to construct artillery positions along the Mississippi River throughout
the spring and summer of 1862, then turned his attention to building
landward defenses. He reasoned that because the Union navy had failed
to take Vicksburg, the next effort would be made by the Union army.

Smith assigned Maj. Samuel H. Lockett, another capable military
engineer, the task of constructing a semicircular line of earthworks around
Vicksburg. Lockett was aghast at the enormity of the task. The terrain was
rugged beyond description; hillsides were covered by dense forests, and
ravines were choked with canebrakes. "No greater topographical puzzle
was ever presented to an engineer," he declared. Lockett labored for weeks
to gain some understanding of how the land lay, which proved to be
nearly vertical in places. The base of the escarpment on the east bank of
the Mississippi is limestone, but the bluffs above are composed of a fine
yellowish soil called loess that erodes in such a way as to produce a maze
of steep, narrow ridges and deep, twisting defiles. The resulting terrain
has no pattern but is simply a jumble of high and low places. It is a strange
landscape found almost nowhere else in North America.[1]

Lockett eventually plotted an irregular line of earthworks that wrung
every possible tactical advantage out of the dizzying landscape. Construction commenced in September 1862 and was well underway when
Pemberton arrived. Picks and shovels were in short supply, but since loess
is soft, the work progressed at a satisfactory pace. Hired or impressed
slaves provided most of the manpower. When completed the semicircular
line was about eight miles in length and anchored on the Mississippi River
both above and below Vicksburg. It was basically a trench and parapet
fronted by a ditch for most of its length. Dozens of artillery positions
were located along the arc, and nine large earthen forts guarded the gaps
where the Southern Railroad of Mississippi and a half-dozen roads passed
through. Thousands of trees were cut down to clear a field of fire for the
defenders and create a vast tangled abatis (the preindustrial equivalent of
barbed wire) to slow attackers and break up their formations. Lockett's
line was an impressive example of military engineering, but many of the
ridges were too narrow to permit a defense in depth. This meant that
if the Confederates were driven out of their works, they would tumble
downhill into the town. The barrier of trenches and forts was both the
first and last line of defense.

In the months to come Smith and Lockett laid out additional positions to protect the Hill City's extended flanks. To prevent Union boats from reaching Yazoo City, fortifications were constructed at Haynes' Bluff, Snyder's Bluff, and Drumgould's Bluff along the Yazoo River twelve to fifteen miles north of Vicksburg. Earthworks also were thrown up at Warrenton and Grand Gulf along the Mississippi River below town. As fall faded into winter the Confederates prepared Vicksburg and its outposts for whatever the Federals might have in mind.

Early in November 1862 Grant and the Army of the Tennessee began moving south toward the Rebel position along the Tallahatchie River. Grant knew that Pemberton depended on the Mississippi Central Railroad for supplies just as much as he did. He also knew that the most vulnerable point on the railroad was the wooden bridge over the Yalobusha River at Grenada, sixty miles south of the Tallahatchie. If that bridge could be destroyed, the Confederate line of communications would be severed, and Pemberton would have to retreat.

On November 27 Brig. Gen. Alvin P. Hovey led seven thousand Union cavalry and infantry across the Mississippi River from Helena, Arkansas, to Friar's Point, Mississippi. Cold rains fell unceasingly and turned the countryside into a sea of mud, but Hovey persevered. When his infantry bogged down, he gambled and sent his cavalry splashing eastward toward the Mississippi Central Railroad. The Union horsemen tore up a section of track a few miles north of the Yalobusha but were unable to destroy the bridge, which not only was too wet to burn but also was guarded by a swelling force of Confederates. On December 7 Hovey withdrew to Helena, his weary soldiers followed by over five hundred refugee slaves, who undoubtedly were in a more upbeat mood.

Hovey's unheralded raid was not a success, but it demonstrated the importance of Grant's authority to make use of Union forces stationed across the Mississippi River in Arkansas and Missouri. Pemberton, by contrast, could not issue orders to Confederates along the west bank of the Mississippi, which would cost him dearly in the months to come. The operation also demonstrated that audacity was not confined to soldiers in gray. Far too much is made of Confederate cavalry raids in the Civil War, especially in the sparsely settled West, where mobile columns appeared without warning and disappeared just as quickly. Union raids also were common in the theater and often were just as dramatic and destructive as their Confederate counterparts, though they have attracted far less attention from historians. Hovey's raid was one of the first Federal strikes deep into enemy territory. It would not be the last.

The incursion awakened Pemberton to the vulnerability of his line of communications. In early December, much to Grant's surprise and delight, the Confederates abandoned their fortifications along the Talla-hatchie River and fell back sixty miles to Grenada. Soldiers and slaves spread out along the south bank of the Yalobusha and constructed new earthworks in sight of the slightly scorched railroad bridge. The Federals trudged southward in the wake of the retiring Rebels.

The campaign was off to a good start, but Grant soon was distracted by rumors of political machinations deep in his own rear. By the fall of 1862 the Mississippi River had been closed for eighteen months. Even though the volume of east-west commerce on the railroads connecting the Midwest and the Atlantic coast grew every year, the importance of the Mississippi as the principal artery of trade for Midwestern merchants and farmers was not only still very real but also had assumed mythic proportions. The Union naval victories in the spring and summer had raised hopes that the river soon would be open to the Gulf, but the failure to take Vicksburg and the apparent Confederate resurgence in the fall were severe blows to Midwestern morale. Congressmen, governors, and editors from Ohio to Iowa demanded that more be done. The result was a classic demonstration of the relationship between political, economic, and military matters in war, particularly civil war.

Maj. Gen. John A. McClernand was an ambitious Democratic politi-cian and a talented amateur soldier from Illinois. He had demonstrated courage and ability at Fort Donelson and Shiloh, but he chafed at being subordinate to Grant. Aware of the growing dissatisfaction in the Midwest with the progress of the war, he saw an opportunity to garner a large measure of military glory and political capital. In mid-1862 McClernand proposed to Lincoln that he raise a force of Midwestern troops and personally lead them down the Mississippi River to Vicksburg. Halleck opposed creating a force outside the normal military channels and giving it to an amateur like McClernand, but Lincoln was frustrated by the sluggish pace of operations in the West after Shiloh. He was willing to experiment with anything that might achieve military success and encourage his supporters in the Midwest.

McClernand got what he wanted, or so it seemed, but at a cost. He earned Halleck's implacable hostility, which was bad enough, and also inadvertently cemented an alliance between Halleck and Grant. During

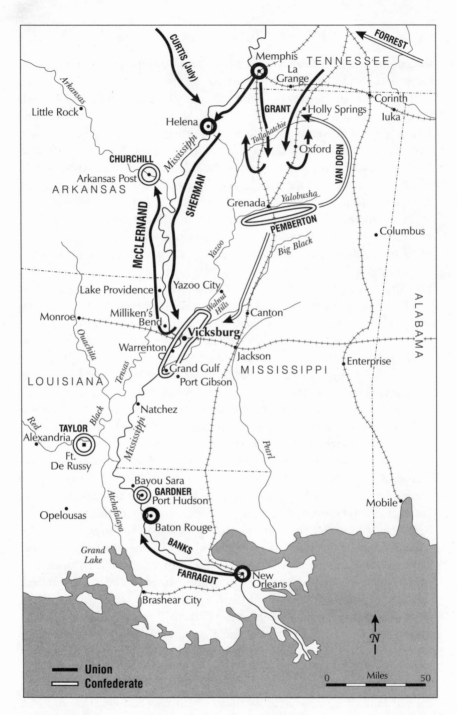

Union operations: November 1862–January 1863

the first year of the war, Halleck had developed a low opinion of his rumpled lieutenant and on more than one occasion had tried to shunt him aside. Halleck now recognized that Grant, a fellow West Pointer, was the only bulwark against McClernand. Lincoln had approved a special operation, at least in principle, but in drafting the orders for that operation, Halleck and Secretary of War Edwin Stanton deftly circumscribed McClernand's authority. He was directed to proceed to the Midwest, raise new regiments, and send them to Memphis. McClernand naturally assumed that he would command the troops he had raised, but Grant's instructions permitted him to use every soldier stationed in or passing through the Department of the Tennessee, which included Memphis. When it came to bureaucratic infighting, McClernand was no match for the general in chief.

Grant was puzzled by talk of another offensive against Vicksburg and asked Halleck for clarification: "Am I to understand that I lay still here while an Expedition is fitted out from Memphis or do you want me to push as far South as possible?" Halleck's reply was cryptic but reassuring: "You have command of all troops sent to your Department, and have permission to fight the enemy when you please." Grant had no trouble reading between the lines. He decided to commandeer McClernand's newly raised regiments and launch a waterborne expedition of his own against Vicksburg, placing Maj. Gen. William T. Sherman in charge of the hastily organized operation. Sherman was tall, talkative, politically naive, and so mercurial that friends and family wondered about his sanity. Although a West Point graduate, his uneven military record did not inspire confidence. Grant, for whatever reason, thought highly of Sherman. Perhaps he recognized Sherman's potential or perhaps simply valued Sherman's patriotism and personal loyalty. The Northern war effort often was hamstrung by personal ambition and political maneuvering (witness McClernand), but Grant trusted Sherman to do his best and what was best for the country.[2]

The expedition was modeled after Grant's successful campaigns against Forts Henry and Donelson. Sherman would pack about thirty-three thousand men (twenty thousand from the Army of the Tennessee and thirteen thousand from the Helena garrison) aboard a flotilla of transports and proceed down the Mississippi and then up the Yazoo River to Haynes' Bluff, about fifteen miles north of Vicksburg. After gaining the high ground the Federals would move inland between Vicksburg and Jackson and cut the Southern Railroad. The new plan had its merits, but once

Sherman went down the Mississippi, he and Grant would be separated by hundreds of miles of Confederate-held territory. They would not be able to coordinate their movements or support one another in a crisis. Pemberton would have the advantage of interior lines, that is, the ability to shift his troops back and forth between Grenada and Vicksburg on the railroads. Nonetheless Grant was cautiously optimistic. He also was in a hurry and ordered Sherman to get underway as soon as possible. In his memoirs Grant was frank about the reason for such haste; "I feared that delay might bring McClernand."[3]

In order for Sherman's descent on Vicksburg to succeed, Grant had to fix the Confederate army in place at Grenada. He decided not to crowd Pemberton until he learned whether Sherman had gained a lodgment at Haynes' Bluff. "The enemy are as yet on the Yalabusha," he informed Sherman in mid-December. "I am pushing down towards them slowly, but so as to keep up the impression of a continuous move."[4]

Grant's approach to the Vicksburg problem had evolved rapidly in only a few months. He no longer was wedded to the idea of an overland thrust across Mississippi or to any particular plan. His thinking at this stage was essentially opportunistic. If Pemberton stood his ground at Grenada, Grant would give the impression of preparing for battle and thus allow Sherman to seize Haynes' Bluff. If Pemberton fell back from Grenada or sent substantial reinforcements to Vicksburg, Grant would force his way across the Yalobusha, pummel Pemberton, and threaten the Hill City from the rear.

Vicksburg was the critical stage in Grant's development as a soldier. During the long, frustrating campaign his characteristic determination and aggressiveness remained as strong as ever, but he demonstrated that he was learning to anticipate difficulties and adjust his plans as circumstances dictated. These skills first appeared during the overland movement across Mississippi, and they marked Grant's evolution from a fighter to a general.

While Sherman crowded men, animals, and stores aboard a fleet of transports at Memphis, Grant continued to advance along the Mississippi Central Railroad. He described his situation to his sister. "I am extended now like a Peninsula into an enemies country with a large Army depending for their daily bread upon keeping open a line of railroad runing [*sic*] one hundred and ninety miles through an enemy's country, or at least through territory occupied by a people terribly embittered and hostile to us." In mid-December the Federals reached Oxford, fifty miles inside Mississippi.[5]

Grant soon received welcome news from Halleck, who directed him to divide the Army of the Tennessee into four corps: the Thirteenth Corps under McClernand, the Fifteenth Corps under Sherman, the Sixteenth Corps under Maj. Gen. Stephen A. Hurlbut, and the Seventeenth Corps under Maj. Gen. James B. McPherson. While Grant did not relish the thought of McClernand as a subordinate, Halleck's order meant that the previously uncertain relationship between the two western generals was clarified. Grant informed McClernand of his reduced authority and of the imminent departure of the Vicksburg expedition under Sherman's command, but McClernand did not receive the message due to disruptions caused by Confederate cavalry raids. This snafu led to confusion and bad feelings in the weeks ahead.

Unaware that anything was amiss, Grant remained with McPherson's and Hurlbut's corps on the Mississippi Central Railroad in northern Mississippi. Sherman prepared to proceed down the Mississippi River with his own corps and that of McClernand, who was still in Illinois and ignorant of the fact that "his" operation was unfolding without him. Grant's hastily formulated two-pronged offensive was proceeding smoothly. Only two days later everything was to change.

Lt. Col. John S. Griffith, a Texas cavalryman, suggested to Pemberton that a raid into Grant's rear might reach the Union supply depot at Holly Springs, about thirty miles north of Oxford. The loss of so much material would slow or even halt the Federal offensive. Pemberton recalled how close Hovey's raid against the Yalobusha River bridge had come to success, and he decided to act on Griffith's suggestion.

Pemberton had placed Van Dorn in command of the cavalry division. He now directed the general to destroy the depot at Holly Springs and spread destruction and confusion in the Union rear. For the only time in the war, Van Dorn was properly matched to an assignment. On December 17 he led thirty-five hundred mounted men across the Yalobusha and swung around to the east of Grant's army. The Confederate column thundered into Holly Springs at dawn on December 20 and quickly overran the unprepared Union garrison. Col. Robert C. Murphy surrendered his fifteen hundred men without putting up much of a fight; he was later dismissed from the army for cowardly and disgraceful behavior.

The jubilant Confederate horsemen were amazed at the cornucopia of clothing, weaponry, equipment, and food that lay before them. "Our whole Division helped themselves to as much clothing as they could wear & carry," wrote Capt. James C. Bates of the Ninth Texas Cavalry. "Almost every man fitted himself out in Yankee uniforms—boots, hats, caps, pants, shirts, overcoats &c & as far as uniforms went we were transformed into Yankee Cavalry. Besides the above we captured not less than 600 or 800 horses & mules—burned some 300 wagon loads of ammunition & after our men had picked out such arms as they preferred instead of their own we destroyed 6,000 or 7,000 stand of Enfield & Springfield Rifles— Six Shooters & Sharp's rifles went almost begging. The fact is I have never seen such destruction of property in so short a time." The orgy of confiscation and destruction continued all day and into the night.[6]

After leaving Holly Springs Van Dorn continued north, his men resplendent in their new blue uniforms. The Confederates reached Bolivar, Tennessee, before turning back. Van Dorn eluded pursuing Union cavalry and returned safely from his twelve-day foray. Each side lost about one hundred men killed and wounded in addition to the large number of Union prisoners captured and paroled at Holly Springs. The operation took place in abysmally wet winter weather that ruined equipment and wore out men and animals.

Van Dorn's raid probably would have been enough to halt Grant in his tracks, but unknown to Pemberton, a second Confederate foray was underway at the same time. Several weeks earlier Pemberton had asked Bragg to do something to distract Grant and relieve the pressure on his northern front. Bragg promised to help. And so it was that about the time Van Dorn rode out of Grenada, another Confederate cavalry force swept into western Tennessee from the east. Beginning on December 15 Brig. Gen. Nathan B. Forrest and twenty-five hundred men rampaged around in Grant's rear for nearly two weeks. The Confederates cut railroads and telegraph lines and generally raised havoc, but they almost stayed too long. At Parker's Cross Roads on December 31, Brig. Gen. Jeremiah Sullivan surprised Forrest and fought him to a draw. After riding three hundred miles in miserable weather, the hard-pressed Confederates fled to the safety of Bragg's lines on New Year's Day, 1863. The spectacular operation cost Union forces over fifteen hundred men, most of them captured and promptly paroled; the Confederates lost about five hundred men, two-thirds of them at Parker's Cross Roads.

This was the only occasion in the Civil War when cavalry alone determined the outcome of a major campaign. When Grant learned of the logistical disaster at Holly Springs and the damage done to the Mobile and Ohio Railroad in Tennessee, he abandoned his attempt to reach Vicksburg by marching overland across Mississippi. Van Dorn had destroyed his forward supply base; Forrest had made it impossible to rebuild that supply base for at least several months. Grant ordered a withdrawal of the Army of the Tennessee. As tens of thousands of Union soldiers, horses, and mules retraced their steps across northern Mississippi, they subsisted in large part on food and forage gathered from farms located within fifteen miles of the railroad. "I was amazed at the quantity of supplies the country afforded," Grant recalled two decades later.[7]

Its commander may have been the last man in the Army of the Tennessee to have gotten the word. Federal soldiers made use of local foodstuffs to supplement their rations throughout the campaign. "We cleen the country pretty well of provisions where we travel although there is plenty to eat in this part of the country," observed Capt. Lewis Eyman of the 116th Illinois. "We take all the cattle and hogs and sheep that we want and that is considerable. There is plenty of them where we have come and lots of sweet potatoes. . . . [N]early everything that we eat we get here in the country as we go along." During the withdrawal, Grant belatedly realized that a mobile army could sustain itself inside the Confederacy by organized foraging, particularly if the foraging took place in a region unspoiled by previous depredations. It was something worth keeping in mind.[8]

While his troops plodded north Grant pondered the advantages of moving the Army of the Tennessee down the Mississippi River to Vicksburg, leaving behind only the minimum force necessary to secure Memphis and Corinth against enemy raids. By returning to a familiar river-based mode of operations, Grant would have a more secure and efficient line of communications. And without a vulnerable railroad to protect, he would have more men available for combat operations. In other words the Army of the Tennessee would have a much shorter tail and much larger teeth. Grant concluded that success lay down the Father of Waters.

Having reached that conclusion Grant realized that he had to warn Sherman not to attack Haynes' Bluff. With the Federals pulling back from Grenada, Pemberton was free to shift his forces to meet another threat from a different direction. What happened next was aptly summed up by Grant in his memoirs: "Pemberton got back to Vicksburg before Sherman got there."[9]

# CHAPTER FOUR

# The First Onslaught

Sherman's expedition pulled away from Memphis on December 20, 1862. "Just leaving the city & streched out before me is one of the grandest spectakles to be seen," stated William Winters of the Sixty-seventh Indiana. Up and down the Mississippi River, as far as the young Hoosier could see, were sidewheelers and sternwheelers "with colors flying & covered with men all dressed in uniforms & cheering each other as they pass, a fitting sight for an artist's pencil." Additional transports jammed with soldiers from the Department of the Missouri joined the expedition at Helena, raising Sherman's strength to about thirty-two thousand men.[1]

South of Helena the armada of sixty transports caught up with the Mississippi Squadron, formerly the Western Flotilla. The new commander of this eclectic mix of ironclads, tinclads, timberclads, mortar boats, hospital boats, and supply boats was Acting Rear Adm. David Porter, back from operations in Virginia. When he took over from Flag Officer Charles Davis, Porter found the vessels worn down by months of campaigning in a subtropical climate. His first priority was to get men and equipment back into fighting trim. He commandeered hotels, evicted the guests, and established hospitals for sickly sailors. He refitted existing gunboats with additional armor, heavier guns, and improved equipment, and ordered the construction of dozens of tinclads, lightly armored small steamboats that could operate in very shallow water. Porter worked tirelessly, ignored bureaucratic procedures, bullied recalcitrant contractors and suppliers, and got things done. By December 1862 the Mississippi Squadron was in better condition than at any other time during the war.

Amid these preparations for what he was certain would be a sustained campaign against Vicksburg, Porter met with Grant and Sherman. The three officers quickly established an effective working relationship. It would take a concerted army-navy effort to capture Vicksburg, and the serendipitous mix of personalities among the top Union officers was of vital importance.

When Sherman asked Porter to explore the Yazoo River and locate a suitable landing site for the army near Haynes' Bluff, the admiral was agreeable. On December 12 Capt. Henry Walke sent a small flotilla up the Yazoo in search of mines (then called "torpedoes") and other obstructions. Disaster struck a short distance above the mouth of Chickasaw Bayou when the ironclad *Cairo* hit two mines and settled to the bottom of the river. No lives were lost, but the reduced flotilla withdrew to the Mississippi River and the operation called off. Walke's abortive reconnaissance-in-force was an unpromising start to Sherman's expedition. Not only did it cost Porter one of his trusty "turtles," but it also alerted the Confederates to the fact that the Yankees were interested in the Yazoo.

A week after the loss of the *Cairo,* Sherman was on his way down the Mississippi River with half of the Army of the Tennessee. His state of mind is something of a mystery. Sherman knew of Van Dorn's raid on Holly Springs and must have realized that Grant's overland campaign had suffered a serious, perhaps even a fatal, logistical blow. Sherman nonetheless behaved as if Grant would continue to advance along the Mississippi Central Railroad and fix Pemberton in place at Grenada as planned. He also assumed that the Rebel commander was unaware of the hastily mounted amphibious expedition. Sherman was wrong on both counts.

Between December 21 and 24 Pemberton received repeated warnings that a large Union army-navy force was moving down the Mississippi, but he did not know where the attack would come. That critical information arrived at the last possible moment and in the most dramatic fashion imaginable. As darkness fell on Christmas Eve, a Confederate army telegrapher named L. L. Daniel stood atop the levee near Lake Providence, Louisiana, and watched a massive convoy churn past his position. The vessels were steaming in column with their running lights aglow and obviously headed toward Vicksburg, only sixty miles below by river. Daniel rushed to his telegraph station. Minutes later the news reached Phillip H. Fall, another army telegrapher stationed on De Soto Point. Fall commandeered a rowboat and braved strong winds and choppy water to reach Vicksburg. He burst into Dr. William T. Balfour's handsome hilltop home, where a Christmas Eve ball attended by General Smith and many of his officers was in progress. Upon being told of the sighting, Smith informed the crowd: "This ball is at an end; the enemy are coming down the river!" Partygoers gathered up their hats and coats and hurried into the night, civilians to their homes, officers to their posts.[2]

On Christmas Day the Union armada tied up along the Louisiana shore west of De Soto Point and landed elements of Brig. Gen. Andrew J. Smith's and Brig. Gen. Morgan L. Smith's divisions. The Federals marched inland and wrecked a section of the Vicksburg, Shreveport, and Texas Railroad between Vicksburg and Monroe. While this expedition was in progress, Sherman received the bad news that the Yazoo River was mined above the mouth of Chickasaw Bayou: a landing at Haynes' Bluff was no longer possible. Chagrined at this unexpected development, Sherman nevertheless was determined to press ahead with his original plan and put his troops ashore on high ground somewhere north of Vicksburg. The most likely place for an attack was the Walnut Hills, a section of the escarpment located between Haynes' Bluff and Vicksburg. The Union armada pulled away from De Soto Point on December 26 and turned into the Yazoo.

On December 19, 1862, President Davis arrived in Vicksburg midway through a tour of the western Confederacy. The trip was intended partly to raise public morale and partly to allow Davis to see for himself how matters stood a thousand miles west of Richmond. The president was anxious about the fate of Vicksburg as well as that of Brierfield, his modest plantation on Davis Bend a short distance downriver. Doubtless he would have been even more anxious had he known that Sherman's host would begin its descent of the Mississippi the very next day.

Davis was accompanied by Gen. Joseph E. Johnston, whom he recently had selected to head the Department of the West, an overarching command that comprised all Confederate military organizations between the Appalachians and the Mississippi River. There had been no guiding hand in the West since Albert S. Johnston's death at Shiloh nine months earlier, and Davis hoped—in vain as it turned out—that Joe Johnston would provide sorely needed direction and coordination. After inspecting the Vicksburg defenses Davis and Johnston traveled to Grenada to meet Pemberton.

The three men discussed ways to bolster Pemberton's ranks with troops from other Confederate armies. There were two possible sources of

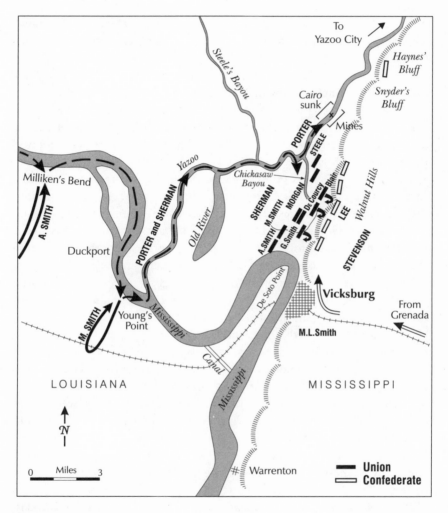

Chickasaw Bayou

additional manpower: Braxton Bragg's Army of Tennessee and Lt. Gen. Theophilus H. Holmes's Army of the Trans-Mississippi. A few days earlier Davis had directed Johnston to transfer Maj. Gen. Carter L. Stevenson's division from Tennessee to Mississippi. That force of about ten thousand men was en route to Vicksburg over the South's rickety and roundabout railroad system while the conference in Grenada was underway, but only a portion of the division would reach Vicksburg in time to confront Sherman. (Stevenson's transfer could not have taken place at a worse time, for it meant that Bragg would fight the battle of Stones River at the end of December against Rosecrans's Army of the Cumberland with a drastically reduced command. Had Stevenson's men been present, Stones River might well have been a Confederate victory.)

Johnston and Bragg opposed any further reduction in strength of the Army of Tennessee. The obvious place to turn for additional reinforcements was the trans-Mississippi, but there were problems. The Mississippi River was a dividing line between Confederate departments. Neither Johnston nor Pemberton could call on Holmes for help; their authority ended at the river's edge. Davis did not hesitate to order Bragg to rush a division to Pemberton, but throughout the lengthy struggle for Vicksburg, he merely urged Holmes to send whatever force he could spare. When Holmes refused to part with a single soldier, citing the critical state of affairs in Arkansas, Davis acquiesced.

Holmes was not being intransigent; his department was in real danger of being overrun by Union forces. On December 7 Holmes's principal army was wrecked at Prairie Grove in northwest Arkansas. This calamity left his western flank wide open to the Federals, who promptly swept down to the Arkansas River. His eastern flank was endangered by the Union presence at Helena and increased naval activity on the Mississippi River. Under the circumstances Holmes could not assist Pemberton without effectively abandoning Arkansas to the enemy, and that was a sensitive matter.

Arkansas already had been abandoned once by the Confederacy, and it was unlikely that its citizens and soldiers would allow it to happen a second time without causing an enormous uproar. In April 1862, following the defeat at Pea Ridge, Van Dorn had moved his army from Arkansas to Mississippi. Acting on his own authority the general took with him all the arms, munitions, machinery, stores, wagons, animals, and steamboats he could lay his hands on in Arkansas, Missouri, northern Louisiana, and the Indian Territory. Political leaders in every corner of the trans-Mississippi raised a howl of outrage. Nowhere was public confidence more deeply shaken than in Arkansas, where Gov. Henry M. Rector threatened to secede from the Confederacy unless his state was defended. The new Department of the Trans-Mississippi was created, a makeshift army was cobbled together in Arkansas, and the political crisis eased, but thereafter Confederate forces in the trans-Mississippi would not, could not, be transferred eastward without the approval of the department commander and the consent of political leaders.

The military situation in Louisiana, while not so politically sensitive, was even less promising. A small Confederate army led by the very capable Maj. Gen. Richard Taylor harassed Union occupation forces in southern Louisiana, but it was too weak and too far away from Vicksburg to be of much help. The rest of Louisiana was practically defenseless; barely a corporal's guard could be found north of Alexandria.

Van Dorn's abandonment of the trans-Mississippi in the spring of 1862 was the logical culmination of the Confederate policy of draining manpower from the states west of the Mississippi to bolster armies in Virginia, Tennessee, and Mississippi. That policy had run its course by the end of 1862. Pemberton would have to make do with what he had.

While playing host to Davis and Johnston in Grenada, Pemberton learned that Grant was falling back in the aftermath of Van Dorn's raid on Holly Springs and that Sherman was moving down the Mississippi. Late on December 24 came a telegram from Smith with the shocking news that Sherman was only hours away from Vicksburg. Pemberton immediately began to shift troops from Grenada to Vicksburg by rail, just as Grant feared he would. As each contingent of Confederate soldiers rattled into the Hill City, Smith, an experienced engineer with a good eye for ground, hurried them north to fill the gap between Vicksburg and Haynes' Bluff. It seemed fairly obvious to him that with the Yazoo River blocked by mines above Chickasaw Bayou, the Federals had little choice but to advance toward the Walnut Hills.

Sherman's decision to strike at the Walnut Hills instead of Haynes' Bluff probably was the correct one, but every course of action open to the Union commander was fraught with immense difficulties. The land along the lower Yazoo River was wooded, low, and usually wet. In the mid-nineteenth century it was laced by meandering streams and dotted with sloughs and shallow lagoons. Clearings were few and far between. It was a bad place to maneuver an army or fight a battle.

Sherman had hoped to steam up the Yazoo, land his army at the foot of Haynes' Bluff, and quickly seize the high ground from the astonished defenders. An attack against the Walnut Hills was an altogether different proposition. Simply getting from the alternative landing site along Chickasaw Bayou to the foot of the heights involved slogging through a truly dismal swamp. Nonetheless Sherman was optimistic that he could reach the bluffs before the enemy barred his path.

The Walnut Hills were neither fortified nor occupied on December 26, when the Federals approached Chickasaw Bayou, but that soon changed. Their peculiar terrain presented the Confederates with exceptional tactical advantages. The primary line of defense was a terrace or shelf that runs along the base of the bluffs. Its western face rises ten to twenty feet above the swampy lowland. The upper portion of Chickasaw Bayou meanders directly below the terrace for much of its length. The combination of natural parapet and moat formed an almost insurmountable barrier to an attacking force. Running along the terrace and atop the bluffs were two parallel roads that connected Vicksburg and Haynes' Bluff. These permitted the defenders to move laterally to any threatened point along the escarpment. Sherman would have had to search long and hard to find a less promising place to make an assault.

Pemberton accompanied President Davis to Jackson and saw him off, very likely with a sigh of relief, then continued on to Vicksburg, where he demonstrated his peculiar hands-off style of command. Pemberton permitted General Smith to remain in overall command of the rapidly unfolding tactical situation. Smith knew his personal limitations and assigned responsibility for defense of the Walnut Hills to Brig. Gen. Stephen D. Lee, a West Point graduate recently transferred from the Army of Northern Virginia. Lee had fewer than three thousand men on December 26, but over the next three days troops trickled in by rail from Pemberton's main force at Grenada and Bragg's army in Tennessee. By the time Sherman launched his final assault on December 29, the Confederates numbered about six thousand.

Lee put his troops to work clearing fields of fire and constructing rifle pits, trenches, and artillery redoubts across the most likely avenues of approach. To buy as much time as possible, he sent a substantial force down into the bottomlands to harass and delay the Federals. Between December 26 and 28 Sherman's thirty-two thousand troops disembarked from their transports and slowly pushed through the bottomlands toward the Walnut Hills. Skirmishes, some approaching the size and intensity of small battles, erupted with increasing frequency as the Federals forced the Confederates back. The leading Union regiments were only a few hundred yards from the main fortifications by nightfall on December 28. Sherman ordered a general attack for the next day.

Brig. Gen. George W. Morgan, a senior division commander, was dismayed at the obstructed approaches to the Confederate position and the existence of only a single rickety bridge across Chickasaw Bayou. When he expressed his doubts about the wisdom of a head-on attack, Sherman snapped that "we will lose 5,000 men before we take Vicksburg, and may as well lose them here as anywhere else." It was a remark that would haunt the voluble general, who all too often said or wrote exactly what he was thinking. Morgan gave the order to go forward, though under protest. He was not the only Union officer who was appalled at what was about to happen. "General, do I understand that you are about to order an assault?" asked Col. John F. De Courcy. When Morgan said yes, De Courcy gasped: "My poor brigade!"[3]

After an artillery bombardment that had little effect on the entrenched defenders, Sherman's infantry advanced just before noon on December 29. The fighting was most severe on the Union left, where parts of three brigades led by Brig. Gen. Frank P. Blair, Brig. Gen. John M. Thayer, and Colonel De Courcy struggled across Chickasaw Bayou and established a shallow bridgehead at the base of the terrace. Col. James A. Williamson's Fourth Iowa actually captured an outlying section of the Confederate earthworks, but the Federals eventually were driven back across the bayou. Morgan watched helplessly as his men were "mowed down by a storm of shells, grape and canister, and minie-balls which swept our front like a hurricane of fire." The assault, he wrote later, "was as valiant as it was hopeless." De Courcy's premonition of disaster was correct; his brigade suffered by far the heaviest casualties.[4]

A short distance to the right a force comprised of Col. Daniel W. Lindsey's and Col. Lionel A. Sheldon's brigades approached Chickasaw Bayou but did not attempt to cross. The troops traded gunfire with the entrenched Confederates for a time, then withdrew into the dense woods that covered the bottomlands. Farther to the right, near the center of the Union formation, Col. Giles A. Smith's brigade performed in similar fashion. Only the men of Lt. Col. James H. Blood's Sixth Missouri showed the kind of grit that might have carried the day. The Missourians waded across the bayou but were unable to advance any farther because of intense Rebel fire and a complete lack of support. They huddled under the shelter of the east bank until nightfall, then returned to their own lines. The attacking force on the right of the Union line, led by Brig. Gen. Andrew J. Smith, withdrew after failing to penetrate a barrier of felled trees. The assault was a complete failure.

Darkness brought a drenching rain and plummeting temperatures. "A night commenced, such as God forbid, I may never live through again," recalled Sgt. Paul Reichelm of the Third Missouri. "Before leaving the river bank we had been ordered to leave *everything behind* which could impede our movements in any way. Thus blankets, oil-cloth, haversack, canteen and even overcoats had been left, and here we stood with nothing on our bodies but the thin blouse and pants . . . exposed to the merciless cold and howling storm. . . . The rain did not stop until morning—the storm raging with unbroken fury, and when daylight *at last* dawned upon the pitiful scene we found ourselves in a swamp—(every inch of which stood under water) stiff blue and teeth rattling, scarcely able to walk, and many totally unable to speak!" No one knows how many wounded men perished during the dismal night.[5]

Sherman wisely decided not to renew the attack on December 30. He later insisted that his men were in good spirits and ready for another go at the Rebels, but exactly the opposite was true. Casting about for some way to retrieve the situation, Sherman returned to his original idea of a landing at Haynes' Bluff. He was encouraged when Porter informed him that a solution to the problem of mines in the Yazoo River had been found: Ellet had fashioned a huge wooden rake that extended over the bow of the ram *Lioness*. As the device swept through the water, it detonated or dislodged the mines in the boat's path. *Lioness* was the world's first minesweeper.

Perhaps a belated thrust at Haynes' Bluff would have succeeded, though it seems likely that the Confederates, fully alert and growing more numerous every day, could have countered a landing simply by shifting troops northward to match Sherman's progress up the river. No one will ever know. On the morning of December 31, a dense fog blanketed the bottomlands. Porter's vessels could not move. The next day rain fell in torrents. With the elements against him, Sherman gave up and ordered a withdrawal. Thousands of wet, cold, and demoralized soldiers crowded back aboard their transports and returned to the Mississippi River. "Well we have been to Vicksburg, and it was too much for us, and we have backed out," Sherman confessed to his wife.[6]

The clash along the muddy banks of Chickasaw Bayou was a costly affair. Union losses amounted to 1,776 men: 208 killed, 1,005 wounded, and 563 missing, 332 of whom were captured by the Confederates. Eighty percent of the casualties—1,439 men—fell in the assault of December 29, and most of them belonged to Morgan's division, especially De Courcy's brigade. Confederate losses were far lower: 187 killed, wounded, and missing.

Sherman deserved much of the blame for the Union defeat. He convinced himself, despite evidence to the contrary, that Grant was continuing to advance on Pemberton at Grenada. After rushing away from Memphis and tearing down the Mississippi, Sherman inexplicably shifted into a more measured mode of operations upon reaching Vicksburg. He wasted a day before entering the Yazoo, then allowed several more days to slip away while his men floundered around in the swamps. The attack, when it finally got underway, was a poorly organized frontal assault that had no realistic chance of success. Sherman may not have lost five thousand men at Chickasaw Bayou, but it was not for lack of effort. The Union repulse was a dismal end to his first independent command and to Grant's hope of a quick knockout blow. Sherman did not duck responsibility, at least not immediately. "I reached Vicksburg at the time appointed, landed, assaulted, and failed," was how he summed up the operation to Halleck. In his postwar memoirs, however, Sherman attempted to shift much of the blame for the debacle to his subordinates, particularly George Morgan.[7]

The Confederates, naturally, were exhilarated at the outcome of the battle. Nearly everyone in gray performed capably. Pemberton acted decisively, Smith hurried men and equipment to the right spot, Lee handled the tactical situation admirably, and regimental commanders demonstrated pluck and initiative. The only negative aspect of the victory was that it focused Pemberton's attention on the area north of Vicksburg and confirmed his belief that a static defense was the correct approach to holding the Hill City.

On December 30, the day after Chickasaw Bayou, McClernand arrived in Memphis and discovered that Sherman had gone down the Mississippi River ten days earlier with "his" army. McClernand set out in pursuit, correctly convinced that he had been outmaneuvered by a clique of West Pointers. He caught up with Sherman at Milliken's Bend and learned of the repulse. The next day, January 4, 1863, McClernand assumed command of what he called the Army of the Mississippi. For the next few weeks he acted as though he was an independent army commander, which is precisely what he considered himself to be. Due to the breakdown in Union communications, McClernand was unaware that he now was merely the senior corps commander in the Army of the Tennessee.

Another assault against the Walnut Hills was out of the question, so McClernand, Sherman, and Porter decided to attack the Confederate position at Arkansas Post (or the Post of Arkansas), an old settlement along the lower Arkansas River. A short time earlier Confederate forces at the mouth of the Arkansas had captured an unescorted Union transport on the Mississippi River carrying coal and ammunition. McClernand had been contemplating an attack on Arkansas Post for some time. Following the loss of the transport, he decided to descend on that position with his entire force in order to eliminate the threat to the Union line of communications on the Mississippi River. As the operation got underway McClernand informed Samuel Curtis in St. Louis that he was about to barge into the Department of the Missouri. Curtis welcomed the strike because of his concern for the Union enclave at Helena, located about sixty miles northeast of Arkansas Post. Most of the town's once-substantial garrison had been "borrowed" by Sherman on his way down the Mississippi and now was part of McClernand's army.

When the Union gunboats and transports steamed away from Vicksburg under a cloud of sooty smoke, the Confederates were elated and relieved. Everyone assumed the defeated Yankees were retiring to Memphis to regroup. "I hope the rascals have found the taking of Vicksburg impractable and have returned to their northern dens," exclaimed a Confederate artilleryman as the last of the vessels vanished from sight.[8]

Arkansas Post was garrisoned by about five thousand Confederate soldiers under the command of Brig. Gen. Thomas J. Churchill. Most were dismounted Texas and Arkansas cavalrymen whose ranks had been reduced by disease; fewer than three thousand men were healthy enough to carry a weapon, and most of them were equipped with short-range carbines and shotguns instead of rifles. The key to Arkansas Post was Fort Hindman, a square earthen structure located on the northwest side of a hairpin curve in the Arkansas River (a mirror image of the situation at Vicksburg). The fort had only three heavy guns but was partially covered with an inch of iron plating backed by heavy timbers. The Confederates had no ironclad vessel in Arkansas, but they had an ironclad fort.

When Churchill detected the Union armada approaching Arkansas Post, he called upon department headquarters in Little Rock for support. Theophilus Holmes was prone to dither in a crisis, and this he promptly commenced to do, informing Churchill that no reinforcements were available but nevertheless ordering him to "hold out till help arrived or all dead." Then he reversed himself and promised Churchill that help was on the way. Churchill had served under Holmes long enough to understand that he was on his own and prepared to defend his position as best he could with what he had.[9]

Two hundred winding river miles above Chickasaw Bayou, the Union force turned west into the Arkansas River and proceeded another fifty miles upstream. About four miles below Arkansas Post the transports nosed into the north bank of the river and disgorged men, animals, equipment, and stores. On January 10 over thirty thousand Union soldiers slogged upstream around the hairpin bend. Progress was slow, and there was a good deal of confusion and countermarching. McClernand had hoped to outflank the Confederate fortifications by swinging inland, but the back swamp (the lower ground away from the river) proved impassable, so he sent his men directly toward the enemy position across the natural levee (the slightly higher ground along the river). By late afternoon the Federals were within sight of Fort Hindman's landward defenses, a line of rifle pits extending westward from the fort to Post Bayou, a distance of about seven hundred yards. In front of the Confederate earthworks was an abatis of tangled trees and a shallow ditch.

Shortly after noon on the next day, January 11, the ironclads *Baron De Kalb, Cincinnati,* and *Louisville,* supported by the timberclads *Lexington* and *Black Hawk* (the latter with Porter aboard), closed in on Fort Hindman and opened fire. The hail of heavy shot and shell stripped away the fort's iron plating and pounded it into a shapeless mass of rubble. When the fort surrendered around four o'clock, Porter turned his attention to the Confederate troops on the landward side. He directed the tinclads *Rattler* and *Glide* and the ram *Monarch* to squeeze past obstructions in the river and fire into the exposed rear of the Rebel position.

While Porter's gunboats hammered Fort Hindman, McClernand's troops stormed the fortifications. Sherman's Fifteenth Corps was deployed on the Union right and McClernand's Thirteenth Corps (led by Morgan) on the left. Because the approach to the Confederate line was constricted between the river and the swamp, only about one-third of McClernand's men got into the fight. The brunt of the battle was borne by the divisions of Brig. Gen. Frederick Steele and Brig. Gen. Andrew J. Smith.

The attack began in fine style, with massive infantry formations surging across the muddy plain. A soldier in the Twenty-fifth Iowa recalled every

man in his regiment "running with all his might half drunk with excitement and yelling as loud as possible, but this fierce looking array did not
stop the rebel balls." When the long lines of blue-clad troops came within
range of the Confederate defenders, a "blaze of fire flashed like lightning"
along the top of the earthen parapet. The storm of bullets, buckshot, and
canister felled hundreds of Federals and brought the advancing lines to a
halt. For a few terrible minutes it seemed like Chickasaw Bayou all over
again. But the Union troops reformed, sought such shelter as could be
found, and continued the assault. By late afternoon thousands of Federals
had reached the shelter of the ditch in front of the parapet.[10]

About this time Fort Hindman ceased firing and Porter's tinclads
began shelling the Confederate infantry from behind. White flags unexpectedly fluttered into view along the battered parapet. Although they
were unauthorized, the damage was done. Firing sputtered out as puzzled
Confederates lowered their arms. Seizing the moment Union troops
scrambled over the parapet and disarmed the defenders before they could
change their minds.

The battle of Arkansas Post was "as fierce an engagement of six hours as
has occurred during the war," wrote a Texas soldier. He did not exaggerate
by much. At a cost of 1,092 casualties—140 killed, 923 wounded, and
29 missing—the Union army and navy had overrun a stoutly fortified
Confederate position and captured 4,791 prisoners, roughly one-fourth
of the total Confederate strength in Arkansas, Missouri, and the Indian
Territory. At least 60 Confederates were killed and 75 wounded; only a
few hundred managed to escape through the swamps and bring the grim
tidings to Holmes in Little Rock.[11]

"Vicksburg is going to be a hard nut to crack, but I think our affair
at the Post of Arkansas will help some," wrote Sherman. He was right.
The loss of Arkansas Post struck the reeling Confederate establishment
in the trans-Mississippi a heavy blow. It removed the only potential threat
to the Union line of communications on the Mississippi River, cost the
Rebels men and supplies they could not afford to lose, and opened the
Arkansas Valley to invasion. The defeat also extinguished any lingering
hope that Jefferson Davis might work up the political courage to order
Holmes to send reinforcements to Vicksburg. With Missouri gone and
Arkansas and Louisiana going, the security of the Hill City now depended
on Confederate resources east of the Mississippi.[12]

In the afterglow of his first victory, McClernand wanted to continue
up the Arkansas River to Little Rock. He lost sight of the fact that his

objectives were the capture of Vicksburg and the reopening of navigation on the Mississippi River, not the conquest of the trans-Mississippi. Low water in the Arkansas proved to be a more formidable obstacle than Fort Hindman, however, and McClernand concluded that Little Rock was not within his grasp. He sent a raiding force up the White River in eastern Arkansas and settled down to await developments. The Army of the Mississippi, also known as the Thirteenth and Fifteenth Corps of the Army of the Tennessee and with both a defeat and a victory to its credit, was temporarily stalled in Arkansas.

When Grant learned of the Union repulse at Chickasaw Bayou, he hurried preparations to move McPherson's corps down the Mississippi River to join Sherman. A few days later came word that McClernand had assumed command of Sherman's expedition and veered off to the west. Grant angrily informed Halleck that McClernand had "gone on a wild goose chase to the Post of Arkansas." He ordered the wayward general to return to the Mississippi at once and reminded him that the capture of Vicksburg was the sole purpose of the expedition. The "wild goose chase" message caused an uproar in Washington and gave Halleck the opportunity he had been waiting for. He directed Grant to relieve McClernand and either replace him with Sherman or assume command in person. Grant chose the latter.[13]

Sherman, meanwhile, informed Grant that there were sound military reasons for the attack on Arkansas Post. This information, combined with a fuller understanding of the magnitude of the Union victory, caused Grant to tone down his criticism of McClernand. Sherman concluded his letter with a plea for Grant to take personal command of the expedition. He need not have worried. Grant already was on his way, arriving at the mouth of the Arkansas River on January 18 and assuming command from a very unhappy McClernand. The short-lived Army of the Mississippi was no more, but the Army of the Tennessee was about to return to Vicksburg.

# CHAPTER FIVE

# Dark Winter

The Army of the Tennessee returned to Vicksburg at the end of January 1863. McClernand's and Sherman's corps disembarked at Young's Point, Milliken's Bend, and other locations on the west bank of the Mississippi above De Soto Point; McPherson's corps landed farther upstream near Lake Providence in extreme northeast Louisiana. The weather was abysmal. Cold rain fell for days on end and transformed the low-lying landscape into a vast swamp. Soldiers pitched their tents atop the narrow levee or on the occasional islands of slightly higher ground that dotted the waterlogged countryside.

The result was an archipelago of misery. Wells and latrines were impossible, so soldiers drew drinking water and relieved themselves at random along the muddy shorelines. Illnesses of every description swept through the camps. "Some have the chills & a good many the diareah & none of them seemed to be in very good spirits," opined William Winters of the Sixty-seventh Indiana. Hundreds of men died within weeks. With so little land above water, the living shared the high ground with the dead. "The levee for long distances is full of *new made graves*," reported Cyrus F. Boyd of the Fifteenth Iowa. "This is a hard place for a sick man. He must have plenty of *grit or die*." On one occasion the river rose over the levees and forced thousands of men and animals back aboard the transports, which tied up to treetops or steamed around aimlessly until the land reappeared.[1]

The situation gradually improved as the Federals adjusted to their amphibian existence, but throughout February and March, newspapers in the Midwest received a stream of mildewed letters from dispirited soldiers telling of the dismal state of affairs. Editors and politicians far from the scene fulminated about military incompetence and demanded that changes be made. The chorus of complaints eventually reached the highest levels of the Lincoln administration.

By this time Halleck had overcome his initial doubts about Grant and was solidly in his corner. Stanton, however, was not yet convinced Grant was the man for the job. It requires some effort to recall that in early 1863—roughly halfway through the war—Grant's record was decidedly mixed. His early victories at Forts Henry and Donelson had been followed by the near-disaster at Shiloh, the fiasco at Holly Springs, and the failure at Chickasaw Bayou. Equally disturbing were persistent reports of alcoholism. With the Army of the Tennessee stuck in the mud in front of Vicksburg, Stanton wanted an independent observer to report on the progress of the campaign and on the qualities of the commanding general. The man he chose was Charles A. Dana, a trusted official in the War Department.

When Grant learned what Stanton was up to, he decided to make Dana an unofficial member of his staff. Instead of observing matters from the outside, a pleasantly surprised Dana found himself very much part of the inner circle and soon shed all traces of objectivity. He sided with Grant against McClernand and convinced Stanton (and possibly Lincoln as well) that despite the often discouraging outcome of military and naval activities in front of Vicksburg, it was only a matter of time before the general succeeded in wresting control of the Father of Waters from Confederate hands. And during the dreary, wet winter of 1862–63, time was what Grant needed more than anything else.

While his soldiers suffered in their cheerless tent cities and his staff converted Stanton's spy into one of their own, Grant wrestled with the problem that had confounded Sherman: how to come to grips with the enemy. The Confederates were in plain sight but seemed hopelessly out of reach. Grant somehow had to get his army to the top of the bluffs on the east side of the Mississippi. But how?

When the Union army reappeared in front of Vicksburg, every Confederate soldier from Pemberton to the lowliest private was surprised. Watching the enemy spread out across the drowned Louisiana countryside, the Rebels grew perplexed. "What their purpose is no one seems to be able to fathom," wrote Sgt. Edward T. Eggleston, though he noted the "general supposition" among his fellow Mississippi cannoneers that the Federals intended to march downstream, cross the Mississippi River, and approach Vicksburg from the landward side.[2]

Sergeant Eggleston was correct. Grant had tentatively decided on a course of action even before he reached the vicinity of Vicksburg. He wanted to move his army down the west side of the Mississippi River and cross to the east side below the Hill City. For the time being, however, such a move was impossible. The alluvial plain of the Mississippi was awash as a result of the winter rains, and the spring floods would only make matters worse. Stymied by nature as much as by the Confederates, during the first three months of 1863, Grant explored a variety of options that offered at least some possibility of immediate success. Nonetheless he never lost sight of the opportunities presented by a move to the south. As Sergeant Eggleston suggested, it was the obvious course of action.

Grant had to face the fact that the Army of the Tennessee, rushed south in such haste in December and January, was marooned on the Louisiana shore until April at the earliest. Local roads were submerged. If he was to move the army anywhere during the first quarter of the new year, he would have to make use of the expanse of water extending for miles in all directions across the Mississippi Valley. Fortunately the presence of Porter's Mississippi Squadron and a fleet of transports gave Grant enormous potential mobility. How could he make the most of his command of the water?

The most direct course of action would have been to crowd every-body back aboard the transports, race around De Soto Point, and storm Vicksburg. The Confederates had anticipated this possibility, however, and had constructed defenses along the Hill City's waterfront. Because an amphibious assault against a fortified shoreline was beyond the capability of nineteenth-century armies, Grant did not seriously consider such a move.

An only slightly less direct approach would have been to rush the transports past Vicksburg and disembark the army downstream on the east bank. It did not require military genius, however, to realize that the Confederate batteries would inflict fearful carnage on a stream of fragile boats packed with men and animals. And even if such a passage somehow succeeded, there was no way to maintain a reliable waterborne line of communications. Every transport that attempted a supply run to Memphis would have to pass Vicksburg twice. Confederate artillerymen inevitably would destroy a certain percentage of the targets that appeared in their sights. Grant would run out of transports long before Pemberton ran out of shells, and his army would be isolated deep in enemy territory with shrinking stocks of food, forage, and ammunition.

A possible solution to the problem posed by the Vicksburg batteries was the abandoned canal across the base of De Soto Point. If it could be completed, transports could drop downstream without running the gauntlet of fire. The canal had an enthusiastic supporter in a very high place. Abraham Lincoln was fascinated by engineering projects. Ever sensitive to political developments or personal quirks that affected military matters, Halleck informed Grant of the president's interest. For both military and nonmilitary reasons, Grant put four thousand soldiers from Sherman's corps and two thousand freedmen to work scooping mud out of the half-drowned canal. Porter had more experience with water than the president or the generals, and he did not believe the Mississippi would flow through the canal, which was badly sited. Moreover, he was convinced that the Confederates would simply move artillery down from Vicksburg to cover the lower end of the canal.

As work on the canal progressed, the Confederates placed several guns on the opposite bluffs and waited for Union working parties to come within range. In early March the dam at the waterway's upper end gave way and filled it with water. Sherman's men labored for weeks to construct another dam and clear out the mess. Two steam dredges were brought down from the Midwest and put to work. Making rapid progress at first, when they came within range of the Confederate guns they were driven off, just as Porter had predicted. Toward the end of March Grant became disillusioned with the canal, but he kept the project alive partly to please Lincoln and partly to give Pemberton something to worry about. Sherman summed up the situation in a letter to Curtis: "Our canal here don't amount to much."[3]

At the same time, Grant put McPherson's troops to work creating a navigable route through a network of rivers and bayous in the bottomlands of northeast Louisiana. Lake Providence, 40 miles (75 by river) north of Vicksburg, was connected to the Red River, 120 miles (190 by river) to the south, by a serpentine passage consisting of Bayou Baxter, Bayou Macon, the Tensas River, and the Black River (not to be confused with the Big Black River in Mississippi). If this route could be opened up to light-draft steamboats, Grant could float some or all of his men below Vicksburg without exposing them to the dangers of a desperate dash past the Confederate guns on the Mississippi.

McPherson's men cut the levee between the Mississippi and Lake Providence and began clearing a channel through narrow, cypress-choked Bayou Baxter. It was an immensely difficult task, and progress was slow.

Nevertheless Grant had more confidence in the Lake Providence project than in any of the other schemes to bypass Vicksburg. As late as March 23 he intended to send McPherson's corps to the Red River via this roundabout route through the interior of Louisiana.

While these engineering projects were underway, heavily laden Confederate steamboats continued to shuttle back and forth on the Mississippi and Red Rivers. Porter decided to send a portion of the Mississippi Squadron into the Vicksburg–Port Hudson corridor and halt this commerce. He directed nineteen-year-old colonel Charles R. Ellet (son of Charles Ellet, mortally wounded at Memphis) to pass Vicksburg in the ram *Queen of the West* and patrol the river beyond. Ellet was to capture or destroy every vessel he met and generally raise havoc with Rebel commerce. The admiral was reluctant to send down any of his trusty but cumbersome "turtles," fearing that if the underpowered ironclads went below Vicksburg, they would never get upriver again. The *Queen of the West* was lightly armed but sturdy and fast. Porter was confident she could run away from any danger.

The operation got off to an auspicious start. At dawn on February 2 the *Queen of the West,* covered from bow to stern with bales of cotton for protection, sped past the surprised Confederate gunners at Vicksburg and disappeared downstream. For a few exhilarating days it seemed that Ellet might single-handedly sever Confederate ties to the trans-Mississippi. On his initial foray downriver he captured and burned three steamers loaded with supplies for Port Hudson. On February 5 Ellet returned safely to the downstream side of De Soto Point, which was occupied by Sherman's canal diggers.

As Porter had hoped, the *Queen of the West*'s presence caused an uproar and brought river traffic to a halt. When news reached Natchez that a Yankee gunboat was on the loose, every vessel on the waterfront raised steam and fled up the Red River. A citizen of Vicksburg assayed the effect of the lone Federal ram. "The worst that has befallen this place, and perhaps the entire Confederacy, since the arrival of the Yankee army on the peninsula across the river, is the interference of our communication with Red River."[4]

A few days later Ellet set out on a second raid down the Mississippi with orders to "burn, sink, and destroy" everything of military value he encountered. Despite the bold tone of his orders, Porter cautioned the youthful colonel to watch out for the Confederate gunboat *William H.*

*Webb,* rumored to be fitting out somewhere up the Red. Ellet reached the mouth of the Red on February 14 and promptly captured another Confederate steamboat. From the crew he learned of several other vessels huddled for protection under the guns of Fort Taylor (later renamed Fort De Russy), about forty-five miles up the shallow, unpredictable river. Ellet rashly decided to dash up the Red and capture or destroy the boats. When the *Queen of the West* came under fire from Fort Taylor, she ran aground and was disabled by a shot through her steam lines; jubilant Confederates seized the ram before she could be destroyed. In the confusion Ellet and some of his crew managed to escape on the previously captured steamboat.[5]

Three nights before the *Queen of the West* approached Fort Taylor, Lt. Cmdr. George Brown took the new ironclad *Indianola* past Vicksburg without injury. The *Indianola*'s crew was understrength and inexperienced, but the ironclad could make better than two knots against the current, unlike the slower "turtles," and Porter decided to send her down the river on the chance she could safely return upstream in an emergency. He expected that a miniature flotilla composed of a powerful ironclad, a speedy ram, and one or two captured steamers would give the Union navy effective control of the Mississippi between Vicksburg and Port Hudson. Somewhere below Vicksburg Brown encountered Ellet and learned of the loss of the *Queen of the West.* Shaken by the news, Brown nonetheless continued downstream and briefly reestablished a one-boat Union blockade of the mouth of the Red River. Ellet, meanwhile, returned to De Soto Point to face Porter's wrath.

Maj. Gen. Richard Taylor, commanding the Confederate District of Western Louisiana, was a bold and energetic officer. He regarded the *Indianola* not as a threat, but as a tempting target. While his engineers refloated and repaired the *Queen of the West,* Taylor hatched a plan to capture or destroy the Union ironclad and regain control of the Vicksburg–Port Hudson corridor.

Commander Brown also considered the *Indianola* to be a sitting duck. After a week at the mouth of the Red, he picked up rumors that Taylor was planning an attack on his isolated vessel. Brown abandoned the blockade and headed up the Mississippi. He elected to keep the coal barges lashed alongside his ironclad for protection against the captured *Queen of the West*'s reinforced bow. The barges were an immense drag, though, and the *Indianola* made slow progress against the current. On the evening of February 24, Brown sighted smoke astern. A few hours later the *William*

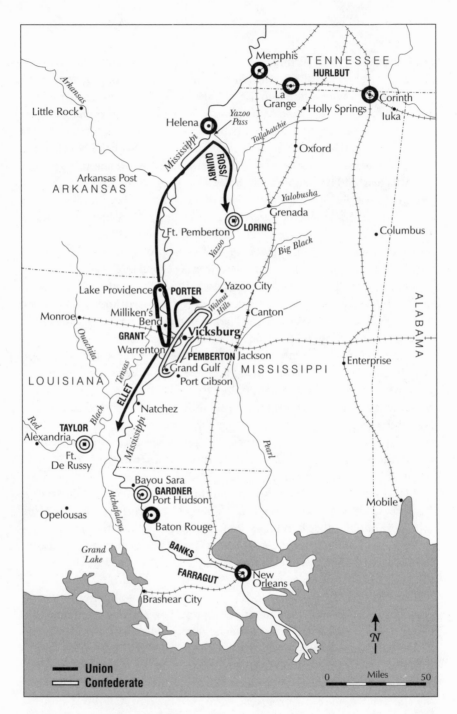

Union operations: February–March 1863

*H. Webb, Queen of the West,* and a pair of smaller vessels approached out of the gloom. The Union ironclad was only about twenty-five miles from the lower end of the canal at De Soto Point, but Brown knew the jig was up. He turned downstream and cleared for action.

The makeshift Confederate squadron was manned by army volunteers and commanded by Maj. Joseph L. Brent, a former attorney serving as Taylor's chief of ordnance and artillery. Despite a complete lack of experience in maritime warfare, Brent pitched right in to the fight; it was Plum Run all over again. The speedy Confederate vessels rammed the unwieldy ironclad, tore away the coal barges, and smashed a hole in her stern. Brown surrendered after ninety minutes; his gunners fired few shots and failed to seriously damage any of the Confederate boats. The crippled ironclad settled to the bottom in about ten feet of water near Davis Bend, where Joseph Davis and his younger brother, Jefferson, had their plantations. Fewer than a dozen sailors and soldiers were killed or wounded in the fight, but nearly every member of the *Indianola*'s crew, including Brown, was captured.

Undoubtedly amazed at his victory, Brent led his boats upstream to Vicksburg to have their battered bows repaired. Meanwhile a Confederate salvage crew boarded the *Indianola* to determine whether the vessel could be refloated. The following day, February 26, Brent returned to the wreck with news that a second Union ironclad was approaching. With his boats leaking like sieves, the major could not risk another fight and withdrew down the Mississippi to the sanctuary of the Red.

Toward evening, a dark, low-lying vessel slowly rounded Davis Bend and halted a short distance above the wreck of the *Indianola*. Abandoned, alarmed, and possibly inebriated, the salvage crew set the captured vessel afire and fled into the woods. The last opportunity to put a Confederate ironclad into service on the Mississippi River had passed.

The craft that so unnerved the Confederates was no ironclad at all, rather a clever ruse. Two days earlier, when Porter heard the sound of gunfire below Vicksburg, he correctly surmised that the enemy was engaging the *Indianola*. Unfortunately there was little he could do; all of his rams, timberclads, and tinclads were committed to operations upstream. Although anxious about the fate of the *Indianola*, Porter was unwilling to risk sending more of his precious ironclads into an uncertain situation without a proper escort. Instead he decided to float a dummy vessel downstream. He hoped that the Confederates would be fooled into thinking that the *Indianola* was being reinforced and would withdraw.

How much faith Porter had in this hare-brained scheme is not known, but his carpenters quickly assembled a three-hundred-foot raft around a coal barge and topped it with a casemate, wheelhouses, smokestacks, and guns, all crudely made of logs and lumber. The entire contraption was coated with tar and the words "Deluded People Cave In" were painted on the wheelhouses in huge letters. A national flag flying from the stern along with smudgepots to produce smoke completed the disguise. Porter reported with pride that the ersatz gunboat required less than twelve hours' labor and cost the taxpayers only $8.23.

That night the newest Union "ironclad" was towed to the tip of De Soto Point and released. The Vicksburg batteries fired dozens of shots at the strange craft but did her no serious damage. The barge drifted into an eddy near the lower end of the canal and began going around in circles, but Sherman's soldiers pushed it back into the current. It glided downstream and finally came to rest on a mudflat less than a mile from the *Indianola*. The ruse worked beyond Porter's wildest dreams and embarrassed the Confederates. But it could not disguise the fact that both of the vessels sent to interdict traffic on the Mississippi and Red Rivers, one an expensive new ironclad, had been lost.

For three weeks Ellet and Brown halted the flow of supplies between the two halves of the Confederacy, but bad luck, questionable decisions, and a vigorous enemy response scuttled the Union initiative. "My plans were well laid, only badly executed," Porter explained to Secretary Welles. "I can give orders, but I can not give officers good judgement." On the other side Taylor and Brent demonstrated what could be accomplished with an aggressive and opportunistic defense. Though they landed only a glancing blow against the Union naval juggernaut, it was enough to secure Confederate control of the Vicksburg–Port Hudson corridor for another six weeks.[6]

While rams and ironclads battled for control of the Mississippi River below Vicksburg, two curious operations were taking place north of the city. In earlier times a maze of streams formed a continuous navigable passage through the bottomlands between Memphis and Vicksburg. The northern entrance to this byzantine waterway was Yazoo Pass, a stream that branched off from Moon Lake, an old channel of the Mississippi River roughly opposite Helena, Arkansas. Water flowed from Moon Lake through Yazoo Pass, the Coldwater River, the Tallahatchie River, and finally the Yazoo River before returning to the Mississippi just above

Vicksburg. In 1856 a levee was constructed across Yazoo Pass to facilitate draining and clearing the rich alluvial soil in that portion of the Mississippi Valley. It occurred to Grant that if the levee at Yazoo Pass was cut, a joint army-navy expedition could move through the web of waterways and reach Haynes' Bluff from the north. It would be an extremely roundabout flanking movement, but it might work.

The Yazoo Pass route offered another potential benefit as well. The spring campaigning season was approaching, and Grant was worried about the safety of his dwindling force in the Department of the Tennessee. Three of his four corps were present in the vicinity of Vicksburg, while only Hurlbut's Sixteenth Corps was stretched between Memphis and Corinth. Van Dorn's attempt to recover northern Mississippi the previous October had failed by a slim margin; a future offensive might succeed. Grant wanted the Yazoo Pass expedition to make a short side trip and burn the railroad bridge across the Yalobusha River at Grenada, the same span that Hovey's raid had failed to destroy a few months earlier. With the bridge gone Pemberton could not use the Mississippi Central Railroad to support a northward thrust.

This was the last time in the campaign that Grant seriously misread his opponent. Pemberton never considered for a moment the sort of bold counterstroke the Federals feared. After his discussions with Jefferson Davis and Joseph Johnston in December 1862, Pemberton was content to remain on the defensive and react to Grant's moves. He was comfortable with his expanding arc of fortifications and had no intention of going anywhere.

Union pioneers blew up the levee at Yazoo Pass on February 3, 1863. The Mississippi River poured into the old channel and inundated the swampy countryside as far as the eye could see. Lt. Col. James H. Wilson, the military engineer in charge of this phase of the operation, reported that water surged through the breach "like nothing else I ever saw except Niagara Falls. Logs, trees, and great masses of earth were torn away with the greatest ease. The work is a perfect success."[7]

By February 24 the torrent of water had subsided somewhat, and Union gunboats and transports began passing through the levee into the old channel. The naval force under Lt. Cmdr. Watson Smith consisted of the untried ironclad *Chillicothe,* the "turtle" *Baron De Kalb,* six tinclads, a ram, and fourteen light-draft transports carrying Brig. Gen. Leonard F. Ross's division from McClernand's corps. The success of the operation depended upon reaching Haynes' Bluff before the Confederates realized what was happening, but Smith proceeded at a snail's pace. The flotilla took four days to negotiate the fourteen miles between the Mississippi and the Coldwater and another six days to steam thirty miles down the Coldwater to the Tallahatchie. Though the circuitous route offered serious difficulties to navigation, and overhanging trees played havoc with smokestacks and superstructures, Smith's lack of urgency is inexplicable.

The natural levees along the streams stood above the water, and the Union soldiers and sailors encountered substantial numbers of Southern civilians. "Truly we are in an enemy country," observed Surgeon Henry C. Huntsman of the Fifth Iowa. "Most of the houses seem deserted and where citizens have been sitting about their doors a sullen silence prevails, no expression or evidence of welcome to our troops." Another Iowan, Andrew F. Sperry of the Thirty-third Regiment, was struck by the very different reaction of the slaves, who saw the Federals as liberators, not invaders, and received them with "the most extravagant expressions of wonder and joy."[8]

Weeks before the Union operation got underway, the indefatigable Isaac Brown of *Arkansas* fame warned Pemberton that the Yazoo Pass route was a back door to Vicksburg. When Brown learned on February 9 that the Federals had cut the Mississippi River levee, he hurried upstream from Yazoo City with every available soldier and sailor and began felling trees into the narrow channel. Despite Smith's deliberate approach and Brown's exertions to render that approach even more deliberate, the Union flotilla inched forward. By early March spring had arrived, and sailors and soldiers aboard the gunboats and transports had a clear view of the bluffs forming a green wall against the eastern sky.

Pemberton had mirrored Grant's strategic moves by shifting most of his army from Grenada to Vicksburg during December and January. He left only Maj. Gen. William W. Loring's division behind to hold the fortified Yalobusha River line against Hurlbut's corps in western Tennessee. When Brown sent word that a Union force was approaching via the Yazoo Pass route, Pemberton directed Loring to move westward along the south bank of the Yalobusha and block the enemy advance. Loring personally led one of his brigades down from the bluffs into the waterlogged alluvial plain.

A short distance west of Greenwood, Loring constructed an earthen fort near the point where the Yalobusha and Tallahatchie join to form the Yazoo. Fort Pemberton was barely above river level and initially contained only two heavy guns, but it was surrounded by swamps, which made an infantry assault impossible. Loring brought a derelict ship up from Yazoo City and sank her in the narrow channel next to the fort. The wreck was the *Star of the West*. Two years earlier Pres. James Buchanan, in the waning days of his administration, had chartered the *Star of the West* and sent her to deliver supplies to Fort Sumter in the harbor of Charleston, South Carolina. Confederate batteries fired the first shots of the Civil War on January 9, 1861, and drove the unarmed merchant vessel away. Now after various adventures the *Star of the West* lay on the muddy bottom of the Tallahatchie, hundreds of miles from the sea.

Loring's men were putting the finishing touches on Fort Pemberton when the leading Union vessels came into view. Had Commander Smith moved more quickly, he would have reached the site before the fort was completed. On March 11, 13, and 16 Smith engaged Fort Pemberton with his two ironclads. Because of the narrow channel and the location of the fort, the Union vessels had to attack head-on, which effectively made them stationary targets for the Confederate gunners.

The *Chillicothe*, like most of the second-generation river ironclads, was poorly designed and even more poorly constructed by corrupt or careless contractors. The iron gunport covers and the wooden backing of her armored casemate soon buckled under repeated blows from solid shot, and she was forced to withdraw. Despite this unexpected problem, Smith still might have taken Fort Pemberton had he simply steamed ahead with one or both of his ironclads and pulverized the small earthwork at close range, but he was not Farragut or Porter. While Smith dawdled, Loring strengthened Fort Pemberton and brought in additional men and guns from Grenada. Union reinforcements arrived as well, and another half-hearted effort was made to capture the Confederate fortifications, but to no avail. The back door to Vicksburg via Yazoo Pass was sealed shut. Soon the battered flotilla of gunboats and transports was on its way back to the Mississippi. Because of the initiative demonstrated by Brown and Loring, the Confederates had achieved a tidy tactical and moral victory.

The end of the Yazoo Pass expedition, one way or another, could not come soon enough for the thousands of soldiers jammed aboard the transports. Officers were assigned cabins, but enlisted men were herded onto the decks and expected to make the best of it. Soldiers on the lower decks shared their living space with mules and horses; those on the upper decks were exposed to the wind and rain. Fires were not permitted for obvious reasons, so men tried to cook their rations by placing meat and dough near fireboxes, boilers, steam pipes, or anything else that radiated heat. Sanitation was a nightmare aboard overcrowded boats lined up bow to stern in narrow, sluggish streams. "In some respects it was the hardest of our soldiering," wrote Andrew Sperry. "Diarrhea was universal, almost unanimous. Few of us remained in as good health as usual, and many contracted diseases to whose sad end the lonely grave-yard on the bare Helena hills, within the next few months bore witness."[9]

Though the Yazoo Pass expedition was a failure, most of the Union participants, soldiers and sailors alike, considered their escape from the miasmatic bottomlands to be a victory of sorts. "When our boat reached the Mississippi river, we fired a 'grand salute' of all the muskets on board, and the one six-pound brass field piece on the bow, as a kind of greeting to the noble river," recalled Sperry. "Cramped up as we had been for almost six weeks, on the narrow rivers in the swamps, it gave us a great feeling of relief, to come out again on the broad Mississippi, where there was room enough to breathe."[10]

Even while the ill-fated Yazoo Pass expedition was underway, Porter decided to try another route that he believed might enable a joint army-navy expedition to reach the Yazoo River north of Haynes' Bluff. A vast amount of water had poured through the cut in the Mississippi River levee at Yazoo Pass, and the admiral reasoned that the water level in the bayous that laced the bottomlands had risen enough to float gunboats and transports through streams that were not normally navigable.

On March 12, while Smith and Loring dueled at Fort Pemberton, Porter explored the downstream portion of the Yazoo Pass route. He made a personal reconnaissance up Steele's Bayou, which flows into the lower Yazoo River opposite the mouth of Chickasaw Bayou (the scene of Sherman's disastrous assault the previous December). Information gleaned from maps and helpful slaves indicated that the upper portion of Steele's Bayou connects with Black Bayou, which leads to Deer Creek, which in turn reaches the Rolling Fork, which flows into the Big Sunflower, which enters the Yazoo River about ten miles above Haynes' Bluff. Once in the Yazoo the Union expedition could turn north and take Yazoo City and Fort Pemberton from the rear or turn south and operate against Haynes' Bluff. The serpentine route was about 130 miles in length.

Porter secured Grant's agreement for a joint army-navy reconnaissance-in-force up Steele's Bayou. By this time Grant may have been a bit leery of Porter's schemes, but he was impressed by the admiral's energy. The two men were alike in their approach to the Vicksburg problem, determined to maintain the initiative, probe for weaknesses, and seek opportunities. Both also intuitively understood that if Pemberton remained passive behind his fortifications, which he seemed content to do, it was only a matter of time before they found the solution.

On March 14 five "turtles" and assorted smaller vessels, with Porter in personal command, steamed up the Yazoo River and turned north into Steele's Bayou. Grant accompanied the expedition for thirty miles. Satisfied that at least the first part of the route was practicable, Grant returned to the Mississippi River. He sent Sherman after Porter with as many troops as could be crammed aboard the few available light-draft transports. (The army had only a limited number of such vessels, and most of them were immobilized on the Coldwater and Tallahatchie Rivers awaiting the outcome of the impasse at Fort Pemberton.)

The pace of the expedition slowed when Porter turned into Black Bayou, a narrow stream that apparently had never been navigated by anything larger than a rowboat. The ironclads cleared their own path by ramming trees to loosen the roots, then backing up and pulling them down with hawsers. Overhanging branches were a constant hazard to stacks and upper works, and decks soon were swarming with snakes, raccoons, and other local fauna. Porter posted sailors with brooms to sweep the unwelcome visitors overboard. Despite these difficulties the gunboats made steady progress, an indication of what might have been accomplished by the Yazoo Pass expedition had it possessed a commander as vigorous as Porter. The flotilla reached Deer Creek and turned north toward the confluence with the Rolling Fork. The natural levees bordering Deer Creek were high and dry, and for the first time the Union sailors encountered signs of civilization.

By March 19 the Confederates finally grasped what Porter was trying to do. Up to this point the Federals had been opposed only by Lt. Col. Samuel W. Ferguson, who did everything possible to harass the Yankees but whose command strength was too small to have much effect. Brig. Gen. Winfield S. Featherston hurried his brigade from Haynes' Bluff to the confluence of Deer Creek and the Rolling Fork to reinforce Ferguson. The Confederates proceeded most of the way on flatboats and barges towed by steamboats. Lacking artillery they attempted to stop the Union ironclads with axes and muskets.

Porter was within two miles of the Rolling Fork when he encountered a tangle of felled trees blocking the channel. Volleys of rifle fire erupted from the swamps on either side of Deer Creek and drove the sailors inside their boats. Porter attempted to sweep the woods with grapeshot and canister but found that the height of the natural levees rendered his guns almost useless. Stymied, he sent to Sherman for help. But while waiting for the Union infantry, whose light-draft transports were twenty miles to the rear, Porter grew impatient and decided to take on the Confederates himself. He sent a landing party ashore equipped with rifles, pistols, cutlasses, and a pair of howitzers. Demonstrating a good grasp of tactics and terrain, the sailors seized the highest ground in the vicinity—an Indian mound—and drove the Rebels away from Deer Creek.

The ironclads resumed butting their way forward. By the next day they were nearly seventy miles from their starting point at the mouth of Steele's Bayou and only a few hundred yards from the Rolling Fork. That was as far as they got. Confederate reinforcements arrived with a battery of field artillery that forced the Union sailors back to the safety of their ironclads. When the Rebels began dropping cypresses into Deer Creek behind the ironclads, Porter realized that he was in serious trouble. He sent a second courier—a slave from a nearby plantation—to Sherman, then he put his men on half rations, made ready to repel boarders, and prepared to blow up the ironclads if all else failed. When Sherman learned that the admiral and his flotilla were trapped, he disembarked Col. Giles A. Smith's brigade and sent it forward on foot and then dispatched the transports back to the Mississippi to bring up additional troops. Colonel Smith made good time along the natural levee of Deer Creek and reached Porter late on the afternoon of March 21. His eight hundred men soon cleared away the Confederates and, with the help of the sailors, cleared away the trees as well.

Porter had nearly lost the heart of the Mississippi Squadron to a few hundred Confederate soldiers in a swamp. Drained by the harrowing experience, he ordered the withdrawal of the gunboats to continue, despite the presence of Union infantry. The channel was clear by midnight and the boats resumed creeping backward the next day, with Smith's men moving along the banks to keep the enemy at bay.

But Colonel Ferguson, who was far more aggressive than Featherston, had not yet given up hope of trapping the gunboats. After six miles the flotilla encountered another barricade of felled trees and a hail of bullets from Confederates who had circled around the slow-moving vessels. Smith readied his troops for a fight when, in the nick of time, Sherman arrived with reinforcements and scattered the Rebels. "I do not know when I felt more pleased to see that gallant officer," Porter reported to

Welles of his meeting with Sherman. A week later the transports and gunboats, much the worse for wear, emerged from the wilderness and resumed their stations on a more appropriate body of water.[11]

By the end of March 1863 both the Yazoo Pass and Steele's Bayou operations were effectively over. Temporarily demoralized by the dual setbacks, Porter concluded that Grant should return to Memphis and attempt to reach Vicksburg by a more traditional overland approach from Tennessee. Grant too was disappointed by the litany of failures, but he understood that a return to Memphis was impossible. People in the North would interpret a withdrawal from Vicksburg as an admission of defeat, and there was no reason to expect that a second overland campaign would be any more successful than the first. The Army of the Tennessee and the Mississippi Squadron would stay and find a way to achieve victory.

But victory, when it came, would not take place north of Vicksburg. Grant was certain that his initial assessment of the situation was correct. He now returned to the idea of moving his army down the west side of the Mississippi River and crossing somewhere below Vicksburg. Winter had given way to spring, and the long Southern summer was approaching. The Mississippi was finally beginning to drop. In a few weeks the land on the Louisiana shore would emerge from the spring floods and the roads would be firm enough to support an army on the march.

But before Grant could put his plan into motion, he had to take into account developments in southern Louisiana. While Sherman's soldiers at the lower end of the De Soto Point canal watched in amazement, a massive warship steamed up the Mississippi and dropped anchor just out of range of the Vicksburg batteries. Admiral Farragut had returned.

# CHAPTER SIX

# Detour in Louisiana

Shortly after he approved McClernand's proposal to raise an army and lead it against Vicksburg, Lincoln selected Maj. Gen. Nathaniel P. Banks to replace Benjamin Butler as commander of the Department of the Gulf. Banks was a former Speaker of the House of Representatives and a powerful force in the Republican Party. He had been appointed a major general at the outbreak of the war despite a complete lack of military training or experience. Like many "political generals," Banks demonstrated serious shortcomings in the field, though he was not without ability, and he was destined to play a key role in the struggle for the Mississippi River.

The appointments of McClernand and Banks were connected. Lincoln was frustrated by the sluggish pace of events in the West in the summer and fall of 1862. He hoped that ambitious politicians in uniform would energize the struggle to open the Mississippi River. Halleck was less certain. His doubts about Banks were magnified by geography. The Department of the Gulf consisted of the southeastern corner of Louisiana and several smaller coastal enclaves in Florida, Mississippi, and Texas. Separated by a thousand miles of ocean from the North, Banks would be both isolated and independent. Halleck had whittled McClernand down to size, but Banks was a far more formidable figure. Not only was he politically untouchable, but as one of the more senior generals in the army, Banks outranked practically everybody, including Grant. Resigned to making the best of an unpromising situation, Halleck showered Banks with advice and encouragement. "The President regards the opening of the Mississippi River as the first and most important of all our military and naval operations," intoned Halleck in one of many such letters, "and it is hoped that you will not lose a moment in accomplishing it."[1]

Banks reached New Orleans on December 15, 1862, after a passage down the Atlantic coast and across the Gulf of Mexico. He was followed by a stream of ships bearing reinforcements for the Union occupation force in Louisiana. The last of these troops did not dribble in until February 1863, but Banks lost no time forming the twenty-five thousand Union soldiers in Louisiana into the Nineteenth Corps. He divided the corps into four divisions commanded by Maj. Gen. Christopher C. Augur and Brig. Gens. William H. Emory, Cuvier Grover, and Thomas W. Sherman. The Nineteenth Corps was generally known as the Army of the Gulf.

On December 17, one week before Sherman arrived in front of Vicksburg, Banks reoccupied Baton Rouge. It was his first and, for a long time, only offensive move. Within days of arriving in Louisiana, Banks became mired in the chaos left by his predecessor. This was precisely the sort of thing that Halleck feared would happen, but it was unavoidable.

Banks bore a greater array of responsibilities than any other Union general. In addition to serving as commander of the Department of the Gulf, he also was military governor of occupied Louisiana. And if that were not enough, he was charged by President Lincoln with the task of "reconstructing" that state's civilian government. This meant that in addition to opening the Mississippi River and maintaining order in Louisiana, Banks was expected to create a new Unionist state government to replace (or, more accurately, to compete with) the Confederate state government, which had fled from Baton Rouge to Opelousas. This was an extraordinarily complex assignment, one without precedent in American history.

While the new commander wrestled with everything from banking laws to race relations and struggled to comprehend the labyrinth of Louisiana politics, his soldiers, mostly New Yorkers and New Englanders, adjusted as best they could to garrison duty in an exotic culture. The mild winter weather gave no hint of the searing heat and suffocating humidity to come or of the subtropical maladies that would decimate the Federal ranks. The most exciting event that transpired during the winter undoubtedly was the accidental fire that gutted the Gothic-revival state capitol in Baton Rouge.

During the first three months of 1863, Banks surprised everyone, perhaps even himself, with his accomplishments. He established a reasonably effective and honest civil administration, launched the process of political reconstruction, raised a substantial force of black troops (which he named the Corps d'Afrique), strengthened fortifications throughout the department, and accumulated a stockpile of stores and munitions for future operations. Despite a stream of increasingly strident messages from

Halleck urging him to move upriver and cooperate with Grant, who by this time was floundering in the mud around Vicksburg, Banks correctly concentrated on getting his own house in order before marching off into the unknown.

When he turned to the business of opening the Mississippi River, Banks discovered the limitations of Union military power in deepest Dixie. Because of the need to man fortifications and maintain order in occupied territory, he could safely put only about three-fifths of his twenty-five thousand troops in the field, and he was not certain how long he could keep them there. The general had only a handful of shallow-draft steamboats capable of transporting men, animals, and supplies through Louisiana's maze of navigable streams and lakes. The vast majority of such craft plying the western rivers were in Union hands, but nearly all of them were north of Vicksburg. Though Farragut's warships controlled several key waterways in the Department of the Gulf, the lack of transports prevented Banks from fully exploiting this advantage. Union mobility was further hampered by a lack of cavalry mounts and draft animals. Few horses and mules survived the long sea voyage from the North, and few could be found in occupied Louisiana, which had been stripped bare of military resources by the Confederates.

The former Speaker of the House was no military genius, but he recognized, as his superiors in Washington did not, that he lacked the resources to carry out a sustained campaign against the formidable Confederate stronghold of Port Hudson, the geography of which is similar to that of Vicksburg. The low-lying land on the west side of the Mississippi River is a continuation of the alluvial plain that bedeviled Grant one hundred miles to the north. The east side of the river is bordered by the familiar line of bluffs, sixty to eighty feet high. Though the topography of Port Hudson is not as spectacular as that of Vicksburg, the yellowish loess soil erodes in the same irregular fashion, producing the same peculiar landscape of plateaus and ravines.

The hamlet of Port Hudson no longer exists, but in the mid–nineteenth century it overlooked a bend where the Mississippi made a 110-degree curve around a swampy headland called Thompson Point. Port Hudson was the western terminus of an antique short-line railroad that ran to Clinton, a prosperous town nineteen miles to the northeast. Unfortunately for the Confederates, thirty-five miles of dirt roads lay between Clinton and the nearest station on the New Orleans, Jackson, and Great Northern Railroad. Without a rail connection to the eastern Confederacy,

Port Hudson was largely dependent on a vulnerable waterborne supply line to the trans-Mississippi Confederacy via the Red River.

The Confederate position was initially commanded by Brig. Gen. Daniel Ruggles, who established the first river batteries; then by Brig. Gen. William N. R. Beall, who laid out the initial landward fortifications; and finally by Maj. Gen. Franklin Gardner, who arrived on December 27, 1862. Gardner had been a classmate of Grant at West Point and was a veteran of the Mexican War, Seminole War, and frontier duty. Like Pemberton, he was a Northerner (in his case a New Yorker) who had married a wealthy Southern woman and cast his lot with the Confederacy. Gardner's brother was a Union officer, but his brother-in-law, Alfred Mouton, was a Confederate general and his father-in-law, Alexandre Mouton, had served as governor of Louisiana, a U.S. senator, and president of the Louisiana Secession Convention. In his own way Gardner was as well connected politically as McClernand or Banks.

Gardner established a busy regimen of drill and work for the Port Hudson garrison, which varied in size from twelve to sixteen thousand men during the winter of 1862–63. Port Hudson's initial landward defenses were designed only to ward off an attack from Union-occupied Baton Rouge, sixteen miles to the south, but when Banks approached Port Hudson from the opposite direction in the spring of 1863, Gardner extended the defenses around to the east and north. The completed semicircular line of earthworks was four and a half miles in length and enclosed the hamlet and the river batteries. The fortifications were less elaborate than those at Vicksburg and consisted primarily of a parapet fronted by a ditch and abatis.

Belles and balls were absent from Port Hudson, but the daily routine of garrison life was enlivened from time to time by the arrival of distinguished visitors. In March 1863 Lt. Gen. Edmund Kirby Smith inspected the garrison before heading west to assume command of the Department of the Trans-Mississippi from Theophilus Holmes. Smith moved the department headquarters from Little Rock to Alexandria because of the latter's location on the Red, which by the spring of 1863 had become one of the more important rivers in the Confederacy. A week later Sterling Price arrived in Port Hudson and announced that he too was on his way to the trans-Mississippi to liberate his home state of Missouri from Federal oppression. Both generals exhorted Gardner's men to keep open the corridor between the two halves of the Confederacy. The presence of so many starry collars in such an obscure place demonstrated that with the Federals in possession of the shore opposite Vicksburg, Port Hudson was the last secure Confederate crossing point on the Mississippi.

While Banks plowed through paperwork in New Orleans and Gardner dug in at Port Hudson, Farragut learned of the loss of the *Queen of the West* and the *Indianola* inside the Vicksburg–Port Hudson corridor. Never one to sit idly by while there was work to be done, the admiral decided to take his warships past Port Hudson and reestablish the blockade of the Red River. Farragut discussed the matter with Banks and pointed out that because Port Hudson was supplied by river, he might be able to isolate the place and compel its garrison to evacuate. Banks then would be able to join Grant and commence operations against Vicksburg. Farragut's plan appealed to Banks, for it promised a relatively bloodless solution to the vexing problem of Port Hudson. The only difficulty was the matter of getting the Union warships past the Confederate guns, but the admiral had done that sort of thing three times (once at Forts Jackson and St. Philip and twice at Vicksburg), and he was confident of success. To make success a little more certain, Farragut requested that Banks demonstrate against Port Hudson from the landward side and distract the garrison.

Banks set out from Baton Rouge for Port Hudson at the head of twelve thousand men, but he failed to consider that his inexperienced soldiers had been cooped up inside ships and fortifications since joining the army and were unfamiliar with campaigning. The march proceeded at a snail's pace and was marked by confusion and disorder. When the time came for Farragut to make his move, the floundering Union column was still several miles short of the Rebel earthworks. "Banks had as well be in New Orleans or at Baton Rouge for all the good he is doing us," snapped Farragut when he learned of the situation.[2]

Farragut was determined to proceed with or without Banks's assistance. He felt that the safest route for his warships was the deep channel running close to the east bank of the river. Because of the thickness of the Confederate earthworks, Farragut believed that the heavy guns could not be depressed sufficiently to fire on targets passing directly under the bluffs. He left the cumbersome ironclad *Essex,* the mortarboats, and assorted oceangoing ships behind to protect New Orleans and Baton Rouge. He intended to take only seven vessels past Port Hudson. As usual, he would command in person aboard *Hartford.*

A few hours after sunset on March 14, 1863, the Union flotilla weighed anchor and steamed toward the guns of Port Hudson. The Confederates had detected the forest of masts assembling downstream and were on full alert. At 11:22 a rocket blazed into the sky above Port Hudson: enemy ships approaching. Bonfires illuminated the river, and the first of six hundred large-caliber shells rained down on the Union vessels. A Confederate soldier recalled that "the whole atmosphere appeared to be full of the screaming, exploding heavy bombs." The noise could be heard in the outskirts of New Orleans, one hundred miles to the southeast.[3]

*Hartford* and *Albatross*, lashed together for protection and additional motive power, led the way. Navigating the Mississippi River in an ocean-going vessel was a tricky proposition in daylight; it was next to impossible when the main channel was obscured by darkness and smoke and the pilots were distracted by explosions, flashes of light, hails of shrapnel and splinters, and shouts and screams. Upon reaching the bend around Thompson Point, *Hartford* failed to swing to port quickly enough and went aground on the east bank. After several heart-stopping moments the combined engines of the two ships pulled her free. The two ships churned through the bend, hugging the east bank all the way, and emerged from the maelstrom with only minimal damage and casualties.

The rest of the Union flotilla fared less well. *Richmond* and *Genesee*, also lashed together, were done in when the *Richmond* lost power after a Confederate shell tore through her hull and smashed the steam valves. The smaller *Genesee* was unable to maintain headway against the current. "We were, for a few minutes, at the rebels' mercy," reported Cmdr. James Alden of the *Richmond*. "Their shell were causing great havoc on our decks; the groans of the wounded and the shrieks of the dying were awful. The decks were covered with blood." The pair of ships swung sharply to port and headed back downstream. This maneuver precipitated a disastrous chain reaction.[4]

By now visibility was severely limited, and *Monongahela* and *Kineo* were misled by the sight of *Richmond* and *Genesee* turning to port. Assuming that they were approaching the bend in the river, *Monongahela* and *Kineo* turned as well and went aground on Thompson Point. After a desperate struggle punctuated by the crash of shells tearing through rigging and hulls, the pair pulled themselves off the bar, but the damage had been done. *Monongahela*'s overheated engines shut down. With *Kineo* unable to push both ships against the current, the crippled pair drifted to safety in the wake of *Richmond* and *Genesee*.

Bringing up the rear was the venerable *Mississippi*, Matthew Perry's flagship during his famous visit to Japan in 1854. On her quarterdeck was a promising young lieutenant named George Dewey, who would lead his own squadron to victory in Manila Bay thirty-five years later. Blindly following *Monongahela* and *Kineo,* the huge paddlewheeler also turned to port prematurely and plowed into the mud of Thompson Point. She soon was burning furiously and her captain ordered her abandoned. As the flames gradually consumed the *Mississippi,* she floated free and drifted downstream, ablaze from waterline to mast tops. A tremendous explosion took place when the fire reached her magazine. Capt. Homer B. Sprague, a dozen miles away with Banks's army on the far side of Port Hudson, wrote that the blast lit up the night sky "from horizon to horizon with a fiery splendor. The stars sank in an ocean of flame. For ten seconds the lurid glare filled the sky; then came a moment of dense blackness; and then, a crash so loud and deep that the earth shook for a hundred miles, and it seemed as if all the thunder of the past five hours had been concentrated in one terrific peal." The shattered hull of the old warship disappeared into the river for which she was named.[5]

Because most of the Union ships passed the Confederate batteries twice, naval casualties at Port Hudson were more severe than on previous occasions. About seventy-five Union sailors were killed or wounded; thirty-seven crewmen from the *Mississippi* were captured. Confederate losses were about twenty-five killed, wounded, and missing. Some of the Rebel casualties were infantrymen struck by Union shells that sailed over the edge of the bluffs and landed far to the east in camps and earthworks.

For the first time since entering the Mississippi River eleven months earlier, Farragut had failed to get the heart of his squadron past an enemy position. Disappointed but undaunted he pressed ahead with only *Hartford* and *Albatross.* Confederate steamboats fled in all directions, spreading the dreadful news that Union warships once again were loose between Vicksburg and Port Hudson. Farragut dropped anchor off the lower end of the De Soto Point canal on March 20. For the rest of the struggle for the Mississippi River, Grant and Banks would be in direct, though sometimes tenuous, communication via the Union navy.

Farragut intended to ask Porter for reinforcements, but the commander of the Mississippi Squadron was up Steele's Bayou and temporarily out of touch. When Ellet learned of Farragut's predicament, he offered the services of two of his rams. As the sun rose on March 25, the rams raced around De Soto Point into a hail of artillery fire from the Vicksburg batteries. *Lancaster* was sunk and *Switzerland* was struck in a boiler, but she drifted downstream to the safety of Farragut's warships, whose engineers repaired the damage. When a frazzled Porter finally emerged from Steele's Bayou, he was heartened to learn that Union warships had returned to the Vicksburg–Port Hudson corridor. He urged Farragut to descend the Mississippi as quickly as possible and reestablish the blockade of the Red. "It is death to these people," he wrote his foster brother; "they get all their supplies from there."[6]

Farragut needed no urging. He bid farewell to the Hill City on March 28, and the odd trio of *Hartford, Albatross,* and *Switzerland* dropped downstream. Despite the minuscule size of his flotilla, Farragut was determined to interdict or at the very least disrupt Confederate river traffic and do whatever he could to help Banks operate against Port Hudson. The Union flotilla anchored off the mouth of the Red on April 1. A short time later Farragut approached Port Hudson and dispatched a courier to Banks. The courier floated past the Confederate guns in a skiff disguised as a log. He carried the information that Grant hoped to send McPherson's corps from Lake Providence to the Red River as soon as a sufficient number of light-draft transports and barges became available. (All such vessels presently were involved in the Yazoo Pass and Steele's Bayou operations.) Upon reaching the Red, McPherson would move downstream to the Mississippi and land at Bayou Sara, a short distance above Port Hudson. He then would cooperate with Banks in reducing that Confederate bastion.

Purely by coincidence Banks had settled on a plan that dovetailed nicely with Grant's proposed course of action. Not long after arriving in Louisiana, Banks had received an intriguing suggestion from Brig. Gen. Godfrey Weitzel, who was stationed at Brashear City (now Morgan City) about seventy miles southwest of New Orleans. From his location in south-central Louisiana on the east bank of the Atchafalaya River, Weitzel had a different geographical perspective on the situation. He suggested that the best way to link up with Grant was not to attack Port Hudson, but to avoid it altogether and slip into the Vicksburg–Port Hudson corridor from the west via Alexandria. Once in Alexandria, Banks would be able to interdict the flow of supplies on the Red River, much of which went to Port Hudson. He also would be within cooperating distance of Grant.

Weitzel had discovered the strategic possibilities offered by the unusual X-shaped confluence of the Mississippi and Red Rivers. The Mississippi approaches the confluence from the northeast; the Red the from the northwest. At the confluence, generally referred to as the mouth of the Red, some of the current of the Red enters the Mississippi and flows southeast past Port Hudson, Baton Rouge, and New Orleans to the Gulf of Mexico. Much of the current of the Red, however, veers off to the south just before the meeting and forms the Atchafalaya River. (For the geographically challenged the Atchafalaya might be thought of as the misnamed lower portion of the Red.) The Atchafalaya is a broad, navigable stream that flows almost due south through a vast swamp of the same name and reaches the Gulf of Mexico about 130 miles west of the Mississippi. West of and parallel to the Atchafalaya is Bayou Teche, a smaller stream that meanders along the edge of the waterlogged alluvial plain. The land west of Teche is generally high and dry, with roads suitable for the passage of an army all the way north to Alexandria.

With civil and political affairs in occupied Louisiana beginning to take shape, Banks decided to do as Weitzel suggested. He would move as many men as possible to Brashear City, cross the Atchafalaya River, then turn north and advance up the west side of Bayou Teche to Opelousas, sixty miles south of Alexandria. The few available transports would accompany the army on Bayou Teche, though Banks expected his men and animals to live off the land as much as possible. Smaller warships of the West Gulf Blockading Squadron would ascend the Atchafalaya, clear away Rebel forts and gunboats, and secure the army's line of communications with Brashear City. From Opelousas Banks would decide whether to press on to Alexandria or return to the Mississippi River. It was a good plan with significant strategic potential.

Halleck, meanwhile, continued to remind Banks of his mission. "The President expects that you will permit no obstacle to prevent you from co-operating with [Grant] by some movement up the Mississippi River," he wrote Banks, with obvious exasperation, at the beginning of February. "Of such vital importance is this cooperation that nothing but absolute necessity will excuse any further delay on your part." At the end of February Halleck adopted an ominous tone, warning Banks that there was "much dissatisfaction here at the delay" in moving against Port Hudson.[7]

Banks was about to move, but not as Halleck expected. At the end of March he ferried two divisions of the Army of the Gulf to the west bank of the Mississippi River. Grover's division floated down Bayou La-fourche from Donaldsonville to Thibodaux, then rattled westward on the Opelousas and Great Western Railroad to Brashear City. Emory's division traveled all the way from Algiers to Brashear City on the same rickety railroad. Thomas Sherman's division and part of Augur's division remained behind to safeguard New Orleans and Baton Rouge against the possibility of an attack by the Port Hudson garrison. Banks was right to be prudent, but he overestimated Gardner, who demonstrated even less initiative than Pemberton.

On April 11 the Union force at Brashear City, now sixteen thousand strong and with Banks in personal command, crossed the Atchafalaya River and advanced north along the west bank of Bayou Teche past fields green with sugar cane. The Union offensive against the southern flank of the Vicksburg–Port Hudson corridor finally was underway.

The Bayou Teche country is the heart of French-speaking Acadiana. It was defended by Richard Taylor and a small force of about three thousand Confederates. Taylor had helped Thomas J. Jackson drive Banks out of Virginia's Shenandoah Valley the previous spring, and he yearned to do the same in his native Louisiana, but the Confederate policy of siphoning men and material from the trans-Mississippi left him without sufficient strength to strike a blow. As evidence mounted that Banks was planning a movement northward from Brashear City, Taylor constructed a line of earthworks on either side of Bayou Teche four miles north of Patterson-ville (now Patterson). The left end of the Confederate line rested on Grand Lake, part of the Atchafalaya Swamp, the right on a marsh. The gunboat *Diana* provided artillery support from Bayou Teche, which bisected the fortifications. This elongated complex was named Fort Bisland.

Banks launched a bold two-pronged attack against Taylor's line on April 12–14. While Emory's division deployed in front of the Confederate earthworks and engaged in an exchange of artillery fire, Grover's division carried out an amphibious envelopment of the Confederate left flank. The handful of transports shuttled back and forth across Grand Lake, slowly ferrying thousands of Union soldiers past the eastern extremity of Fort Bisland. The troops went ashore near Franklin, well behind the Confederate position. Taylor was caught completely off guard by Banks's audacity. When he learned that the Federals were in his rear, Taylor abandoned Fort Bisland in the middle of the night, burned the *Diana,* and hurried north. The Rebels fought their way past Grover at a curve in Bayou Teche named Irish Bend and narrowly escaped being cut off. The sharp clashes at Fort Bisland and Irish Bend cost each side about six hundred casualties. Had not the shortage of transports delayed Grover's movement on Grand Lake, the entire Confederate force might have been trapped. For Banks, the victory at Fort Bisland, however incomplete, was an auspicious beginning to the campaign.

After being flushed out of Fort Bisland, Taylor retreated northward up the west side of Bayou Teche. Banks followed close behind. The two

Union forces sever the Vicksburg–Port Hudson corridor

forces skirmished occasionally, but there was little Taylor could do to slow the Union juggernaut. As Confederate morale plummeted, one-third of Taylor's men deserted, many in hopes of protecting their families and possessions from the invaders. Banks reached Vermillionville (now Lafayette) on April 17 and Opelousas on April 20. The governor, legislators, and bureaucrats of the Confederate state government packed up for the second time and fled to Shreveport in the far northwest corner of Louisiana. Taylor retreated to Alexandria. It was the Shenandoah Valley all over again, except this time the roles were reversed.

The Confederate retreat was on the verge of becoming a rout when Banks unexpectedly broke off the pursuit. The Army of the Gulf paused in Opelousas for two weeks while its commander rushed back to New Orleans by steamboat and railroad in order to deal with his myriad civil and political responsibilities, a sure sign that he was wearing too many hats. During this initial phase of the campaign, Farragut's courier arrived and informed Banks of Grant's intention to send McPherson's corps in his direction. Banks was elated. Everything seemed to be coming together even better than he had anticipated. He informed Grant that his forces would be in Alexandria on the Red River in the very near future.

Banks was as good as his word. He returned to Opelousas on May 4 and sent the Army of the Gulf hurrying north toward Alexandria. The Union column fairly raced across the level Louisiana countryside; Weitzel's brigade, for example, covered ninety miles in three days. Unable to halt or even delay the onrushing Federals, Edmund Kirby Smith had no choice but to abandon Alexandria and the entire lower Red River Valley, including Fort Taylor (De Russy). Thousands of panicked civilians departed along with the soldiers, many of them herding their slaves toward Texas for safekeeping. Smith followed the refugee Confederate state government up the Red to Shreveport, with Taylor and the remnant of his army following behind as a rear guard. Farragut described the exodus as a "general stampede."[8]

During the advance from Brashear City to Alexandria, a distance of 150 miles but considerably longer by the meandering roads of the day, the soldiers of the Army of the Gulf consumed or destroyed huge amounts of food and forage and confiscated much-needed boats, wagons, and draft animals. Banks, like Grant before him, discovered that certain bountiful areas of the Confederacy were capable of supporting an army on the march. Whether the troops knew or cared about the emerging Union policy of waging war against Southern resources is uncertain, but

there was a growing conviction in the ranks that Southerners, regardless
of political allegiance, should suffer for the sin of secession. Foraging
degenerated into vandalism, and the fertile Bayou Teche country was
devastated. The Federals liberated about six thousand slaves, many of
whom joined in the orgy of destruction.

While Banks moved overland toward Alexandria, a part of the West Gulf
Blockading Squadron under Lt. Cmdr. Augustus P. Cooke was busy on
the Atchafalaya River. Cooke's mission was to advance in concert with the
army and open navigation of the river to Union shipping. Having failed
to halt Banks, Taylor sought to stop Cooke. On April 14, the day the
Confederates fought their way out of the trap at Irish Bend, the *Queen
of the West* made a surprise night attack against four Union vessels on
Grand Lake. It was a bold but futile gesture. A barrage of gunfire set the
Confederate boat afire, and she blew up with a heavy loss of life.

With the well-traveled ram finally out of the way, Cooke steamed
northward through the Atchafalaya Swamp. On April 20 the Union flotilla
approached Butte-a-la-Rose (now Butte la Rose) and made short work
of Fort Burton, a tiny redoubt mounting only two old guns. On May
1 the *Arizona* and *Estrella* emerged from the Atchafalaya and cautiously
entered the Red. No Confederate vessels were in sight. The two gunboats
turned downstream toward the Mississippi, where the *Hartford, Albatross,*
and *Switzerland* maintained their lonely vigil. Cooke reported to a greatly
relieved Farragut that the Atchafalaya was open to the Gulf of Mexico.
Port Hudson was bypassed. The admiral received more good news a few
days later when Porter appeared at the head of a flotilla of ironclads from
the Mississippi Squadron. Porter announced that Grant had crossed the
Mississippi River below Grand Gulf. Then he steamed up the Red to
meet Banks at Alexandria.

The Army of the Gulf marched into Alexandria on May 7, six days
after Cooke reached Farragut. Banks was immensely pleased with his
six-week campaign into central Louisiana. For the first time in the war,
he had carried out a major military operation without experiencing defeat
or disaster. "Our success has been splendid," Banks boasted to his wife.
"All say it is the cleanest, the best conceived and best executed campaign
of the war." That was an exaggeration, but Banks deserved considerable
credit for the success of the Bayou Teche campaign. He directed a large
and complex operation that required cooperation between the army and
navy. He overcame weak but spirited resistance and gained his objective,
Alexandria. Faced with daunting logistical problems he partially subsisted

his mobile command on the Louisiana countryside, doing so *two weeks before* Grant's far more celebrated use of the same method in Mississippi. In the process Banks devastated a large swath of Louisiana and gobbled up or destroyed immense amounts of food that otherwise would have gone to Confederate forces. Finally, by rampaging through central Louisiana when he did, Banks kept Taylor and Smith occupied and made it possible for Grant to move down the west side of the Mississippi River without interference. Upon reaching the Red River Banks was poised to carry out joint operations with Grant against either Vicksburg or Port Hudson. This was the high point of his military career.[9]

Even Halleck was impressed. "The operations of your army have been truly brilliant and merit high praise," he told Banks. Never one to compliment without nagging, Halleck again urged Banks to unite with Grant as soon as possible and gain possession of the Mississippi. "It is worth to us forty Richmonds."[10]

That is exactly what Banks wanted to do, but it was not to be. Unlike Sherman at Chickasaw Bayou, McClernand at Arkansas Post, and Grant at Vicksburg, Banks did not have a sufficient number of transports in the Department of the Gulf to carry his army long distances over water. This was the reason why his troops had marched over two hundred miles from Brashear City to Alexandria instead of cruising up the Atchafalaya River on a convoy of steamboats. (Even the movement of Grover's single division across Grand Lake during the fight for Fort Bisland had stretched Union transportation to the limit.) After pausing at Opelousas Banks eagerly continued on to Alexandria because he believed that Grant was moving McPherson's corps south from Lake Providence on a large number of light-draft transports and barges. Banks was confident that his transportation problems would be solved when this mobile amphibious force joined his land-bound army on the Red.

But by the time Banks reached Alexandria, the strategic situation in the lower Mississippi Valley had changed dramatically. When he rode into the town, Banks was delighted to find a half dozen Union ironclads tied up along the waterfront, but when he conferred with Porter, he received a tremendous shock. Porter announced that Grant and his entire army—including McPherson's corps—had crossed to the east side of the Mississippi River and was marching *away* from Banks into the interior of the Magnolia State. Banks was stunned by the news. What had happened? Where was Grant going? And what was Banks to do?

# CHAPTER SEVEN

# River of No Return

During the night of March 28, 1863, thunderstorms raised havoc in the Union camps and anchorages opposite Vicksburg. Perhaps the spectacular display of nature's might cleared Grant's head, for the next morning he made the fateful decision that left Banks high and dry at Alexandria six weeks later. He ordered McClernand to move his Thirteenth Corps down the west side of the Mississippi River from Milliken's Bend to New Carthage, midway between Vicksburg and Grand Gulf, where he was to prepare to cross the river. The exact landing site on the east bank was yet to be determined, but once across McClernand would march south to Port Hudson or north to Vicksburg as circumstances dictated. The rest of the army would follow.

Sherman and McPherson had serious reservations about the projected movement; the former even sent Grant a letter stating his objections (thus putting them on record in case of disaster). McClernand, however, enthusiastically supported the plan. For months he had schemed to regain command of the expedition, but his intemperate letters to Stanton and Lincoln had not had the desired effect. Despite his bitterness at being superceded, McClernand had dutifully carried out Grant's directives during the winter and spring. Now ironically he was the only corps commander to demonstrate enthusiasm for the operation that would elevate Grant to the top tier of Union generals and relegate McClernand to the sidelines.

The most serious problem Grant faced was logistical. In order for the operation to succeed, he needed a reliable means of moving supplies across the soggy Louisiana countryside. The roads were not yet firm enough to carry the hundreds of vehicles needed to support a force the size of the Army of the Tennessee. A solution seemed to be at hand in the form of Walnut Bayou. The army's line of march would be the winding road that ran atop the natural levee alongside the bayou; the line of supply would be the bayou itself.

Union engineers laid out a canal from Duckport on the Mississippi River (between Young's Point and Milliken's Bend) to a back swamp about a half mile inland. The nameless, meandering streams in the swamp flowed into Walnut Bayou, three miles farther inland. When the canal was completed and the bayous cleared of obstructions, the result was a narrow, serpentine waterway, thirty-seven miles in length, that connected the Mississippi above Vicksburg with New Carthage below. On April 13 the Mississippi River levee was cut and water surged through the canal and into the bayous. A procession of dredges, tugboats, and heavily laden barges entered the passage and set out for New Carthage. Everything was going according to plan. Then came an unexpected setback. The high water in the Mississippi that had plagued the Federals all winter suddenly fell and stranded the vessels. Disappointed and disgusted, Grant ordered the Walnut Bayou route abandoned. Like every other Union engineering project in the bottomlands, it had come to naught.

While Grant explored other means of moving supplies, the operation went forward. McClernand's corps began slogging south on the Walnut Bayou Road on March 31. It was the most difficult advance of the war. The spring flood was receding earlier than expected, as the Duckport Canal–Walnut Bayou fiasco demonstrated, but the land was far from dry. Pioneer troops, aided by ordinary soldiers and freedmen, constructed dozens of bridges and miles of causeways and corduroy roads (tree trunks laid crossways across the roadbed like railroad ties). The work was arduous and progress was slow. "The road was all but impassable," recalled an Ohio soldier named Owen J. Hopkins. "It lay through a vast bog, intersected by numerous bayous half flooded with water. The heavy artillery wheels cut through the slime and the mud, making the path a perfect mortar bed through which we waded knee deep, and where the hubs of the wheels often disappeared out of sight." The morass would have stopped most Civil War armies in their tracks, but McClernand's Midwesterners pushed on and reached New Carthage on April 6.[1]

The movement of such a large force could not be kept secret from the Confederates for long, so Grant attempted to distract Pemberton. While McClernand headed south Grant sent Maj. Gen. Frederick Steele's division of Sherman's corps in the opposite direction. Steele left Milliken's

Bend on April 2 and steamed upriver to Greenville, Mississippi, about seventy miles north of Vicksburg. The Federals destroyed half a million bushels of corn and carried off over a thousand animals. They also liberated more than a thousand slaves. Steele returned to Milliken's Bend on April 24. The primary purpose of the Greenville expedition was to divert Pemberton's attention away from McClernand, but it also reflected a shift in the policy of the Lincoln administration. "The character of the war has very much changed within the last year," Halleck informed Grant. "There can be no peace but that which is forced by the sword." Henceforth the army was to bring the war home to Southern civilians by enforcing emancipation and seizing or destroying all items of possible military value.[2]

A few months earlier Halleck had directed Grant to enroll freedmen into military service. Grant accepted the new policy without hesitation and made it clear that he expected everyone under his command to "especially exert themselves in carrying out the policy of the Administration, not only in organizing colored regiments and rendering them efficient, but also in removing prejudice against them." During the spring of 1863 swelling numbers of black troops began drilling at Milliken's Bend under the watchful eye of Brig. Gen. Lorenzo Thomas, the adjutant general of the U.S. Army.[3]

In a similar fashion Grant accepted the new policy of expanding the war to include Southern social and economic institutions. "Rebellion has assumed that shape now that it can only terminate by the complete subjugation of the South or the overthrow of the Government," he informed Steele. "It is our duty therefore to use every means to weaken the enemy by destroying their means of cultivating their field[s], and in every other way possible." Steele was to seize or destroy everything of military value in his path, including food, animals, and slaves, which is exactly what he did.[4]

The Confederate response to the Greenville expedition was all that Grant could have hoped for. Pemberton ordered Stephen Lee to halt Steele's depredations. While Lee entered the bottomlands north of Vicksburg in search of the Federals, who had long since returned to Milliken's Bend, McClernand moved closer to New Carthage. The unheralded Greenville expedition was a success both as a raid and as a diversion.

Steele's expedition was followed by two coordinated Union operations that dispersed Confederate military forces and left Pemberton more distracted than ever. Hundreds of miles to the northeast, Rosecrans launched a daring effort to sever Bragg's line of communications and compel the Confederate Army of Tennessee to abandon its namesake state. In mid-April he sent Col. Abel D. Streight and an infantry brigade mounted on mules toward the Western and Atlantic Railroad between Atlanta and Chattanooga. After a grueling running battle with Nathan Bedford Forrest's cavalry across northern Alabama and Georgia, Streight and his command were compelled to surrender. Forrest's hard-fought victory saved Bragg but weakened and possibly even doomed Pemberton. Though the Federals failed to reach the railroad, they drew Forrest all the way to Georgia and left his men and animals worn to a frazzle. The most effective Confederate cavalry commander in the West would play no further role in the struggle for Vicksburg.

With Forrest fully occupied by Streight and his mule-mounted soldiers, Maj. Gen. Stephen A. Hurlbut, commanding Grant's Sixteenth Corps from Memphis, launched a raid of his own against Pemberton's line of communications. On April 17 Col. Benjamin H. Grierson and seventeen hundred cavalrymen left La Grange, Tennessee, and headed south through the gap in the Confederate defensive perimeter created by Forrest's absence. Grierson's objective was the Southern Railroad of Mississippi, two hundred miles inside Confederate territory. His command reached the railroad at Newton Station, sixty-five miles east of Jackson, on April 24. The men tore up tracks and telegraph wires and burned bridges and water towers. But instead of returning to Tennessee, Grierson continued south and reached Baton Rouge on May 3. The Federal horsemen met no significant opposition on their sixteen-day, 475-mile odyssey through he heart of the Confederacy. Losses came to four men killed, sixteen wounded, and seventeen missing.

Grierson's raid was the most spectacular Union cavalry operation of the war. It began as a strike at Pemberton's line of communications but evolved into an extremely successful diversion. The true importance of the raid was not the amount of damage inflicted on the Southern Railroad, which was relatively minor, but the uproar Grierson created within Pemberton's department and, more to the point, within Pemberton's head. The Rebel commander assumed personal control of the effort to stop Grierson. For the better part of two weeks, while the main body of the Army of the Tennessee was on the move across his front, Pemberton focused his attention on a few regiments of Federal cavalry in his rear.

As winter passed into spring, Pemberton gradually lost touch with the constantly changing tactical situation in his department, particularly along the Mississippi River. This was in part a problem of his own making. During Grant's abortive overland campaign from the north, Pemberton had assumed operational command of his forces in the field, but thereafter he established his headquarters in Jackson, forty miles east of Vicksburg, where he was free to immerse himself in paperwork. During the first four months of 1863, the Confederate commander visited the Hill City only occasionally. For nearly all of that period, Grant was closer to Vicksburg than Pemberton.

After five months of parrying Union thrusts, Pemberton was showing signs of strain. "Enemy is constantly in motion in all directions," he informed Secretary of War James Seddon, using words that revealed both exasperation and confusion. Steele's Greenville expedition kept Pemberton's attention focused on his immediate right flank above Vicksburg, the scene of almost continuous Union activity since the battle of Chickasaw Bayou. Grierson's raid shifted his attention around to his far right flank and rear. Distracted by these pinpricks, Pemberton was slow to sense that the bulk of Grant's army was flowing south through Louisiana toward his untested left flank. "So far enemy has gained nothing toward opening the Mississippi," he declared in early April. While that complacent message hummed over the telegraph lines to Richmond, McClernand's soldiers were spreading out along the levee at New Carthage.[5]

Pemberton did have some reason for optimism. A large number of Union transports steamed up the Mississippi in April. Pemberton tentatively concluded that Grant might have given up after the failure of the Yazoo Pass and Steele's Bayou operations and that the annoying cavalry raids were designed to mask a Union withdrawal. "I think most of Grant's forces are being withdrawn to Memphis," he reported, undoubtedly with a heartfelt sigh of relief. It was wishful thinking at its finest.[6]

If Grant was indeed pulling back, Pemberton thought it likely that much of the Union force opposite Vicksburg would join Rosecrans in Tennessee. Joseph Johnston shared this view and approved Pemberton's decision to send part of his command to bolster Bragg. (Pemberton intended to return the equivalent of Carter Stevenson's division, which Davis and Johnston had borrowed from Bragg back in December 1862 to reinforce Vicksburg.) His subordinate's interpretation of Union activities was reasonable and also accounted for the fact that the Federal camps west of De Soto Point were not as crowded as had been the case a short time earlier. The obvious conclusion was that Grant's soldiers were returning north from whence they had come.

A large number of Union transports were, in fact, heading for Tennessee, but they were empty. Rosecrans was experiencing logistical problems, and Halleck directed Grant to release the smaller steamboats that could operate most effectively on the Ohio, Cumberland, and Tennessee Rivers, the vessels used to carry troops into the bayous north of Vicksburg. In early April dozens of boats, many of them much the worse for wear, pulled away from Young's Point and Milliken's Bend and churned northward. The Union logistical redeployment unintentionally acted as yet another diversion and misled Pemberton into thinking that he had outlasted Grant.

While Pemberton insisted that all was well, Brig. Gen. John S. Bowen began to suspect otherwise. A West Pointer and one of Pemberton's best officers, Bowen commanded the Confederate outpost south of Vicksburg at Grand Gulf. When he learned that a Federal force of unknown size was gathering at New Carthage about fifteen miles to the north, he sent Col. Francis M. Cockrell's brigade of Missouri infantry across the Mississippi River to find out what was going on. Cockrell and his men discovered what the Federals had been up against since the beginning of the campaign. "Most of the route lay through a vast sheet of water covering the surface of both woods and fields, from knee to waist deep," recalled a Missouri soldier. After floundering across the flooded Louisiana countryside for a week, Cockrell encountered strong Union detachments several miles south of New Carthage. He gathered as much information as he could, then reported to Bowen that something big was underway. Bowen in turn informed Pemberton that the Federals appeared to be moving down the west side of the Mississippi River in force. But Pemberton dismissed his subordinate's warning with three fatal words: "Much doubt it."[7]

With the Walnut Bayou route impractical because of low water, Grant had no choice but to attempt to send supplies down the Mississippi River to New Carthage directly under the Confederate guns. He realized that it would be next to impossible to maintain McClernand's corps, much less the entire army, for any length of time by such a perilous route, but he hoped to slip enough material past Vicksburg to keep the men and animals at New Carthage alive until he could arrange something better.

Grant informed Porter that he intended to run transports loaded with food and forage past Vicksburg. If most of the boats survived the passage,

McClernand's command not only would have enough to eat for several more days but would also have a means of crossing the river. Grant was concerned about the possibility that Confederate gunboats might dash out of the Red River, evade Farragut's tiny flotilla, and destroy the transports after they reached New Carthage. He asked Porter whether a pair of ironclads could accompany the transports downstream. The admiral was agreeable as always, but he warned Grant that once the ironclads went below Vicksburg, "we give up all hopes of ever getting them up again." The "turtles" made about six knots moving with the current, which permitted them to pass Vicksburg in less than half an hour. Moving against the current, however, they would be under fire for well over an hour, probably closer to two. The plodding ironclads would be nearly stationary targets for the Confederate gunners, who only a few days earlier had demonstrated their skill by perforating the *Switzerland* and *Lancaster.* The newer ironclads were slightly faster than the "turtles," but they had a disturbing tendency to disintegrate under fire.[8]

Grant hesitated. What if Sherman and McPherson were right? Perhaps he was taking too great a risk by moving south. A few days after directing McClernand to head for New Carthage, Grant ascended the Yazoo River on one of Porter's ironclads to see for himself whether a more powerful thrust against the Haynes' Bluff–Walnut Hills fortifications might succeed. The sight of miles of earthworks convinced Grant that a second assault would fare no better than the first. He informed Porter: "After the reconnaissance of yesterday I am satisfied that an attack upon Haynes' Bluff, would be attended with immense loss of life, if not with defeat. This, then, closes out the last hope of turning the enemy by the left." The moment of self-doubt was over. Grant now was certain that the only course of action left to him was to cross the Mississippi below Vicksburg. The Army of the Tennessee would go south.[9]

And so would most of the Mississippi Squadron. Grant had asked for two ironclads to accompany the transports, but after thinking the matter over, Porter concluded that a more substantial naval force would be necessary. Moreover Secretary of the Navy Welles had instructed Porter to lead the Mississippi Squadron into the Vicksburg–Port Hudson corridor as soon as possible so that Farragut could return to New Orleans and resume active command of the West Gulf Blockading Squadron. Porter decided to dash past Vicksburg with his ironclad flagship, *Benton;* four "turtles," *Louisville, Pittsburg, Mound City,* and *Carondelet;* two new ironclads, *Lafayette* and *Tuscumbia;* and the captured ram *General Price.*

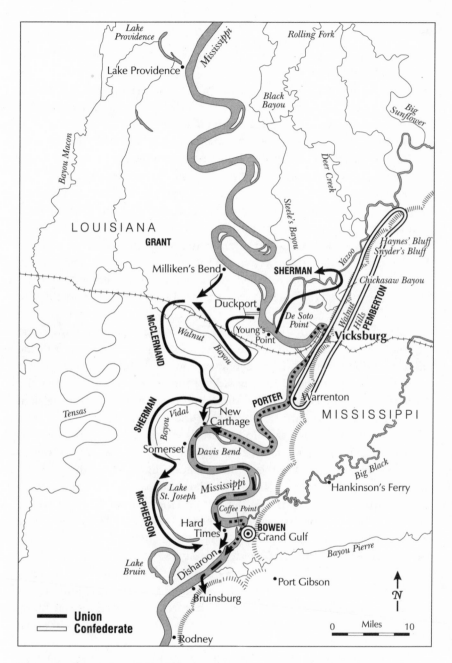

Grant moves south through Louisiana

The eight gunboats would be accompanied by three transports loaded with food and forage and covered with bales of cotton and hay. Barges filled with coal and additional stores would be lashed to the gunboats and transports. To ensure that his instructions would be carried out to the letter, Porter would lead the flotilla aboard *Benton*.

The most dramatic episode in the long struggle for Vicksburg, and one of the most spectacular episodes in the entire Civil War, began two hours after dark on April 16, when the heart of the Mississippi Squadron got underway. The darkened vessels crept around the tip of De Soto Point, hugging the west bank. Union soldiers climbed trees for a better view and sailors crowded the upper decks of the vessels left behind. Grant, accompanied by wife Julia and their children, watched from a transport. Sherman waited near the lower end of the canal in charge of a tiny flotilla of his own: four rowboats manned by his soldiers strung across the broad river. If the worst happened, he was prepared to rescue survivors floating downstream.

Porter was in the pilothouse of the *Benton* at the head of the single line of boats. After rounding De Soto Point undetected, he muttered to the pilot that "the rebels seem to keep a very poor watch." Moments later a flare blossomed on the Vicksburg side of the river. Fires erupted as the Confederates torched vacant buildings and lit barrels of tar and bales of cotton soaked in turpentine to illuminate and silhouette their targets. But not a shot was fired, and the Union vessels continued downstream.[10]

On this particular night a ball was underway in one of Vicksburg's finest residences. Many of the artillery officers in charge of the river defenses were in attendance. When the alarm sounded, the officers bade their partners good night and rushed out into the unearthly orange light of burning tar and cotton. Six minutes ticked by—six critical minutes during which many of Porter's boats slipped past the silent batteries opposite De Soto Point—before the first Confederate gun roared into action. A few minutes more and the crash of heavy artillery and the rattle of musketry were all that could be heard. Billows of smoke from the fires and dozens of heavy guns settled on the river and obscured the scene. Muzzle blasts and shell explosions illuminated the sulfurous cloud from within like heat lightning.

All order in the Union line was soon lost as the captain or pilot of each vessel called for full speed and set his own course past the Confederate guns. Some boats steered toward the middle of the river and raced downstream as fast as their engines and the current could carry them;

others lost their way in the smoke and veered back and forth across the broad stream. Several of the unwieldy "turtles" slipped out of control in unseen eddies and spun round and round as the current carried them to safety. Gunners aboard the ironclads could see almost nothing because of the smoke, but that did not prevent them from contributing to the hellish scene. They fired over one hundred large-caliber rounds into Vicksburg, smashing buildings with shot and shell and spraying the waterfront with grapeshot.

Despite being taken by surprise, the Confederate gunners fired over five hundred rounds and scored perhaps seventy hits. The hail of heavy shot and shell smashed armor, sprung beams and planks, severed steam lines, and riddled stacks and wheelhouses. A near disaster occurred when the *Lafayette* briefly went aground on the east bank directly in front of a Rebel battery. She was struck nine times at pointblank range before pulling free. Several shots smashed through one side of the huge vessel and out the other but failed to damage her engines and guns.

Only one unlucky transport and a coal barge failed to rush, spin, or drift past the Confederate batteries. The civilian crew of the *Henry Clay* abandoned their burning vessel when they might have been able to douse the fire. The pilot was made of sterner stuff and stayed at his post until the end. He jumped into the river and was rescued by Sherman's rowboat patrol. The transports *Silver Wave* and *Forest Queen* made it through.

Porter assembled his battered boats below Vicksburg. To his great relief he discovered that every surviving vessel was still operational, or soon would be, and that only twelve sailors had been wounded during the fiery passage. The next morning the flotilla tied up along the levee at New Carthage to the cheers of McClernand's troops. Carpenters and engineers prepared the gunboats for their next encounter.

Grant was as relieved as Porter, but he would need more than two transports to ferry his army across the Mississippi. He ordered a second passage on the night of April 22. This time there would be no panicky civilian crews. Six transports manned by army volunteers were packed to the rafters with stores and protected with logs, cotton bales, bags of flour and oats, and barrels of salted meat. Each boat was lashed to two barges loaded with additional supplies. The fragile boats would sprint past Vicksburg as fast as possible; there would be no attempt at keeping formation or executing maneuvers under fire.

A few hours after dark on April 22, the transports *Tigress, Empire City, Moderator, Anglo-Saxon, Horizon,* and *J. W. Cheesman* rounded De Soto

Point. The Confederate sentries were alert and the artillerymen were at their posts. Flares and bonfires illuminated the scene as before, and guns rained shot and shell on the transports as soon as they came within range. The volume of fire was twice as great as had been the case six nights earlier, partly because the gun crews were in a higher state of preparedness and partly because they did not have to keep their heads down. The unarmed Union transports did not shoot back.

Once again the river in front of Vicksburg was filled with light and noise. "It was the most magnificent display of fireworks ever witnessed by man," recalled William E. Strong aboard the lead transport, *Tigress*. "It seemed as though Heaven and Hell had turned everything loose to destroy us. I can never forget it, nor can I describe it. Only those who faced this terrible concentrated fire, or who witnessed it from Vicksburg or the headquarters boat, can have the faintest idea of its beauty." Because the transports had no guns, there was little smoke on the river, and the Union soldier-sailors had a clear view of Vicksburg. "The streets of the city were filled with citizens," continued Strong, "and hundreds of ladies, dressed in white, had congregated on the slope of a bluff called 'Sky Parlor Hill.' The gunners at work could be distinctly seen, and a newspaper could have been read with ease from the hurricane-deck of the 'Tigress.'" A lifetime of civilian habits was hard to put aside, even at such a moment, and Strong noticed that the officers around him checked their pocket watches against the clock in the Warren County Courthouse as they sped past. It was 12:20 A.M. Vicksburg time.[11]

If Vicksburg could be seen clearly from the transports, the transports could be seen with equal clarity from Vicksburg. Bathed in the now-familiar flickering orange light, the transports had the advantage of speed, though the barges slowed them down considerably. But they took a terrific pounding nonetheless. The *Tigress* was hulled and went down in shallow water near the lower end of the canal. All of the other boats were damaged, some seriously, and half of the barges were sunk or cut adrift and lost. Two men were killed and six were wounded. The five surviving boats reached New Carthage at dawn.

When the sun rose on April 17, 1863, the Confederacy was sundered. "I regard navigation of the Mississippi River as shut out from us now," Pemberton telegraphed President Davis. "No more supplies can be gotten from Trans-Mississippi department." This was a logistical catastrophe not only for Pemberton but for the entire Confederacy. Soldiers from

David D. Porter. Vicksburg National
Military Park (VNMP).

USS *Cairo*. VNMP.

(*Above left*) Ulysses S. Grant. VNMP.

(*Above right*) John C. Pemberton. VNMP.

(*Left*) John A. McClernand. VNMP.

css *Arkansas*. VNMP.

Nathaniel P. Banks. U.S. Army
Military Institute (USAMHI).

Franklin Gardner. USAMHI.

Orion P. Howe (standing) of the Fifty-fifth Illinois. VNMP.

(*Opposite top*) Shirley house. VNMP.

(*Opposite bottom*) Mine explosion
beneath Third Louisiana Redan. VNMP.

(*Top*) Coonskin's Tower. VNMP.

Grant and Pemberton meet to
discuss surrender terms. VNMP.

Vicksburg to Virginia depended on supplies from Louisiana and Texas via the Red River. Those supplies no longer would arrive because the Vicksburg–Port Hudson corridor had ceased to exist in any meaningful way.[12]

Pemberton also recognized that Grant now had the means to cross the Mississippi River below Vicksburg whenever and wherever he chose, but he did little to prepare for such an eventuality. After sending a second infantry brigade to Grand Gulf, which doubled Bowen's strength to about forty-two hundred men, Pemberton's attention was captured by alarming reports of a Federal cavalry force rampaging unopposed through Mississippi. Grierson's raid was underway. From the Union perspective the timing could not have been better.

Grant's gambles were paying off. The arrival of the heavily laden transports and barges at New Carthage solved his pressing logistical problems, at least in the short run. McClernand's men and animals would not starve for another week or two. More important, the transports gave him the capability to ferry troops across the Mississippi River and gain a foothold on the east bank. The immediate questions were where to cross and what to do on the other side.

Grant made his way down to New Carthage on April 18 to discuss the situation with McClernand and Porter. By this time all four divisions of the Thirteenth Corps had crowded into the New Carthage area. Two divisions of McPherson's Seventeenth Corps were on their way down from Lake Providence to Milliken's Bend and shortly would begin marching south on the Walnut Bayou Road. Sherman's Fifteenth Corps remained behind for the time being, but it would follow in due course. There was not enough dry ground around New Carthage to serve as a staging area for tens of thousands of men and animals and hundreds of wheeled vehicles. Another crossing point would have to be found.

The next day McClernand's corps marched south from New Carthage in two columns, one atop the Mississippi River levee, the other a short distance inland on the Bayou Vidal Road (essentially a continuation of the Walnut Bayou Road). When Bowen learned that Porter's gunboats were below Vicksburg, he recalled Cockrell's brigade to Grand Gulf, lest it be cut off. This was another break for Grant, for it meant that McClernand advanced without meeting any resistance. It also meant that Bowen no longer received reliable information about what was happening on the Louisiana side of the river.

McClernand's two columns reunited at Somerset, a landing on the

Mississippi River eight miles below New Carthage. When Somerset also proved inadequate as a staging area, McClernand sent a reconnaissance force around Lake St. Joseph to Hard Times, the next landing downstream. The road along the oxbow lake was firm and the Federals reached Hard Times without any difficulty. The landing was high, dry, and spacious. Opposite Hard Times the Big Black River flows into the Mississippi from the east. The wide, turbulent confluence of the two streams is Grand Gulf. The remains of a small town of the same name were located on the east bank of the Mississippi a short distance below the mouth of the Big Black. It had been burned by Farragut earlier in the war, but good roads led from the charred waterfront into the interior of Mississippi. Grant considered this to be an ideal place to land.

On April 28 the seven transports, all more or less repaired, carried three of McClernand's divisions down the Mississippi from Somerset to Hard Times; the fourth division marched around Lake St. Joseph on the route taken by the reconnaissance force. The next day two of McPherson's divisions reached Hard Times by the same road after an arduous march from Milliken's Bend. By the evening of April 28, half of the Army of the Tennessee was crowded along the west bank of the Mississippi sixty-three roundabout overland miles below Milliken's Bend.

Three miles downstream at Grand Gulf, Bowen watched the smoke from hundreds of campfires darken the sky over Hard Times. He had repeatedly warned Pemberton that the Federals were moving in his direction with overwhelming force. Now he tried again to get the Confederate commander to understand what was happening: "I advise that every man and gun that can be spared from other points be sent here."[13]

That was the very thing Grant feared most. Grand Gulf was only thirty miles south of Vicksburg by road. If Pemberton woke up and sent Bowen enough men to defend the towering bluffs behind the ruined town, it would be Chickasaw Bayou all over again. In order to buy as much time as possible, Grant asked Sherman to make a strong demonstration against the Confederate positions north of Vicksburg. Sherman quickly packed Brig. Gen. Francis Blair's division aboard ten transports and churned up the Yazoo River, with whistles blowing and bands playing. After two days of noisy skirmishing in front of the Haynes' Bluff–Walnut Hills fortifications, Sherman returned to Young's Point and sent two of his three divisions down the Walnut Bayou Road toward New Carthage and Hard Times. Whether this demonstration had the desired effect on Pemberton is uncertain, but it revealed Grant's determination to do everything possible to distract and confuse his opponent.

While Sherman put on a show north of Vicksburg, Grant prepared to cross the Mississippi River at Grand Gulf. He believed Porter's gunboats could hammer the Confederate fortifications into submission, just as they had done at Arkansas Post. Porter was less certain, regarding Grand Gulf as "the strongest place on the Mississippi." He was right to be cautious. Bowen and his men had worked feverishly to prepare Grand Gulf to withstand a naval attack. Fort Cobun was a massive earthen structure with walls forty feet thick located partway up the bluff north of the ruined town and mounting several heavy weapons. Fort Wade, located just below the town, held a mammoth 100-pound Blakely rifled gun and other heavy weapons.[14]

Despite his misgivings Porter agreed to throw everything he had at Grand Gulf. On the morning of April 29, thousands of McClernand's soldiers crowded aboard transports and barges. The vessels pulled away from Hard Times and gathered behind a long peninsula named Coffee Point. There they waited for word from Porter that his ironclads had silenced the Confederate guns. When it was safe to proceed, the transports would cross the river to Grand Gulf, disembark the troops along the charred waterfront, and hurry back to Hard Times for reinforcements.

Grant watched from a small tugboat while Porter led his seven ironclads against the Confederate forts in the last major ship-vs.-shore engagement on the western rivers in the Civil War. Fighting raged at such close range that nearly every shot found its target. The "turtles" *Louisville, Mound City, Carondelet,* and *Pittsburg* pounded Fort Wade and silenced its guns. They swung around and laboriously made their way upstream where *Benton* (with Porter aboard), *Lafayette,* and *Tuscumbia* were slugging it out, nearly muzzle to muzzle, with Fort Cobun. The unearthly din caused by discharging guns, exploding shells, and iron shot striking iron plate was beyond description. To mesmerized spectators on both banks, the black-painted ironclads seemed to glide like wraiths through swirling clouds of smoke and dust.

After six hours of the most intense fighting ever to take place on the Mississippi River, Porter called a halt in order to rest his crews and assess the damage. The ironclads chugged over to the west bank, where surgeons, engineers, and carpenters did what they could to repair men and machines. The *Benton* and *Pittsburg* were struck forty-seven and thirty-five times respectively but stayed in the fight to the end. As luck would have it the poorly built *Tuscumbia*, a particularly large target, received over eighty hits and lost armor plates, port shutters, and an engine. At least twenty-four Union sailors and soldiers (the latter serving as volunteers aboard the gunboats) were killed and another fifty-six wounded.

Although Porter had no way of knowing, his ironclads gave worse than they got. The Union flotilla fired over twenty-three hundred large-caliber rounds into the Confederate earthworks (Bowen thought the number was closer to three thousand). Both forts were heavily damaged, and every gun but one was destroyed, dismounted, or buried under heaps of dirt. Bowen lost three men killed and fifteen wounded; one of the dead was Col. William Wade, the chief of artillery. After the ironclads withdrew, the Confederates struggled to repair their forts and remount their guns.

The standoff at Grand Gulf presented Grant with another opportunity to demonstrate his growing mastery of mobile warfare. Porter reported that only one or two enemy guns remained in operation, but the general decided that landing at Grand Gulf was too dangerous. McClernand's men returned to Hard Times and disembarked. Late in the afternoon, at Grant's request, Porter led his battered ironclads back toward Grand Gulf and began a desultory bombardment of the fortifications. While this twilight engagement was in progress, the empty transports and barges swung around Coffee Point and slipped past Grand Gulf in the gloom. After half an hour, the ironclads followed the transports down the river.

The soldiers of McClernand's and McPherson's corps left Hard Times and resumed their southward march across the base of Coffee Point, out of range of the Confederate guns. After midnight the Union army and navy reunited at Disharoon plantation, seven miles below Hard Times and four miles below Grand Gulf. Pemberton was outflanked, though he did not yet know it. That same night, while the Federals gathered at Disharoon, the befuddled Confederate commander telegraphed a plaintive query from his headquarters in Jackson: "Is anything going on at Vicksburg or Grand Gulf?"[15]

A short distance downstream from Disharoon on the east bank of the Mississippi was an insignificant landing named Bruinsburg. A Union patrol crossed the river and encountered a slave whose name, unfortunately, was never recorded. The man informed his interrogators that a road led inland from Bruinsburg to Port Gibson and that there were no Confederate soldiers nearer than Grand Gulf. A cavalry regiment normally patrolled this stretch of the east bank, but Pemberton had sent the horsemen in futile pursuit of Grierson four days earlier.

During April, Grant moved down the west side of the Mississippi River in search of an opening to exploit. Cautious at first, he became bolder and more opportunistic as the operation unfolded. When New Carthage and Somerset proved unsatisfactory as staging areas, he moved on. Hàrd Times was a suitable place to concentrate for a crossing, but Grand Gulf was too tough a nut to crack, so Grant pressed on to Disharoon. He was prepared to continue south to Rodney when he learned of the obscure road that ran up the bluffs from Bruinsburg. All that mattered now was to get the Army of the Tennessee across the Mississippi River as rapidly as possible. Grant and McClernand worked through the night to ensure that everything was in readiness for the morrow. Aboard *Benton* Porter sat in his tiny cabin and wrote a letter to Secretary Welles telling of the battle at Grand Gulf. Just before closing he added, "We land the army in the morning on the other side, and march on Vicksburg."[16]

# CHAPTER EIGHT

# The Odds Are Overpowering

If only Matthew Brady or one of the many talented combat artists of the Civil War such as Edwin Forbes or Alfred Waud had been present on April 30, 1863, they would have captured for posterity one of the most sublime moments in American military history as the Army of the Tennessee crossed the Mississippi River. With paddlewheels churning the muddy water and flags snapping in the breeze, gunboats and transports, some of them with barges lashed alongside, pulled away from Disharoon and cautiously approached Bruinsburg. "The decks were covered with anxious soldiers," recalled an Indiana volunteer, "guns were cleared for action, and the crews were at quarters." Grant and Porter shared the cramped pilothouse aboard the *Benton*. Tension mounted as the vessels neared the east bank and all eyes watched the tree-lined shore for signs of the enemy.[1]

Such anxiety was for naught, and the Union soldiers and sailors were relieved to find only a lone citizen at the tiny landing to greet them. (This unfortunate man was detained aboard an ironclad to prevent him from informing Confederate authorities that the invasion of Mississippi had begun.) A band aboard the *Benton* struck up "The Red, White, and Blue," and cheers rang out as the vanguard of the Army of the Tennessee went ashore unopposed.

During the day twenty-four thousand men and sixty guns were ferried across without incident. After months of frustration and failure, Grant finally was on the east side of the Mississippi River. He recalled the moment in his memoirs: "When this was effected I felt a degree of relief scarcely ever equalled since. Vicksburg was not yet taken it is true, nor were its defenders demoralized by any of our previous moves. I was

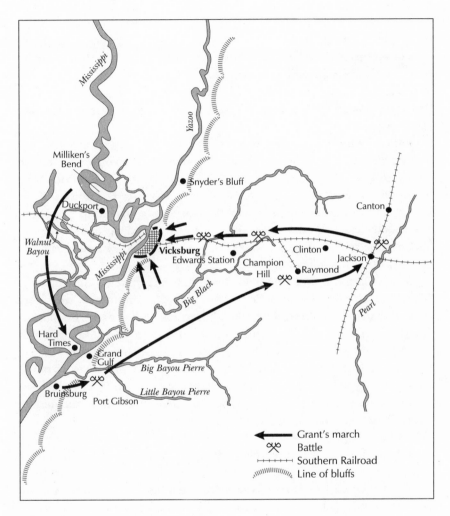

Grant moves on Vicksburg

now in the enemy's country, with a vast river and the stronghold of Vicksburg between me and my base of supplies. But I was on dry ground on the same side of the river with the enemy. All the campaigns, labors, hardships and exposures from the month of December previous to this time that had been made and endured, were for the accomplishment of this one objective." Although many obstacles lay ahead, everyone from the commanding general to the lowliest private seemed to share the same sense of relief and exhilaration. When the time came to move inland, the Federals took up the line of march with firmness of purpose and buoyant spirits.[2]

John McClernand's Thirteenth Corps led the way, as it had since leaving Young's Point four weeks earlier. James McPherson's Seventeenth Corps followed. The long blue column headed toward the bluffs looming in the distance two miles east of Bruinsburg. Charles B. Johnson of the 130th Illinois noted that the road wound past "quiet farmhouses and cultivated fields, through pretty wooded groves and up quiet lanes, all bearing the marks of peace, and resting in supposed security from the inroads of invading armies."[3]

A merciless sun and clouds of dust made the march a difficult one. The Federals were laden with sixty rounds of ammunition and more rations than they could stuff into their haversacks and pockets. Lt. Samuel C. Jones of the Twenty-second Iowa recorded the method by which infantrymen carried a part of their foodstuffs: "The bayonets were placed on their guns and run through the meat, so each man had his extra ration of meat fixed on his bayonet. Then at a right shoulder shift, we proceeded on our march." Soldiers in other units did the same and, as Lieutenant Jones observed, "the whole army could be seen for miles, worming its way over that vast flat country with the bayonets gleaming in the sunshine, and the ration of meat in its place. It was picturesque and beautiful to behold."[4]

When the Federals reached the top of the bluffs, a panoramic view of the Mississippi Valley opened before their eyes. A short distance from the road, rising above fields of corn, was Windsor, one of the largest and most ornate mansions in the South. For many of Grant's soldiers Windsor's towering Corinthian columns must have epitomized the opulence associated with Southern aristocracy. McClernand established his headquarters in the grand house. Less exalted Federals rested in the shade of the oaks lining the drive.

While his men assembled atop the bluffs, McClernand made the decision to push on through the night toward Port Gibson in hopes of securing the bridges across Bayou Pierre. By now word of the Federal presence was spreading like wildfire across the countryside. McClernand was concerned that Confederate forces from Grand Gulf would block the Bruinsburg Road, the most direct route from Windsor to Port Gibson, so he chose a more southerly and roundabout route that he hoped would allow him to reach his objective without a fight. The march inland resumed late in the afternoon. The Federals tramped three miles south from Windsor to Bethel Church, then turned east onto the Rodney Road. Darkness settled over the fields and scattered woodlands, and the pace of the march slowed. Sgt. Charles A. Hobbs of the Ninety-ninth Illinois recorded his experience that night. "As we pass along an old darkey gives us his blessings, but fears there will be few of us ever to return. The moon is shining above us and the road is romantic in the extreme. The artillery wagons rattle forward and the heavy tramp of many men gives a dull but impressive sound. In many places the road seems to end abruptly, but when we come to the place we find it turning at right angles, passing through narrow valleys, sometimes through hills, and presenting the best opportunity to the Rebels for defense if they had but known our purpose."[5]

Grant feared that he might have to fight his way ashore, so he took only infantry and artillery across on the first day. Cavalry and supply wagons were temporarily left behind in Louisiana as were hundreds of horses belonging to field officers. Grant and a few other high-ranking officers rode on mounts seized from unlucky Mississippi farmers, but at this early stage of the operation, most officers trudged inland on foot alongside their men. Because no cavalry was available for scouting purposes, a platoon from the Twenty-first Iowa trotted ahead to act as an advance guard for the Union column on the Rodney Road. The Iowans were instructed to "go forward until fired upon by the enemy." Shortly after midnight on May 1, the Iowans crossed Widows Creek and cautiously approached the A. K. Shaifer house, thirteen miles by road from Bruinsburg. The house was ablaze with light and the yard was full of people.[6]

Back at Grand Gulf Bowen had watched helplessly as the Union fleet passed his batteries and slipped downstream on the evening of April 29. Another officer might have been content to sit inside his fortifications and await the reinforcements Pemberton had promised to send, but Bowen acted quickly to counter the Federal threat to his downstream flank. He

dispatched two brigades—a force of about twenty-five hundred men—
to block the roads leading inland from Bruinsburg and Rodney to Port
Gibson.

Hurrying south from Grand Gulf on the morning of April 30, the
Confederates found the picturesque town of Port Gibson abuzz with
rumors that the Federals were coming ashore at Bruinsburg. About three
miles west of Port Gibson, the Confederates reached good defensive
positions on both the Bruinsburg and Rodney Roads. Brig. Gen. Edward
D. Tracy placed his Alabama brigade, recent arrivals from Vicksburg,
across the Bruinsburg Road just as McClernand had feared. A short
distance to the south, near Magnolia Church, Brig. Gen. Martin E. Green
deployed his brigade of Mississippians and Arkansans astride the Rodney
Road, directly in McClernand's path. He also sent pickets forward to the
Shaifer house near Widows Creek. The two roads are some distance apart
and separated by the densely wooded valley of Centers Creek. Bowen
made an appearance, approved what his subordinates had done, and
returned to Grand Gulf. The Confederates bedded down for the night in
full expectation of meeting the enemy with the rising sun on May 1.[7]

The ground occupied by Bowen's men was ideal for defense. A maze of
flat-topped ridges and steep-sided ravines run in all directions. Although
most of the high ground was cultivated and dotted with buildings, the
deep ravines were choked with an almost impenetrable mass of cane,
vines, and trees. Visibility from the ridge tops is excellent, but as historian
Edwin C. Bearss so vividly describes, "upon descending into the ravines
the jungle closed tightly about, so that each man's world became a tiny
green-walled room only a few yards across." In the fight to come, the
rugged terrain and tangled vegetation would work to the advantage of the
Confederates and prevent the Federals from bringing their overwhelming
superiority in manpower and firepower into full play.[8]

The hours slowly passed, and tension among the soldiers of both
armies mounted as the inevitable clash neared. Shortly after midnight
on May 1, Green decided to check on his pickets at the Shaifer house. He
was amused to find the women of the home frantically loading a wagon
with their most valuable household items. The general assured them that
the Yankees were miles away and would not make an appearance before
daylight. Just then the stillness of the night was shattered by an exchange
of gunfire between Green's pickets and McClernand's advance guard of
Iowans. The Federals had arrived ahead of schedule. The terrified women
leaped into their wagon and whipped the animals toward Port Gibson.

Green ordered his pickets to contest the advance, then rode hard to Magnolia Church to alert his brigade. The Confederates waited nervously as the sound of skirmishing drew ever closer, straining to catch a glimpse of the approaching Federals in the moonlight. Lt. John S. Bell of the Twelfth Arkansas Sharpshooters Battalion recalled: "We could hear the enemy forming, and it was so still we could hear every command given. Our men had orders not to fire until word was given. Soon we could see their line of skirmishers coming down the road and could hear them say there was no one here, it was only a cavalry scout. When they were within 50 yards the word 'fire' was given." Volley after volley of musketry ripped the night, and the fight was on.[9]

The sound of gunfire electrified the troops at the head of the Federal column. Infantry regiments hurried past the Shaifer house and deployed for battle on either side of the Rodney Road. Artillery batteries rumbled up and roared into action. Despite the darkness and the smoke, a spirited exchange of fire continued until around three o'clock in the morning. For the remainder of the night, an uneasy calm prevailed as soldiers of both armies rested on their arms.

As soon as it was light enough to see, Union troops began to move in force toward Magnolia Church. McClernand massed the three divisions of Brig. Gens. Alvin P. Hovey, Eugene A. Carr, and Andrew J. Smith in front of Green's brigade. McClernand sent Brig. Gen. Peter J. Osterhaus's division to confront Tracy's brigade on the Bruinsburg Road to his left. The Bruinsburg and Rodney Roads are connected by a lane running north from the Shaifer house, which permitted the Federals to shift forces back and forth between the roads as needed, a luxury the Confederates did not have. The ensuing battle of Port Gibson consisted of two simultaneous but separate clashes: the main fight on the Rodney Road and a smaller but no less intense struggle to the north on the Bruinsburg Road.

The three Union divisions began a slow and deliberate advance on either side of the Rodney Road. Despite a "galling fire of shell and musketry," the Federals reached Magnolia Church without too much difficulty and engaged in a deadly firefight at close range with Green's Confederates. The once peaceful hilltop around the church became a killing field. Bowen arrived from Grand Gulf at the hottest stage of the fight and informed Green that reinforcements were on the way. But heavily outnumbered and hard pressed in front and on both flanks, Green's soldiers were unable to hang on. The Confederates gave way around ten o'clock and fell back a mile and a half. Roughly halfway between Magnolia

Church and Port Gibson, the Confederates were greeted by the welcome sight of a column of troops approaching from the east.[10]

Arriving on the field not a moment too soon were Brig. Gen. William E. Baldwin's brigade of Mississippi and Alabama soldiers, which had marched all the way from north of Vicksburg, and Col. Francis M. Cockrell's Missouri brigade from Grand Gulf. Bowen hurried the new arrivals forward on the Rodney Road and formed a new and stronger line on a ridge behind a branch of Centers Creek. With the Confederate left wing restored, Bowen sent Green, whose brigade was sadly depleted after five hours of combat, to support Tracy on the Bruinsburg Road. These and other reinforcements that arrived during the course of the day roughly tripled the number of Rebel troops on the field to between seven and eight thousand.

Grant reached the Shaifer house just after McClernand's successful assault at Magnolia Church. The two generals rode forward on the Rodney Road to inspect the field and survey the spoils of war, which included two 12-pound howitzers, three caissons, three ammunition wagons complete with teams, more than two hundred prisoners, and the colors of the Fifteenth Arkansas. Amid cheers of victory McClernand and Gov. Richard Yates of Illinois, who accompanied his constituents during the opening stage of the campaign, did some campaigning of a different nature. Grant permitted the politicians to demonstrate their oratorical skills for a time, then suggested that the advance be resumed. McClernand exchanged his stump for a saddle and returned to the task at hand.

Early in the afternoon the Federal juggernaut resumed, grinding eastward on the Rodney Road toward Port Gibson. McClernand remained in tactical command, which meant that Grant had little to do except pester his principal lieutenant with suggestions. About this time the leading elements of McPherson's Seventeenth Corps reached the Shaifer house. This gave Grant an opportunity to make himself useful by briefing McPherson on the day's events and deciding where to send the new arrivals.

When McClernand's three divisions resumed their drive eastward along the Rodney Road, they encountered Baldwin's and Cockrell's brigades. Bowen had no illusions about his ability to stop the Federals. The approaching Union formations extended well beyond his flanks, yet he was determined to fight for every inch of ground in the faint hope that additional reinforcements from Vicksburg would arrive in time to keep the Federals out of Port Gibson. As fighting flared all across his front,

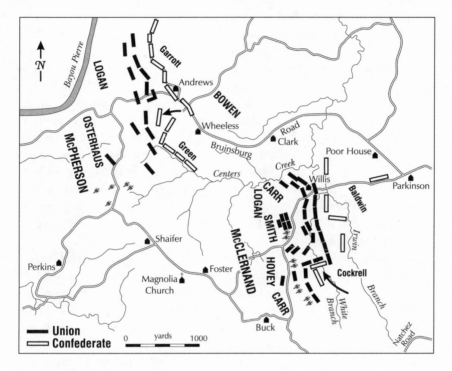

Port Gibson: Afternoon

Bowen detached Cockrell's brigade and sent it around the extreme right of the Union line. The last thing McClernand expected was a Confederate counterattack. Surging out of a maze of ravines south of the Rodney Road, the Missourians caught the Federals by surprise. The Fifty-sixth Ohio gave way, as did the next regiment in line. Rolling up the Federal right flank as they pushed onward, the Confederates next crashed into the Twenty-ninth Wisconsin, whose colonel reported that his men were "hotly pressed with great slaughter."[11]

In the smoke and confusion of battle, Cockrell's men enjoyed initial success, but the Confederates were too few in number to do more than make temporary gains. The Federals recovered and brought the counterattack to a standstill. "Their artillery opened on us with great rapidity," recalled Capt. George W. Covell of the Third Missouri, "and as soon as we got within range the infantry poured the Minie balls into our ranks as thick and fast as hailstones from a thundercloud or rain drops in an April shower." Covell had never before experienced such a heavy fire and later wrote, "The storm of leaden rain and iron hail which was flying through the air was almost sufficient to obscure the sunlight." Cockrell gave up and ordered a withdrawal.[12]

After the survivors of the attack had reached the safety of the Confederate rear, Bowen rode among his fellow Missourians, offering words of praise and encouragement: "I did not suspect that any of you would get away, but the charge had to be made, or my little army was lost." Cockrell's flank attack briefly stalled the Federal advance, but pressure again began to build along the Confederate front. It was now about six o'clock in the evening. Realizing the futility of the situation, Bowen ordered his troops on both roads to retire under cover of darkness to the north side of Bayou Pierre.[13]

While McClernand's principal thrust along the Rodney Road succeeded in forcing the Confederates back toward Port Gibson, his secondary effort along the Bruinsburg Road made little progress for most of the day. During the morning hours Osterhaus's lone division had a difficult time dealing with Tracy's brigade. Whenever the Federals attempted to cross a particularly precipitous ravine cut by Centers Creek, the advancing regiments became entangled in the dense vegetation and either lost momentum, drifted apart, or both. Most Union assaults ground to a halt well short of Tracy's line.

With his formations checked as much by nature as by Confederate fire, Osterhaus resorted to sending waves of skirmishers forward with instructions to wear down the enemy infantry and silence the artillery. Picking their way to within easy range of the Confederates, the Federals found an inviting target in the Botetourt Artillery, the only Virginia unit to participate in the Vicksburg campaign. Exposed on the forward slope of a ridge, men and horses went down at an alarming rate. Then Union artillery found the range and began to shatter gun carriages and limbers with a hail of shot and shell.

Sgt. Francis Obenchain repeatedly sought permission from Tracy to move the battery's caissons to a more secure location. During his third encounter with the general, Obenchain recalled, "a ball struck him on back of the neck passing through. He fell with great force on his face and in falling cried 'O Lord!' He was dead when I stooped to him." Tracy was the first of several Confederate generals to die in the defense of Vicksburg. Col. Isham W. Garrott of the Twentieth Alabama assumed command of the brigade.[14]

Although Tracy was killed early in the action, his brigade held its tenuous position throughout the morning against steadily mounting pressure. Early in the afternoon Green's weary soldiers arrived from the Rodney Road to bolster the sagging Confederate line. But two worn-out brigades could not stop the relentless Federal advance. Osterhaus's troops, supported by a division from McPherson's corps, finally gained the high ground on the north side of Centers Creek. They swept across the Bruinsburg Road and pressed back the Confederate right flank. In desperation Green sent the Sixth Missouri (commanded by Col. Eugene Erwin, a grandson of Henry Clay) forward in a hopeless counterattack to relieve the pressure on Garrott's men, but the lone regiment was driven back with heavy losses. When Green received Bowen's order to withdraw that evening, he retired across Bayou Pierre in the direction of Grand Gulf. The chaotic battle of Port Gibson was over.

Fred Grant, the general's eldest son, accompanied his father throughout the Vicksburg campaign. Despite strict orders to stay well to the rear, he reached the scene of battle in time to witness the closing action. It was an experience that he remembered for a lifetime. "I joined a detachment which was collecting the dead for burial, but, sickening at the sights, I made my way with another detachment, which was gathering the wounded, to a log house which had been appropriated for a hospital. Here the scenes were so terrible that I became faint and ill, and making my way to a tree, sat down, the most woe-begone twelve-year-old lad in America."[15]

The day-long fight cost the Federals 875 casualties: 131 killed, 719 wounded, and 25 missing out of roughly 18,000 troops engaged, mostly from McClernand's corps. The Confederates suffered 60 killed, 340 wounded, and 387 missing, a total of 787 casualties out of somewhat less than 8,000 men engaged.The Rebels fought desperately and made good use of what almost certainly was the most difficult terrain found on any Civil War battlefield, but in the end they were overwhelmed by superior numbers. Bowen summed up the situation in a terse telegram to Pemberton: "We have been engaged in a furious battle ever since daylight; losses very heavy. The men act nobly, but the odds are overpowering." The Missourian did the best he could with what he had, but Grant concentrated more men at the critical point than Pemberton, and that was the difference.[16]

Port Gibson was both a tactical and strategic victory. It not only secured the Union lodgment on the east side of the Mississippi River but also forced the evacuation of Grand Gulf. Pemberton directed Bowen to abandon the town before the garrison was cut off and captured. Early on the morning of May 3, the Rebels spiked the few remaining operational guns, blew up the magazines, and marched out of the battered fortifications. Then they crossed to the north side of the Big Black River and joined the main body of Pemberton's army. Their work of destruction attracted the attention of Union naval forces a few miles down the river at Bruinsburg. The ponderous ironclads slowly worked their way upstream against the current. When Porter reached Grand Gulf and realized that it had been abandoned, he led a landing party ashore and raised the Stars and Stripes over the battered earthworks. Grant's preferred crossing point on the Mississippi River finally was in Union hands. It would serve as a base of operations for the next phase of the campaign.

Pemberton decided that the time had come to move his headquarters from Jackson to Vicksburg. Upon reaching the Hill City he succinctly informed the War Department in Richmond of the day's disastrous events. "Large reenforcements should be sent me from other departments. Enemy's movement threatens Jackson, and, if successful, cuts off Vicksburg and Port Hudson from the east." Pemberton finally saw with terrible clarity the potential consequences of Grant's presence on Mississippi soil.[17]

# CHAPTER NINE

# The Shriek of an Eagle

Grant moved quickly and boldly to exploit his initial success. Since leaving Memphis four months earlier, he had been under strict orders from Halleck to cooperate with Nathaniel Banks in Louisiana. While mired in the mud opposite Vicksburg, Grant had developed plans either to float McPherson's corps from Lake Providence to the Red River or to march McClernand's corps down the east side of the Mississippi River to Port Hudson, depending on circumstances. In recent weeks Grant and Banks had inched closer to one another and exchanged messages via Farragut. A linkup seemed to be in the making.

Recent events changed everything. Rather than send one-third of the Army of the Tennessee on hand to Banks and surrender the tremendous advantage he had gained, Grant decided to advance on Vicksburg with his entire force and leave Banks to fend for himself. He settled on this course of action knowing full well that it would cause anguish in Louisiana and dismay in Washington. The most pressing question for Grant was in which direction to turn. The road north from Port Gibson led directly to Vicksburg, but his keen appreciation of geography argued against this route. After forcing a crossing of the Big Black River, the Army of the Tennessee would be in a narrow triangle of land bordered by the Mississippi River on the west and the Big Black on the east. The rivers would restrict Grant's ability to maneuver, and the deeply eroded terrain would afford Pemberton a succession of natural defensive positions. A series of head-on attacks would bleed the Federal army to death well short of Vicksburg.

Instead of heading straight toward Vicksburg, Grant chose an indirect approach. He decided to move in a northeasterly direction and use the

Big Black River as a shield on his left. (Ironically Pemberton also used the river as a shield or moat as he concentrated his forces for the defense of the Hill City.) Grant's immediate objective was the Southern Railroad of Mississippi. If he could break the railroad somewhere between Vicksburg and Jackson, Pemberton would be cut off from supplies and reinforcements. The Southern had been the target of Grierson's raid, but Grant had no way of knowing whether the Union horsemen had done any significant damage. (They had not.) A drive toward the railroad would take the Army of the Tennessee away from Porter's gunboats on the Mississippi and deep into hostile territory, but the general believed it essential that Vicksburg be isolated. Once that was accomplished he intended to turn west and close in on the Confederate citadel.

Not wishing to advance until his command was united, Grant settled McClernand's and McPherson's corps in the vicinity of Willow Springs east of Grand Gulf and ordered Sherman to join him without delay. Over the next few days the Fifteenth Corps hastened southward through Louisiana from Milliken's Bend, Young's Point, and Duckport to Hard Times. Sherman's troops made good time on roads that had been partially submerged only a few weeks earlier. Because the hard work of corduroying roads and building bridges had been done by McClernand's men in April, the soldiers of the Fifteenth Corps enjoyed the luxury of sightseeing as they tramped along. One Midwesterner described the circuitous route of march: "Sometimes for miles the road was shaded by beautiful live oaks, and catalpas in full bloom, or bordered by a tangled hedge of red and white roses, forming a barricade of beauty eight feet high and more in breadth."[1]

Union troops marveled at the stately homes that dotted the bank of Lake St. Joseph. "These residences, mostly of modern construction and by far the most costly and elegant we had seen in the South, were filled with every appliance of taste and domestic utility," observed a soldier in the Fifty-fifth Illinois. Another infantryman recorded the ill treatment accorded these houses. "The lords of these manors had deserted them in haste, and a few slaves only remained in charge. The troops that had passed before us left proofs of their customary lack of respect for the deserted property of rebels, and at our noon halts groups of tired, dust-covered 'mud-sills' were to be seen seated on satin-upholstered chairs amid roses or in the shade of fig-trees, and eating their bacon and hard-tack from marble-topped tables and rosewood pianos." Devastation followed in the wake of Sherman's corps, and all but a few of the residences along the Union route were burned.[2]

With Grand Gulf now in Federal hands, there was no need for Sherman's men to march all the way to Disharoon and cross the Mississippi River to Bruinsburg. Thus when the Fifteenth Corps reached Hard Times on May 6, the familiar flotilla of gunboats, transports, and barges ferried men, animals, and equipment across the river to Grand Gulf. From there the Federals hastened inland to join their comrades at Willow Springs. The Army of the Tennessee was concentrated in one place for the first time in months.

Grant could not supply his army from Louisiana. He did not, however, immediately sever his line of communications, as is often stated (and as he implied in his memoirs). Instead Grant kept heavily escorted trains of hundreds of wagons moving up behind his army for two weeks after the Bruinsburg crossing. The last such immense train, protected by a full division of Sherman's corps, did not leave Grand Gulf until May 14. Thus the Union "line of communications" existed only when and where trains were actually present.

"I do not calculate upon the possibility of supplying the army with full rations from Grand Gulf," Grant explained to Sherman, who was anxious about the unorthodox logistical situation. "What I do expect," he went on, "is to get what rations of hard bread, coffee, and salt we can, and make the country furnish us the balance." The memory of the bountiful foraging that took place during the withdrawal from northern Mississippi a few months earlier was still fresh in his mind. Beginning at Bruinsburg, where some of the first soldiers ashore commandeered horses for Grant and his staff, the Federals collected food, forage, vehicles, mounts and draft animals, cooking utensils, bedding, and nearly everything else they needed as they moved along. As Grant hoped, the countryside proved perfectly capable of sustaining an army on the march. The only problem was distribution. There was no way to ensure that every soldier received an equal share of the harvest. Some units lived off the fat of the land, while others endured a more Spartan diet, but everyone in blue survived and kept moving on.[3]

Union forces resumed operations on May 7. As Grant prepared to continue his thrust into the heart of Mississippi, he sent a farewell message of sorts to Washington. Informing Halleck of his plans, he added, rather casually, that "you may not hear from me again for several days."[4]

Over a seventeen-day period, from May 1 to May 17, the Army of the Tennessee marched more than two hundred miles, fought five battles, and drove the Confederates into the defenses of Vicksburg. Although often referred to as a nineteenth-century "blitzkrieg," the pace of the Union advance was not particularly fast. The distance and sometimes the direction traveled each day were largely determined by, of all things, the availability of water. No rain fell in central Mississippi during the first half of May, and by the time Grant left Willow Springs, smaller streams were beginning to run dry. Too much water in the soggy bottomlands had hampered Union operations throughout the winter and early spring. Now finally on high (and very dry) ground, Grant found his movements dictated to some extent by a scarcity of water.

Despite this unforeseen difficulty the Federal commander was pleased with the way the operation was unfolding. The view from the ranks was somewhat different. Soldiers were exasperated with the trying conditions of the march and unimpressed with the people and places they encountered in central Mississippi. One infantryman expressed his feelings with a marvelous economy of words: "Water scarce; weather hot; roads dusty; land poor; rations short; houses poor shabby things. Don't like the country." Despite hardships and grumbling Union morale remained high. Officers and men in the dusty blue columns believed that they had the Rebels on the run.[5]

After leaving Willow Springs the Army of the Tennessee moved northeast on a broad front. McClernand's corps was on the Union left, closest to the Big Black River; Sherman's corps was in the center; and McPherson's corps was on the right. This alignment reveals much about Grant's perception of his subordinates and the role that they played during the campaign. It also helps correct the popular image of both McClernand and McPherson.

McClernand is usually depicted as bombastic, egotistic, inept, and reckless. Yet his Thirteenth Corps not only led the march through Louisiana (arguably the most important assignment of the campaign) and was first to cross the Mississippi River, but as the Union army pushed inland it was at all times at the point of danger nearest Pemberton. Contrary to Grant's later claim that he doubted McClernand's fitness for command, he entrusted the energetic and aggressive Illinois politician with a high level of responsibility during the Vicksburg campaign. McClernand had his flaws, but he was the most experienced corps commander in the Army of the Tennessee and boasted an enviable combat record that stretched all the way back to Belmont.

McPherson, a man whom Grant, Sherman, and generations of historians have lionized, was the junior corps commander in Grant's army. In a mere fourteen months he had gone from first lieutenant to major general. This meteoric rise was based largely on his ingratiating personality, which he demonstrated while serving on Grant's staff during the Forts Henry and Donelson and Shiloh campaigns. Due to McPherson's inexperience as a field commander, Grant sought to shield him throughout the Vicksburg campaign by using the Seventeenth Corps in a supporting role whenever possible. Fate, however, would shortly bring McPherson to the fore, and his performance would be less than stellar.

Grant placed Sherman, his most trusted though not necessarily most capable corps commander, in the center as the army pushed inland. In this vital "swing" position the Fifteenth Corps could move left or right to support either McClernand or McPherson as circumstances dictated. Once the army reached a line between Old Auburn and Raymond, Grant planned to wheel to the north and strike the Southern Railroad in the vicinity of Bolton or Edwards Station. Prior to leaving Willow Springs Grant ordered McPherson to make a strong demonstration against Hankinson's Ferry, the point where the road between Port Gibson and Vicksburg crossed the Big Black. He hoped this diversion would keep Pemberton's attention focused south of Vicksburg while the Federals aimed for the railroad to the east.

But Pemberton was on the ball for once. As reports of Union troop movements arrived at his headquarters, he began to suspect that Grant was taking aim at the Southern Railroad. Pemberton shifted his forces northward along the west side of the Big Black, roughly conforming to Federal movements on the east side, but made no attempt to block Grant's progress. His sole aggressive act was an order to Brig. Gen. John Gregg in Jackson to march southwest to Raymond and strike the Federals in flank or rear as they swept past. It is worth noting that while Pemberton called on Gregg to attack Grant with a single brigade of three thousand men, he remained firmly on the defensive behind the Big Black with his main body, about thirty-eight thousand strong.

The morning of May 12 found McPherson's Seventeenth Corps marching northeast on the road from Utica to Raymond. Shortly before ten o'clock a line of Union infantry belonging to Maj. Gen. John A. Logan's division topped a ridge and moved into the valley of Fourteenmile Creek southwest of Raymond. Suddenly artillery and musket fire erupted from

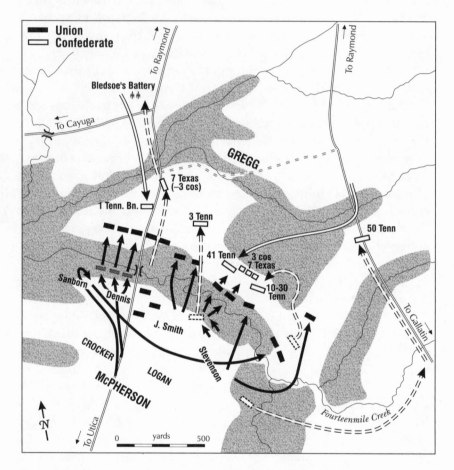

Raymond

the woods lining the nearly dry streambed. McPherson had encountered Gregg's brigade.

Soon after arriving in Raymond, Gregg learned that a Union force was approaching. Eager to strike a blow, he decided to attack. What the combative Gregg did not realize was that the oncoming Federals were the vanguard of the Seventeenth Corps; McPherson's entire command, a force of ten thousand men, was moving in his direction. Unaware that his three thousand troops were outnumbered better than three to one, the Rebel general formed a line of battle on the outskirts of town and opened the ball. After bringing the Union advance to an abrupt halt, Gregg's Confederates emerged from the woods en echelon from right to left and pushed across Fourteenmile Creek. Surprised at the unexpected attack, the line of Federals wavered and broke in places, but Logan rode forward and with "the shriek of an eagle" turned his men back to their places. Smoke and dust obscured the field, and neither commander accurately assessed the size of the force in his front. The ferocity of Gregg's assault compelled the inexperienced McPherson, despite his superior strength, to react to the situation rather than control the battle.[6]

Although the Confederates enjoyed initial success, Union resistance gradually stiffened. As more and more blue-clad troops reached the field, Gregg finally realized that he was facing an enemy force far larger than his own. By early afternoon the Rebel advance ground to a halt and the Federals counterattacked. Union brigades continued to arrive on the field, deploying into line of battle on either side of the road. Several batteries rolled into position on the high ground south of Fourteenmile Creek and roared into action. In piecemeal fashion McPherson's men pushed forward and drove the Confederates back across the creek. The clash at Raymond was unusually confused because of billows of smoke that failed to disperse in the still air and the presence of dense thickets along the stream. Referred to as a "soldier's battle," regimental and company commanders directed the troops more so than general officers. Union strength of numbers gradually prevailed, and the Confederate line began to buckle. Under tremendous pressure the Confederate right flank near the road finally collapsed, and Gregg had no alternative but to retire.

As the Confederates retreated through the tree-shaded streets of Raymond with the Federals close behind, they were unable to partake of a feast prepared for them by the citizens in anticipation of a victory. Rather, much to the townspeople's chagrin, soldiers from Ohio with voracious appetites halted their pursuit and quickly consumed everything in sight.

With the Federals weighed down by fried chicken and lemonade, the weary Confederates escaped to the northeast and bivouacked for the night along Snake Creek. The following day they returned to Jackson. McPherson's troops bedded down in and around Raymond.

The fight at Raymond cost Gregg 73 killed, 252 wounded, and 190 missing, most of whom were from the Third Tennessee and Seventh Texas. In his first engagement as a corps commander, McPherson lost 446 men: 68 killed, 341 wounded, and 37 missing. The young general doubled the size of the Confederate force in his report. This suggests that he was somewhat embarrassed by the fact that Gregg with a lone brigade had held off his corps in the early stage of the battle.

Although a relatively minor engagement by Civil War standards, Raymond had a profound effect on the Vicksburg campaign, for it led Grant to change the direction of his march. After receiving McPherson's exaggerated report of Confederate strength, Grant was reluctant to leave a sizable enemy force in his rear. Instead of wheeling north toward the Southern Railroad with his entire army as originally planned, he decided to continue marching northeast, driving Gregg before him. This movement would bring the Army of the Tennessee within striking distance of the Southern Railroad near Jackson, the state capital and a vital railroad intersection.

Grant was uncertain whether McPherson was up to the task of capturing Jackson. Accordingly he sent McPherson's corps north from Raymond to Clinton on May 13 and turned Sherman's corps northeast through Raymond to Mississippi Springs. In other words the Fifteenth and Seventeenth Corps changed places. McPherson and Sherman would converge on Jackson from the northwest and southwest respectively. To cover the movement on Jackson and fend off any thrusts by Pemberton from the west, Grant moved McClernand's corps away from the Big Black River and into a defensive position between Raymond and Clinton. These developments took the Federals deeper into Confederate territory than originally intended, a development that some in blue found alarming. Grant, however, remained confident.

Late in the afternoon of May 13, as Union columns converged on Jackson from two directions, a train arrived in the capital city carrying Confederate general Joseph Johnston. Ordered to Jackson by President Davis, Johnston was supposed to use his vaunted military skills to salvage the deteriorating situation in Mississippi. Instead he demonstrated the defeatism that blemished his Civil War career. Johnston was apprised of available troop strength and the condition of local fortifications. He concluded with unseemly haste that all was lost, wiring his superiors in Richmond, "I am too late." Instead of fighting for Jackson, Johnston ordered the city evacuated. He directed Gregg to cover the withdrawal, then boarded a train and departed for Canton, twenty-five miles to the north. (The military evacuation was preceded by a civilian exodus. A short time earlier Gov. John J. Pettus had moved the seat of state government to Enterprise near the Alabama state line.)[7]

The previous December Johnston and Davis had inspected the Vicksburg defenses. The president was impressed by what he saw. He considered the fortifications formidable and believed they could never be taken. In his self-serving memoirs Johnston claimed to have warned Davis that the extensive earthworks were an elaborate trap and that if Pemberton's army should become besieged in Vicksburg, it was as good as gone. Whether Johnston made such a prediction at the time is unknown, but from the moment he arrived in Jackson, he acted as if the outcome of the campaign already had been decided.

A much needed heavy rain fell on central Mississippi during the night of May 13. Advancing slowly under cloudy skies the next morning, Sherman and McPherson approached Jackson. For the second time in two days, Gregg found himself in an impossible position confronting an unstoppable foe. He concentrated his meager strength northwest of the city and prepared to delay McPherson's corps as long as possible. Gregg either did not detect Sherman's corps to the southwest or discounted it as a diversion.

Around nine o'clock in the morning of May 14, the leading elements of McPherson's corps encountered Gregg's artillery northwest of Jackson. McPherson deployed his men into line of battle and prepared to attack. After a delay caused by a passing rain shower, the clarion call of bugles sounded the advance. McPherson's men surged forward on a broad front and forced the Confederates back into the Jackson fortifications, a mile to their rear. The fighting was brief but intense, and casualties were numerous on both sides. After pausing to reform, the Federals approached the earthworks only to find that they were empty. The Rebels were gone.

Sherman's troops had an easier time of it. The Fifteenth Corps reached Lynch Creek southwest of Jackson at about the same hour that McPherson's men went into action several miles to the north. The Federals advanced toward the Confederate fortifications until they encountered sporadic artillery fire. Sherman then sent the Ninety-fifth Ohio off to the east in search of a weak spot in the Rebel defenses. After groping through a patch of thick woods, the Ohioans turned north along the tracks of the New Orleans, Jackson, and Great Northern Railroad and cautiously approached a line of earthworks. They were greatly relieved to find the fortifications empty. An elderly black man greeted the Federals, saying: "Ise come to tell you-all that the Rebels is left the city, clear done gone. You jes go on and you will take the city." In disbelief, one Ohioan asked, "Why are the Rebs still firing their battery if they had left the place?" Laughing, the man replied, "Oh! There is only a few cannoneers there to work the guns to keep you back." True enough, the Federals swept down the line of fortifications and discovered only a handful of state troops and civilian volunteers manning the guns in Sherman's front.[8]

Gregg and his sadly depleted brigade, along with stragglers from other units and a pathetic stream of civilians, were well out on the Canton Road to the north when Union soldiers entered Jackson from two directions around three o'clock in the afternoon. Soldiers from McPherson's corps made their way to the center of town and unfurled the Stars and Stripes atop the Mississippi State Capitol. Thousands of blue-clad spectators cheered the sight and tossed their hats into the air. Jackson was the third Confederate state capital to fall into Union hands as part of the vast effort to gain control of the Mississippi River.

In the short but intense clash of May 14, the Federals lost 300 men: 42 killed, 251 wounded, and 7 missing, the great majority from McPherson's corps. Confederate casualties were estimated at about 845 men killed, wounded, and missing. The Federals also captured seventeen pieces of artillery and a substantial amount of military stores.

Grant rode into the Mississippi capital in the wake of his mud-spattered soldiers. He did not intend to tarry long in the city but wanted it neutralized for military purposes. During a two-day orgy of destruction, Union troops tore up railroad tracks, cut telegraph wires, seized whatever stores they could find, and burned all facilities that supported the Confederate war effort. Grant and Sherman visited a textile mill rolling out canvas cloth marked "C.S.A." The commanding general suggested that enough work had been done at the factory. Sherman permitted the women employees to take all the cloth they could carry and then ordered the place burned. With much of Jackson in flames and Johnston's forces withdrawing to the north, Grant turned west toward Vicksburg.

# CHAPTER TEN

# Indecision, Indecision, Indecision

During the two weeks that followed Grant's crossing of the Mississippi River, Pemberton evacuated Grenada and Fort Pemberton as well as Grand Gulf and enlarged the stockpiles of food and ammunition inside the Vicksburg defenses. But while preparing for the worst, he was not yet resigned to a siege. In fact he sought an opportunity to duplicate the victory of the previous December at Chickasaw Bayou. The most promising place to make a defensive stand outside of Vicksburg was the high ground on the west side of the Big Black River. There the Confederates would dig in and repel Grant's attacks. When the bloodletting ended Pemberton would counterattack and drive the weakened Yankee army into the interior of the state, away from the protection and support of Porter's fleet.

Pemberton's ability to carry out this or any other plan, however, was hampered by serious discord among his principal lieutenants. Many of his generals disliked and even distrusted their Northern-born commander; most chafed at his timidity and lack of initiative. Acutely aware of the feelings of his lieutenants, Pemberton dealt with the situation by repeatedly convening councils of war to determine what course of action his officers would support. A defensive stand along the Big Black was tactically sound, but the generals were tired of being cooped up behind earthen walls. Eager to take the field, they recommended that the Army of Vicksburg advance across the Big Black and bring the enemy to battle. A stand-up fight against Grant was the last thing Pemberton wanted, but lacking confidence in his own judgment, he yielded to the wishes of his more aggressive subordinates.

On May 12, the day of the battle of Raymond, Pemberton issued a circular in which he announced "The hour of trial has come!" Appealing to duty, honor, and love of family, he sought to motivate his men. "Soldiers! be vigilant, brave and active; let there be no cowards, nor laggards, nor stragglers from the ranks—and the God of battle will certainly crown our efforts with success." Presumably inspired to accomplish great deeds by such effusive rhetoric, soldiers clad in butternut and gray shouldered their weapons and set out across the Big Black toward Edwards Station, midway between Vicksburg and Jackson.[1]

The Confederate commander plainly did not have his heart in the operation. He left two divisions behind to hold the Vicksburg fortifications—against whom is not clear—and marched to meet Grant with only three divisions, or about twenty-two thousand men. In the fight to come Pemberton would be outnumbered roughly three to two. The thousands of troops sitting on their hands in Vicksburg might have made the difference between victory and defeat.

On May 14 a courier reached Pemberton as he was passing through Bovina and handed him a message from Johnston. It had been composed the previous day, only hours after the general arrived in Jackson. Johnston informed Pemberton that a Union force had reached the Southern Railroad at Clinton, ten miles west of the capital. (The Union force in question was McPherson's corps.) He then directed Pemberton to cooperate with him in crushing the Yankees between two converging columns. Curiously Johnston did not mention that he was about to abandon Jackson to the enemy without a fight and retire in the opposite direction, thereby making a converging attack at Clinton or anywhere else impossible. By the time Pemberton received this message, the situation had deteriorated even further. Jackson was in Federal hands and Johnston was in flight toward Canton. But he knew none of this. When McPherson's soldiers occupied Clinton on May 13 and interdicted railroad traffic to and from Vicksburg, they also cut the telegraph line running alongside the tracks. From that point on Pemberton and Johnston communicated by courier.

The Vicksburg commander dutifully replied to Johnston, "I move at once with whole available force," meaning the three divisions at hand. He pointed out that after months of garrison duty his troops were not in the best condition for a campaign of maneuver. "The men have been marching several days, are much fatigued, and, I fear, will straggle very much." Pemberton also made it clear that if Johnston assumed command, he assumed responsibility as well. "In directing this move, I do not think you fully comprehend the position that Vicksburg will be left in, but I comply at once with your order."[2]

A lack of resolve, however, overtook Pemberton on the road to Edwards Station, where the Army of Vicksburg, or at least the major part of it, was awaiting his arrival. He gradually convinced himself that Johnston's plan was "extremely hazardous" and would have disastrous results. (Pemberton was right, though for the wrong reasons.) Upon reaching Edwards Station he suspended the advance and called another council of war. After reading Johnston's message to his generals, Pemberton expressed his doubts about the projected movement and reminded everyone that "the leading and great duty" of the army "was to defend Vicksburg." In other words he wanted to return to the west side of the Big Black, where earthen ramparts beckoned.[3]

Pemberton's lieutenants favored Johnston's plan of attack (or any plan of attack) and urged Pemberton to press on, but he resisted. Loring, the Army of Vicksburg's senior division commander, stepped forward and offered an alternate plan. Rather than march east toward Clinton (and risk a head-on collision with Grant, something Pemberton obviously dreaded), he proposed that the army march southeast toward Raymond. This would put the Confederates astride Grant's line of communications and compel him to turn about and attack them in a position of their own choosing. (The Army of the Tennessee did not have a line of communications in the usual sense of the term, but the Confederates did not know this.) Impressed, the council voted in favor of Loring's proposal and Pemberton acquiesced. The vaguely defensive nature of the plan undoubtedly had some appeal for him.

Pemberton informed Johnston of the change in plans, explaining less than candidly that his force was insufficient to join in the attack at Clinton. Upon receipt of this and other dispatches the following day, May 15, Johnston reiterated his previous order: "Our being compelled to leave Jackson makes your plan impracticable. The only mode by which we can unite is by your moving directly to Clinton." Johnston, however, had no intention of moving toward Clinton. His repeated instructions were empty words designed to ensure that if anyone was blamed for the loss of Vicksburg, which Johnston clearly believed was both imminent and inevitable, it would be Pemberton. The only result of this exchange of messages was that, instead of uniting their forces or even coordinating their movements, Pemberton and Johnston drifted away from each other. Grant remained free to maneuver as he wished.[4]

Reveille sounded at an early hour at Edwards Station on May 15. As the shrill notes faded, soldiers were in motion, rolling their blankets, kindling fires, and preparing meager breakfasts. Before the Army of Vicksburg could move, though, a problem was discovered: the store of rations and munitions was woefully inadequate. After some confusion a train was sent back to Vicksburg for additional supplies, which then were distributed among thousands of men and the remainder loaded into four hundred wagons, a tedious process that took much of the day. It was not until early afternoon that the army finally began to trudge away from Edwards Station on the Raymond Road, which because of the recent rains was a ribbon of mud. Progress was slow.

After a difficult march of only two miles, the head of the column came to a halt on the bank of rain-swollen Bakers Creek. The bridge was out, washed away by recent rains. Apparently no one at army headquarters had thought to scout the proposed line of march, another instance of poor staff work. Late in the afternoon Confederate cavalry found another bridge a few miles upstream. The column moved up the right side of the stream to the Jackson Road, the main thoroughfare between the capital city and Vicksburg, and finally began crossing the creek. Two miles beyond the bridge the troops reached a crossroads at the base of a rise called Champion Hill. There they turned southwest on the Ratliff Road, and after slogging down the west side of the stream for another two miles, they were back on the Raymond Road.

The soldiers of Loring's division, which led the march, bivouacked on Sarah Ellison's plantation along the Raymond Road around sundown. Bowen's division, next in line, halted a few hours later along the Ratliff Road. Stevenson's division, last in line, did not leave Edwards Station until late in the afternoon and struggled through mud and darkness until long after midnight. The four hundred wagons hauling munitions and rations did not arrive at the crossroads until dawn. The Rebels were exhausted after the long and trying day. When orders to halt finally came, many simply staggered off the road and sank to the ground, asleep within minutes.

The Army of Vicksburg was in open country, no longer safe behind fortifications or rivers. Pemberton and his generals apparently did not give much thought to the possibility that theirs might not be the only military force in the vicinity. John Bowen was one of the few high-ranking Confederate officers to notice a faint glow on the eastern horizon and ponder what it meant. He threw out pickets, placed his regiments in line, and readied his artillery prior to letting his men get some much needed sleep.

The glow that unsettled Bowen was caused by the campfires of the Army of the Tennessee. In contrast to the Confederates, the Federals were well rested and well organized after a day of leisurely marching. By nightfall on May 15, seven Union divisions—about thirty-two thousand men—were camped on a line from Bolton to Raymond, facing west toward Edwards Station. The stage was set for the climactic battle that would decide the fate of Vicksburg.

As the first streaks of dawn appeared in the eastern sky on May 16, a Southern Railroad train bound for Jackson was stopped by Union soldiers in Clinton. (As Pemberton knew that Clinton was in enemy hands, it remains a mystery why he permitted an eastbound train to pass Edwards Station.) The crew was ushered into Grant's presence and, upon being questioned, declared that a Rebel army of about twenty-five thousand men was at Edwards Station poised to attack Grant's rear. (Although the Federals had no way of knowing, this was a remarkably accurate assessment of Confederate strength and intentions.) Grant was elated. For the first time in the long campaign, Pemberton was out in the open. This was the opportunity he had been waiting for since the previous fall, when he first marched into northern Mississippi. Grant set the Army of the Tennessee into motion.

During the morning of May 16, Union forces advanced westward on three roughly parallel roads toward Edwards Station. On the Union left, to the south, two divisions led by Andrew Smith and Frank Blair marched along the Raymond Road toward Edwards Station, the same route that Pemberton was using. On the Union right, to the north, the divisions of John Logan, Alvin Hovey, and Brig. Gen. Marcellus M. Crocker moved over the Jackson Road. Between these columns, on the appropriately named Middle Road, marched the divisions of Peter Osterhaus and Eugene Carr. Grant accompanied McPherson on the Jackson Road, possibly to provide a steadying hand if needed. McClernand was on the Middle Road with strict orders not to bring on an engagement until the army was concentrated. Sherman and two of his divisions lagged a day's march behind, delayed by the work of destruction in Jackson. They would not arrive in time to participate in the fight.

Pemberton, meanwhile, gathered his senior officers for a morning briefing at Ellison's house. Incredibly he was unaware that the Army of the Tennessee was only a few miles away and heading in his direction. Around seven o'clock the distant boom of cannon provided the Rebel commander with the first indication that things were not going according to plan. Minutes later Col. Wirt Adams, whose Mississippi cavalrymen were manning a roadblock to the east, rode up and announced that Yankees were approaching in force on the Raymond Road and driving in his pickets. As Pemberton questioned Adams a courier arrived with Johnston's message of May 15. Scanning the note, Pemberton learned that Jackson was in Union hands and that Johnston still wanted him to proceed to Clinton. Now, with Grant almost close enough to touch, Pemberton decided to comply with Johnston's wishes. He issued orders for the army to reverse course and head for Clinton. Everyone was stunned. It was a surreal moment.

The rear of the Rebel column now became the front, namely the train of four hundred wagons. Much time would be required to turn the wagons around on the narrow road or push them aside and allow the infantry to take the lead. Pemberton, however, did not enjoy the luxury of time. With the sounds of skirmishing steadily intensifying to the east, Loring tried to bring his commander back to reality. He suggested forcefully that the army form a line of battle, "the sooner . . . the better, as the enemy would very soon be upon us."[5]

By now everyone in the Confederate ranks was aware that something unexpected was happening. Except for the troops in Bowen's division, no one was ready for a fight. One soldier observed, "As yet no preparations had been made to make or receive an attack; the artillery was parked, the horses unharnessed, the general staff officers galloped around furiously delivering orders." Such obvious disorganization did not inspire confidence. Lt. William Drennan, a staff officer in Loring's division, observed that Pemberton "gave orders in [an] uncertain manner that implied to me that he had no mature plans for the coming battle."[6]

Adding to Pemberton's woes was his increasingly fractious relationship with his disgruntled subordinates. Drennan recalled an uncomfortable and unprofessional scene featuring Loring, Winfield Featherston, and Brig. Gen. Lloyd Tilghman. "I sat down under a tree and listened to . . . quite an animated conversation the principal topic being General Pemberton. . . . They all said harsh, ill-natured things, made ill-tempered jests in regard to General Pemberton and when an order came from him, the courier who brought it was not out of hearing, before they made light of it and ridiculed the plan he proposed."[7]

By midmorning the situation became more ominous as skirmishing erupted farther north on the Middle Road. Pemberton finally abandoned the idea of joining Johnston. He hurriedly deployed his divisions along a three-mile front on a line running southwest to northeast. The Confederate formation blocked the Raymond Road to the south and the Middle Road to the north. If the Federals advanced on only those two roads, the Rebel line would be tough to break.

The dominant feature on the battlefield is Champion Hill, a partially wooded eminence rising 140 feet above the surrounding area. Winding its way west from Bolton, the Jackson Road abruptly turns south and passes over the bald crest of the hill. A short distance south of the hill, it intersects with the Middle Road and Ratliff Road. From this crossroads it turns back to the west and crosses Bakers Creek en route to Edwards Station and Vicksburg. The Jackson Road bridge across Bakers Creek—the same one the Rebels had used the previous day—was the only escape route should things go badly.

Unbeknown to Pemberton, the most powerful of the three Union columns was advancing undetected along the Jackson Road toward his left flank. Stephen Lee's brigade of Stevenson's division was located on the far left of the Confederate line. Concerned for the safety of his left flank and the unprotected crest of Champion Hill, Lee directed one of his officers to reconnoiter the Jackson Road. A half hour later the officer came riding back, frantically waving his arms and shouting that Union troops were approaching on the road in great strength. Lee realized that the Federals had to be stopped lest they roll up his flank, capture the crossroads, and possibly cut off the army from Vicksburg. In response to the looming threat from the north, Lee shifted his regiments to the left to cover Champion Hill. As the Confederates moved into position on the crest, Federal soldiers on the Jackson Road swung from column into double line of battle. Seeing that the enemy held the commanding hill in their front, Union artillerymen wheeled their guns into position and unlimbered. Bloodshed began in earnest as the guns roared into action.

After surveying the situation Grant ordered an attack. Hovey's and Logan's divisions, ten thousand strong, moved forward in magnificent style with flags flying. The long blue lines extended beyond the Confederate left flank and posed a grave threat to the troops on Champion Hill. To meet this danger Lee shifted his regiments even farther to the west, creating a gap between his brigade and the rest of Stevenson's division, defending the crossroads south of the hill.

Shortly before noon the Federals reached the base of Champion Hill. With a mighty cheer they surged toward the Confederate line. A Georgia

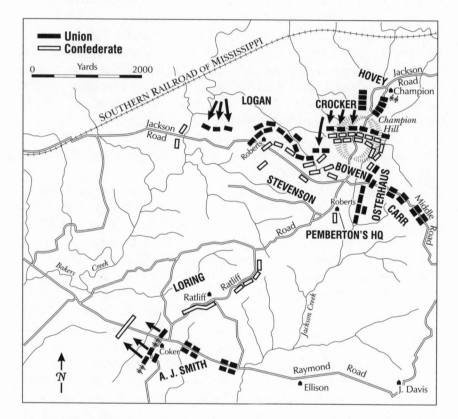

Champion Hill: Afternoon

soldier recalled that "the attack broke upon us with great impetuosity and vehemence, in overwhelming force, and in a manner wholly unexpected and unlooked for." The lines swayed back and forth as charge and countercharge were made. But strength of numbers prevailed, and the blue tide swept over the crest of the hill, driving Lee's men before them. Grant sent a courier on his way with the words, "Go down to Logan and tell him he is making history today."[8]

The Confederates retreated from Champion Hill in disorder. Victorious Union forces captured the crossroads and the Jackson Road escape route over Bakers Creek. Confronted by disaster, Pemberton ordered his two remaining divisions to counterattack. Leaving one brigade to guard the Raymond Road, Bowen and Loring hurried northeast along the Ratliff Road toward the all-important crossroads. Stifling clouds of dust choked the forty-five hundred soldiers of Bowen's division as they swept past the house that served as Pemberton's headquarters. The army commander stood waving his straw hat and urging the men forward. "We passed General Pemberton and staff standing in the road, almost in the edge of action," recalled a Missouri soldier. "His manner seemed to be somewhat excited; he and his staff were vainly endeavoring to rally some stragglers, who had already left their commands."[9]

With characteristic abandon Francis Cockrell led the way with a large magnolia blossom in one hand and a sword in the other. As his Missourians advanced toward the roar of battle, they passed a group of women cheering them on by singing "Dixie." Ephraim Anderson of the Second Missouri recalled, "At the sight of this . . . the boys shouted zealously, and I could not refrain from hallooing just once, expressive of my admiration for the perfect abandon with which these fair creatures gave their hearts to the cause." Bowen's men struck the disorganized Federals near the crossroads. "It was like trying to stop the tide with a broom," as one historian described the futile efforts of Federal soldiers to check the counterattack. The Confederates drove the enemy back three quarters of a mile and regained control of the crossroads and the crest of Champion Hill. Grant was shaken momentarily by the abrupt turn of events but maintained his composure and personally rallied a group of fleeing Federals. Confederate fortune, however, was short lived. Union forces continued to arrive on the Jackson Road and checked Bowen's men. "The battle here raged fearfully," wrote one Confederate, who noted that "one unbroken, deafening roar of musketry was all that could be heard."[10]

Determined to hold the ground thus gained, Bowen sent an urgent plea for reinforcements. Tense moments passed as he waited for support, but Loring's division, supposed to be following directly behind, was nowhere in sight. Loring had been directed onto the wrong road and thus did not arrive in time to capitalize on the initial success. As the Confederates desperately clung to their position on Champion Hill, the ominous cry for ammunition rang out along the line. But no resupply was available, for the ordnance wagons had left the area earlier in the day. Bowen's men scrounged among the cartridge boxes of the dead and wounded in search of ammunition, with little success. Faced with overwhelming numbers in front and on the left, the Confederates began to yield ground inch by inch, hoping all the while that Loring would arrive to even the contest.

All hope was dashed when Osterhaus's and Carr's divisions on the Middle Road finally fought their way to within a few yards of the crossroads. Unwilling to violate Grant's orders not to bring on a fight too soon, the normally aggressive McClernand had delayed an all-out assault until he was certain the time was right. Now his men battered their way behind Bowen's right flank. Risking total envelopment if he remained longer, Bowen ordered his troops to fall back. The Confederate withdrawal turned into a rout as thousands of men streamed through the woods in a race for survival; many even threw away their weapons. The Confederates barely reached the crossroads ahead of the Federals on the Middle Road and suffered heavy losses as they ran through a murderous fire. Unable to stem the tide of panic-stricken men, Bowen rode to inform Pemberton of the disastrous turn of events.

The Army of Vicksburg was faced with destruction, for the Federals controlled not only the vital crossroads but also the Jackson Road bridge across Bakers Creek. At this critical moment Loring finally emerged from the woods and formed a line of battle on a ridge south of the road. Although a difficult subordinate, Loring was full of fight and prepared to attack. No sooner had he issued an order to advance, however, when a member of Pemberton's staff rode up and directed him to fall back on Edwards Station—the day was lost. Confederates soldiers were captured by the score as Union troops swept over the crossroads and pushed after the fleeing gray masses. Stevenson's division was shattered and could not be relied upon for further service, his men falling back on Edwards Station in panic and confusion. Bowen's division, probably the best in the army, also had been badly mauled, and even some of these men evidenced the demoralization that gripped the army. Loring's division alone was in fighting condition, having seen relatively little action, and was ordered to cover the retreat.

Fortunately for the Confederates, fatigue parties had worked throughout the day under the supervision of Samuel Lockett, now chief engineer of the army, to rebuild the washed-out Raymond Road bridge across Bakers Creek. As the water level of the stream subsided, they also were able to make a ford passable for artillery. With only one avenue of escape now open, the Confederates fled westward in disorder. Tilghman was ordered to protect the bridge with his brigade at all costs. He died accomplishing this mission, but his battered brigade, along with the rest of Loring's division, was cut off from Edwards Station. Loring and his men slipped away from the Federals on an obscure country lane and eventually made their way to Jackson by a circuitous route.

Grant's victorious soldiers crossed Bakers Creek late in the afternoon and pushed on in pursuit of the retreating Rebels. About eight o'clock that evening Union troops entered Edwards Station. The scene was illuminated by blazing commissary supplies and quartermaster stores set afire by the retreating Confederates. With the hamlet secured the Federals bedded down for the night for some much-needed rest.

The cost of the Union triumph at Champion Hill was high: 410 men killed, 1,844 wounded, and 187 missing, or 2,441 casualties out of 32,000 men engaged. For the Confederates Champion Hill was an outright disaster. The Army of Vicksburg lost 3,840 men: 381 killed, 1,018 wounded, and 2,441 missing out of the 25,000 soldiers engaged. In addition, twenty-seven pieces of artillery were lost. Twelve of these cannon, along with their caissons and limbers and seven ammunition wagons, were abandoned by Loring's troops as they fled the field.

Deeply shaken by the rout at Champion Hill, Pemberton now sought only to run for the dubious protection of the Big Black River and the Vicksburg defenses. As he rode west through the darkness filled with despair, perhaps he realized, as British general J. F. C. Fuller observed a century later, that "The drums of Champion's [*sic*] Hill sounded the doom of Richmond."[11]

Late that night John A. Leavy, a surgeon with the Confederate army, took pen in hand to jot down his impressions of Champion Hill. "To-day proved to the nation the value of a general," he began. "Pemberton is either a traitor, or the most incompetent officer in the confederacy. *Indecision, Indecision, Indecision.*" He lamented: "We have been badly defeated where we might have given the enemy a severe repulse. We have been defeated in detail, and have lost, O God! how many brave and gallant soldiers." Leavy's sentiments were echoed by hundreds of Confederate soldiers who cursed their unpopular commanding general and declared "It's all Pem's fault."[12]

Throughout the night of May 16, dispirited Confederates crossed the two bridges over Big Black River en route to Vicksburg. East of the stream on low, flat ground, a line of fortifications had been constructed a few weeks earlier to protect the Southern Railroad bridge against possible attack by Grierson's raiders. Pemberton ordered Bowen's division and a fresh brigade of Tennesseans commanded by Brig. Gen. John Vaughn to man the fortifications and hold the bridges long enough for Loring to cross. Unknown to Pemberton, Loring was marching in the opposite direction, away from Vicksburg and the commanding general he so detested.

Dawn on May 17 found Union forces marching away from Edwards Station in pursuit of the reeling Confederates. McClernand's Thirteenth Corps again led the march. As the Federals neared the Big Black, they spotted the enemy posted behind a line of earthworks. McClernand deployed his units astride the road and opened fire on the fortifications with solid shot and shell. Brig. Gen. Michael Lawler moved his brigade into a meander scar, an old river channel, on the Union right. The depression sheltered his men only a few yards in front of the Confederate works. Before more than a fraction of the Union army was on the scene, Lawler decided to take advantage of his advanced position and ordered his troops forward. For once an assault against a fortified position was an unqualified success. The Federals surged out of the depression and fairly raced across the field. They quickly filtered through obstructions and swarmed over the earthworks.

Startled by the sudden attack, the Confederates put up only a brief fight, then broke and ran. The line of defenders disintegrated from left to right as regiment after regiment bolted for the rear. Throwing aside their weapons thousands of demoralized Rebels fled toward the bridges over the Big Black. When a traffic jam developed, many soldiers jumped into the river to swim across, and a few were swallowed by the turbid water. Fortunately for the Confederates the indefatigable Lockett was prepared for just such an emergency. He set fire to both the railroad bridge and the *Dot*, a steamboat moored crossways in the river to serve as an improvised pontoon bridge. With the bridge and boat in flames, the remnants of the Army of Vicksburg fell back toward the Hill City.

Big Black River Bridge was another Confederate calamity. Pemberton lost nearly eighteen hundred men, most all of them captured, along with eighteen guns, six limbers, four caissons, and five flags. Incredibly Federal casualties came to fewer than three hundred killed and wounded.

Pemberton was overwhelmed by despair. He dejectedly told a member of his staff, "Just thirty years ago I began my military career by receiving my appointment to a cadetship at the U.S. Military Academy, and today— that same date—that career is ended in disaster and disgrace." For all practical purpose it was, but it was a disaster that would effect an entire nation.[13]

# CHAPTER ELEVEN

# A Grand and Appalling Sight

The heavy boom of artillery echoed among the streets of Vicksburg on May 16 as the armies clashed at Champion Hill. The ominous rumbling alarmed the citizens of the Hill City as they realized for the first time the proximity of the danger on land. The sound of battle grew louder the following day as the Union army drove the Confederates across Big Black River and into Vicksburg's defenses.

The Sabbath morn dawned bright and clear on May 17. In Vicksburg Emma Balfour, wife of a prominent physician, noted: "The birds are singing as merrily as if all were well. The flowers are in perfection, the air heavy with the perfume of cape jasmine and honeysuckle, and the garden bright and gay with all the summer flowers." Despite the splendor of nature, another woman, Mary Loughborough, whose husband, James, was an officer in Pemberton's army, was filled with anxiety. "Yet in all the pleasant air and sunshine of the day," she wrote with foreboding, "an anxious gloom seemed to hang over the faces of the men: a sorrowful waiting for tidings, that all knew now, would tell of disaster." To Mrs. Loughborough and a host of others soon to be trapped in Vicksburg, "There seemed no life in the city; sullen and expectant seemed the men—tearful and hopeful the women."[1]

Such hope, however, was in vain as the dispirited and disorganized Confederate army poured into Vicksburg that afternoon from the battlefield at Big Black River Bridge. "In all the dejected uncertainty, the stir of horsemen and wheels began," recorded one dismayed citizen. "Wagons came rattling down the street—going rapidly one way, and then returning, seemingly, without aim or purpose: now and then a worn and dusty soldier would be seen passing with his blanket and canteen; soon, straggler after straggler came by then groups of soldiers worn and dusty with the long march."[2]

The stream of stragglers turned into a demoralized mass of humanity that soon filled the streets. Emma Balfour stood in her doorway on that fateful day and watched the drama in disbelief. "I hope never to witness again such a scene as the return of our routed army!" she wrote with trembling hand in the pages of her diary. "From twelve o'clock until late in the night the streets and roads were *jammed* with wagons, cannons, horses, men, mules, stock, sheep, everything you can imagine that appertains to an army being brought hurriedly within the intrenchment." She noted with trepidation, "Nothing like order prevailed, of course, as divisions, brigades and regiments were broken and separated."[3]

Details of the calamitous engagements at Champion Hill and Big Black River Bridge were slowly pieced together by the shocked citizenry of Vicksburg. To those who listened to the woeful details of battle, one fact became apparent. The incisive Balfour, sensitive to the widespread discontentment with Pemberton, recorded the essence of failure with these words, "I knew from all I saw and heard that it was want of confidence in the General commanding that was the cause of our disaster." Late that night, overcome with emotion, she confided to her diary the fears of many in Vicksburg: "What is to become of all the living things in this place . . . shut up as in a trap . . . , God only knows."[4]

On through the long day and into the evening, the weary Confederates made their way back to Vicksburg. The city grew even more crowded when Pemberton ordered the garrisons at Haynes' Bluff, the Walnut Hills, and Warrenton to abandon their positions and hurry to inner works. Officers gradually restored order and directed their men into the landward defenses to meet Grant's rapidly approaching army.

A medley of sounds filled the night air as the Confederates readied the eight miles of fortifications around the city. Officers shouted orders, teamsters whipped their animals, artillerymen wrested their weapons into place, and men cursed and prayed. Many soldiers worked with picks and shovels to repair the damage done to the earthworks by the heavy rains of the preceding few months; others picked up axes and saws and ventured into the forest beyond. Throughout the night the ringing of axes was constant as hundreds, perhaps thousands, of trees were felled to clear fields of fire and form an immense abatis, an essential part of fixed fortifications in the nineteenth century. An abatis was a dense obstruction of felled trees toppled toward likely avenues of enemy approach. The branches were stripped and sharpened, and in some instances telegraph wire was strung among the limbs. Its purpose was to disrupt approaching lines of infantry. Attacking soldiers would be able to worm their way through the tangled obstruction singly or in small groups, but once on the inner side of the abatis and in a clear field of fire, they were easy targets for defenders posted behind stout fortifications. Work continued at a feverish pace, and by sunrise on May 19 Vicksburg was in a good state of defense.

The Confederate left, a high and nearly impregnable ridge, was held by Maj. Gen. Martin L. Smith's division of Louisiana and Tennessee soldiers. The more vulnerable center, which overlooked steeply rolling terrain to the east, was guarded by John Bowen's division of Missouri and Arkansas troops and Maj. Gen. John H. Forney's division of Louisiana, Mississippi, and Alabama soldiers. Carter Stevenson's Texas, Georgia, and Tennessee soldiers, who had performed poorly at Champion Hill, secured the Confederate right, where little action was expected. Roughly twenty-eight thousand Rebels occupied the Hill City's landward defenses, while several thousand more manned the river batteries or performed other duties inside the citadel.

As the Confederates readied their defenses, Union soldiers were hard at work building bridges at four locations across the Big Black River. In stark contrast to their opponents, who labored through much of the night of May 17, the Federals completed their work within hours and, in the glow of huge bonfires, pushed two divisions across the river before bedding down for the night. Sherman's troops threw a pontoon bridge across the Big Black at Bridgeport, a few miles north of the battlefield. "After dark, the whole scene was lit up with fires of pitch-pine," he recalled. "General Grant joined me there, and we sat on a log, looking at the passage of the troops by the light of those fires; the bridge swayed to and fro under the passing feet, and made a fine war picture."[5]

At first light on May 18, the Union army, now over forty thousand strong with the arrival of Sherman's trailing divisions, resumed the advance toward Vicksburg. The roads were littered with discarded blankets, weapons, and accouterments of all description, evidence of Confederate panic and demoralization. The Federals marched with a lively step, confident that they would soon have Vicksburg in hand. As they neared the city, Sherman steered some of his troops north to occupy the empty Confederate defenses at Haynes' Bluff and reestablish contact with the navy's gunboats (and more importantly the army's transports) in the Yazoo River.

Sherman rode to the edge of the Walnut Hills and gazed down on the field at Chickasaw Bayou, where his men had been repulsed in December 1862. He was joined there by Grant, who must have felt a certain degree of relief and pride when Sherman turned to him and said: "Until this moment I never thought your expedition a success; I never could see the end clearly till now. But this is a campaign; this is a success if we never take the town." This was quite an admission from a man who had gone on record at the beginning as being opposed to the whole operation.[6]

Late in the afternoon on May 18, Confederate soldiers watched from behind the security of their parapets as Union troops cautiously approached the Vicksburg defenses. Skirmishing erupted and artillery roared into action on both sides, but the day wore away without any major fighting. That night the soldiers of both armies rested on their arms. Everyone knew that the bloody work at hand would commence with the rising sun and prepared for battle in his own way. William Foster, a chaplain in the Thirty-fifth Mississippi Infantry, captured the varied emotions of the evening in the leaves of his journal:

> That night was a solemn night for the soldier. None but those who have had the experience can tell the feeling of the soldiers heart on the night before the approaching battle—when upon the wings of fond imagination his soul visits the loved ones at home—and while he thinks of a lonely & loving wife whose face he may never look upon again & who may never see his form any more on earth, his heart bleeds & dark forebodings fill his mind. Then when he lies down upon the cold ground & looks up to the shining stars above, the gloomy thought crosses his mind, that it may be the last time he will ever look upon the shining heavens & that those same stars which now look down so quiet upon him, may behold him on the morrow night a lifeless, mangled corpse. If he be a child of God, he will commit his soul to God & implore his protection. If a wicked man he will review the past with remorse & the future with dread & will form a weak resolution to do better from that day if God will spare his life through the battle.[7]

Grant was anxious for a quick victory on May 19. The Rebels clearly were dispirited. They had broken at Big Black River despite having the

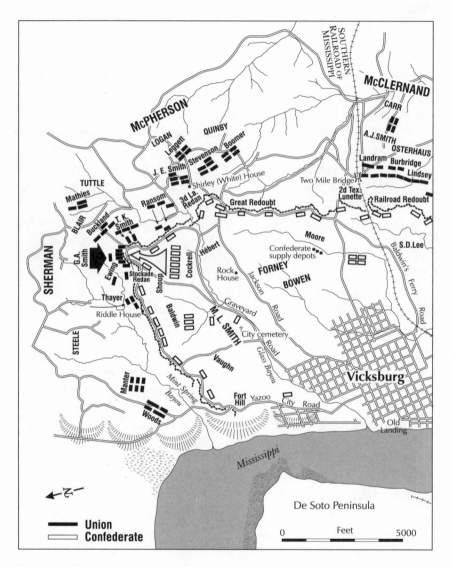

Vicksburg: May 19 attack

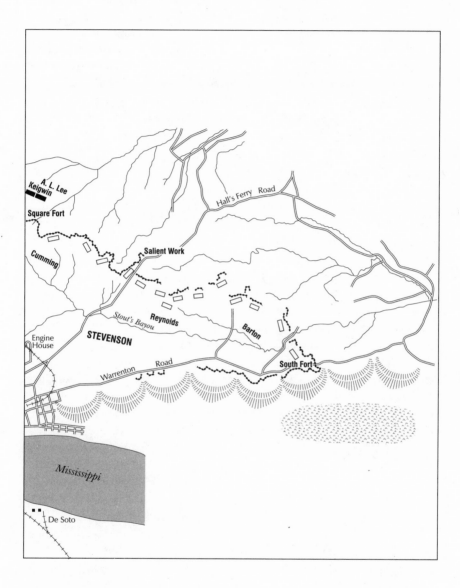

advantage of fortifications; perhaps they would break again. Following a hasty reconnaissance of the Confederate defenses, he ordered Sherman's Fifteenth Corps to make an assault. Union guns bombarded the earthworks with solid shot and shell for four hours in preparation for the attack. Smoke from the guns shrouded the fields and made it very difficult to see. While the artillery hammered away at the enemy's defenses, blue-clad infantrymen steadied their nerves and prepared to face death.

At two o'clock the guns fell silent and Sherman's troops deployed into line of battle astride the ominously named Graveyard Road, which entered the Confederate defenses northeast of Vicksburg. Maj. Gen. Frank Blair's division led the advance. On Blair's right, pushing through a cornfield north of the road, were the men of the First Battalion, Thirteenth U.S. Infantry, one of only two regular-army units then with Grant at Vicksburg. Led by Capt. Edward Washington (grand-nephew of George Washington), the regulars followed their colors into a deep ravine fronting the Confederate fortifications, worked their way through the obstruction of felled trees, and clawed their way up the slope toward Stockade Redan. (A redan is a triangular-shaped fortification, the apex of which faces the enemy. This particular position received its unusual name because it was adjacent to a stockade of poplar logs blocking Graveyard Road.) Braving a murderous fire from the Louisiana and Missouri troops crowded into the redan and the trenches to either side, a handful of regulars reached the ditch in front of the fort and planted their colors on the exterior slope.

Once in the ditch the Federals began digging holes in the slope with their bayonets for the purpose of scaling the bastion's exterior slope. That done, they waited for additional troops to arrive before daring such an effort. A few men from the 83d Indiana and 127th Illinois also reached the ditch, but the Federals still were too few in number to attempt an assault on the redan. Most of the men in Blair's division were pinned to the ground fewer than one hundred yards from the Confederate works. A lethal exchange of fire continued throughout the afternoon.

The summer sun unmercifully beat upon the Union troops pinned down on either side of Graveyard Road. Sweat streamed down the blackened faces of the men, many of whom already had torn their last cartridge, and the desperate cry for ammunition was heard above the din of battle. In the Fifty-fifth Illinois a young musician named Orion P. Howe was one of four men who volunteered to run to the rear and call up a fresh supply of cartridges. Three were killed outright, but Howe, though wounded, managed to reach the rear and reported the desperate situation to Sherman. (Only fourteen years of age Howe was the youngest recipient of the Medal of Honor at Vicksburg.) Boxes of ammunition were run forward and the precious cartridges distributed to the men on the firing line, but to no avail. The assault failed, with the loss of 942 men killed, wounded, and missing, all from Sherman's corps. Confederate casualties came to perhaps 200 killed and wounded.

Among the Federal troops who suffered the greatest loss on May 19 were Captain Washington's regulars, who experienced a casualty rate of 43 percent. Attesting to the fury of battle was the appalling loss among the battalion's color guard. Seventeen flag bearers were killed or wounded while advancing the national and regimental colors toward Stockade Redan. Upon examination that evening the national colors revealed eighteen bullet holes in the cloth and two pieces of canister and one minié ball in the staff; the regimental standard bore fifty-six bullet holes. In recognition of the regulars' heroic performance and terrible loss, Sherman, who had commanded the battalion upon its organization in 1861, directed that the honor "First at Vicksburg" be inscribed on its battleflag. The phrase became the regiment's motto, and members of the descendent unit in the modern army proudly wear the inscription on their shoulder patches to this day.

Undaunted by the failure to capture Vicksburg on May 19, Grant made a more thorough reconnaissance of the Confederate defenses. Union soldiers worked their way closer to Vicksburg, shortening the distance and therefore the time that they would be under fire when they had to go forward again. Three days later, on May 22, Grant hurled his entire force against the city's defenses. Union artillery again roared into action and for four hours bombarded the Confederate works with solid shot and shell, tearing large holes in the earthen fortifications.

As thick smoke again shrouded the field, Union commanders readied their men for the assault. On the right Sherman's troops once more steadied themselves to storm Stockade Redan along Graveyard Road. In the center, east of Vicksburg, the soldiers of McPherson's corps formed a dense column and prepared to strike both the Third Louisiana Redan and the Great Redoubt, two massive earthworks that guarded the point where the Jackson Road passed through the defenses into Vicksburg. (A redoubt is a rectangular-shaped fortification. The Great Redoubt was the largest and most formidable work on the defensive line around Vicksburg.) Farther south, on the left, McClernand's men focused their

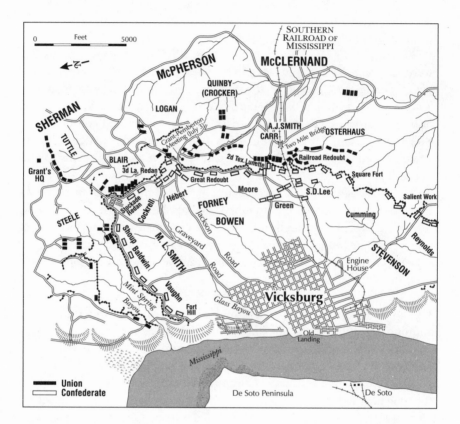

Vicksburg: May 22 attack

attention on the Second Texas Lunette (a crescent-shaped fortification) and Railroad Redoubt, earthworks that guarded the approaches of the Baldwin Ferry Road and the Southern Railroad respectively.

At ten o'clock in the morning, the prearranged time for the assault to begin, the artillery fell silent. Tens of thousands of Union soldiers raised a mighty cheer and moved forward over a three-mile front. Leading Sherman's troops along Graveyard Road were 150 volunteers carrying bundles of cane, planks, and ladders with which to bridge the ditch fronting Stockade Redan and enable the following infantry to scale the bastion's earthen walls. (The building Grant used as his headquarters was dismantled to obtain the materials used to construct the planks and scaling ladders. The commanding general moved into a tent for the duration of the siege.)

Dubbed the "forlorn hope," the volunteers raced along the road with their rifles slung over their shoulders. Scores were killed or wounded, but the remainder somehow managed to reach the foot of the redan, fill the ditch with cane and planks, and place the scaling ladders against the walls. Once again, however, the hail of Confederate rifle and artillery fire kept the supporting infantry at bay. Despite detailed planning and an almost superhuman effort on the part of the volunteers, Sherman's attack was another costly failure. (Of the 122 Medals of Honor awarded at Vicksburg, 78 went to survivors of the "forlorn hope.")

McPherson's troops met a similar fate along the Jackson Road. Charging forward four abreast, the soldiers of Maj. Gen. John E. Smith's brigade braved a murderous fire that knocked down hundreds of men. As the column surged through a narrow cut only one hundred yards from the Confederate line, the pile of dead and wounded Federals formed a roadblock that actually helped check the advance. Despite another heroic effort against desperate odds, none of Smith's men reached the Third Louisiana Redan.

A short distance south of the Jackson Road, the soldiers of Brig. Gen. John D. Stevenson's brigade made their way to a sheltered ravine only two hundred yards from the Great Redoubt. The Federals raised a shout and surged up the steep hill with scaling ladders in hand. The Seventh Missouri (U.S.) led by Capt. Robert Buchanan advanced beneath a green flag emblazoned with a gold harp, symbolic of the men's Irish heritage. Although casualties were high, especially among officers, the Missourians leaped into the ditch and pushed the ladders against the redoubt. For a moment it appeared that McPherson's troops might achieve a breakthrough, but the ladders were not long enough to reach the top of the earthen walls. Discouraged, some soldiers climbed out of the ditch and streamed to the rear through a hail of fire. Others clung to their precarious position despite a barrage of hand grenades tossed into the ditch by the Rebel defenders. Survivors finally made their way to safety under cover of darkness. Here as elsewhere, Union losses were heavy. In one of the many tragic ironies of the Civil War, the Confederate defenders of the Great Redoubt—mostly Irishmen from New Orleans—also flew a green flag. Among them was Capt. David Todd, brother-in-law of Abraham Lincoln. (The president of the United States had two brothers-in-law serving in Confederate gray during the Vicksburg campaign. The other was Brig. Gen. Benjamin Helm, whose brigade was part of Johnston's army in Jackson.)

On McClernand's front farther south the Federals managed to reach the enemy works in force. Shouting "Vicksburg or hell!" scores of men from Brig. Gen. William P. Benton's and Brig. Gen. Stephen G. Burbridge's brigades reached the foot of the Second Texas Lunette. Fighting raged at extremely close quarters. Cpl. Thomas Higgins carried the colors of the Ninety-ninth Illinois to the top of the parapet near the lunette. Both he and his banner were eventually captured. (Higgins was accused by his captors of wearing a metal breastplate, to which the corporal replied, "if I had I would have put it on my rump.") In the maelstrom of battle artillerists of the Chicago Mercantile Battery performed an incredible feat. They hauled a brass 6-pound gun to within thirty feet of the lunette and fired canister at the Confederate defenders. Despite such heroics, the Federals were repulsed with frightful losses.[8]

Only at Railroad Redoubt, a few hundred yards south of the Second Texas Lunette, did McClernand's troops force their way into the Confederate works. Lt. J. M. Pearson of the Thirtieth Alabama described the attack from the perspective of the defenders. "Suddenly the roar of the guns ceased. . . . I sprang to my feet and looked in the direction of the enemy, when they seemed to be springing from the bowels of the earth a long line of indigo a magnificent line in each direction, and they kept for a while the alignment as on dress parade, but moving at the double quick." The lieutenant expressed the thoughts of many when he added, "It was a grand and appalling sight."[9]

Waves of blue-clad soldiers of Brig. Gen. Michael Lawler's and Col. William J. Landram's brigades swept over hilly terrain and poured into the ditch fronting Railroad Redoubt. Clawing their way up the exterior slope,

Sgts. Joseph Griffith and Nicholas Messenger of the Twenty-second Iowa
led a dozen men through a breach in the wall. In a desperate hand-to-
hand struggle, the Iowans forced the Confederates to abandon part of
the fort and took Lieutenant Pearson and some of his troops prisoner.
The Federals appeared on the brink of victory, but McClernand had no
reserves with which to exploit his success. He sent an urgent message
to Grant: "We have part possession of two forts, and the Stars and
Stripes are floating over them." To prevent the Confederates from sending
reinforcements to Railroad Redoubt, McClernand wrote that a "vigorous
push ought to be made all along the line." Although Grant doubted
the veracity of McClernand's claim—for what reason is not clear—he
nonetheless ordered the assaults renewed. Early in the afternoon Union
soldiers again advanced all along the line, though with no more success
than in the morning assaults—the only result was a lengthened casualties
list.[10]

As the Union lines receded across the field on the afternoon of May
22, hundreds of dead and wounded soldiers were left behind. As night fell
the sounds of battle were replaced by the cries of the wounded. Grant's
second and final assault on Vicksburg cost the Army of the Tennessee 3,199
men killed, wounded, or missing. Confederate casualties are not known
with precision but probably did not exceed 500. Fortress Vicksburg had
stood defiant.

Pemberton's men had recovered far more quickly from their shaky
performance at Big Black River Bridge than Grant had expected. As
he contemplated his next move, the Federal commander unaccountably
refused to call a truce to retrieve his dead and wounded, many of whom
had been lying in front of the Confederate works since May 19. Hundreds
of bloated and discolored corpses were emitting a sickening stench in
the ferocious heat. More than one Rebel soldier complained that the
Yankees were trying to stink them out of Vicksburg. On May 25, white
flags appeared along the Confederate line. Many Union soldiers hoped
that the Rebels had decided to give up, but the purpose of the ceasefire was
merely to allow passage of a message from Pemberton imploring Grant
"in the name of humanity" to bury his dead and recover his wounded,
if any remained alive after being forsaken for so long. Grant reluctantly
agreed to a truce of two and a half hours.[11]

While burial details carried out their gruesome task, thousands of other
soldiers in blue and gray mingled between the lines. "There a group of
four played cards," recalled one soldier, "two Yanks and two Rebs, while

others swapped tobacco for coffee." It was almost as if there were no war in progress. At the appointed time, however, the white flags were taken down and everyone ran for cover. The siege of Vicksburg began in earnest that day.[12]

The attack of May 22 precipitated a command crisis within the Army of the Tennessee. The touchy relationship between Grant and McClernand had worsened during the previous few days as a result of several misunderstandings and miscommunications. Then Grant learned that his doubts about the accuracy of McClernand's appeal for help were well founded. Soldiers of the Thirteenth Corps had gained partial possession of only one fort, not two, and even that success was short lived, for the Rebels quickly counterattacked and sealed the breach. When Grant tallied the number of men killed or wounded during the afternoon assault, he considered relieving McClernand on the spot.

McClernand, however, was a capable officer who had performed admirably thus far in the campaign, more so than either Sherman or McPherson, and he enjoyed the respect of his soldiers. Unwilling to do anything that might cause discontent or demoralization in the ranks, particularly after the heavy losses of May 19 and 22, Grant decided to retain McClernand in command of his corps for the duration of the siege, then insist that he take a leave of absence from the Army of the Tennessee.

As it turned out, McClernand inadvertently provided Grant with a reason, or at least a pretext, for his removal. Contrary to standing orders from the War Department, McClernand published a bombastic congratulatory letter in Midwestern newspapers tactlessly lauding the accomplishments of his Thirteenth Corps at the expense of the Fifteenth and Seventeenth Corps. Sherman and McPherson were livid and demanded that Grant take action. By this time the siege of Vicksburg was approaching its end, and Grant concluded that McClernand's departure would have little effect on the outcome. On June 18 he relieved the general for violation of orders and replaced him with Maj. Gen. Edward O. C. Ord, an old army friend and fellow West Pointer but a far less able commander. McClernand appealed to Washington for redress, but Grant's star was in the ascendant, and the Illinois politician-soldier faded from the scene.

# CHAPTER TWELVE

# Outcamp the Enemy

The failure of the costly assaults of May 19 and 22 convinced Grant that the Confederate defenses could not be taken by storm, at least not yet. To avoid another bloodbath he decided to "outcamp the enemy," as he termed it, by laying siege to Vicksburg. "With the navy holding the river, the investment of Vicksburg was complete," wrote Grant in his memoirs. "As long as we could hold our position the enemy was limited in supplies of food, men, and munitions of war to what they had on hand. These could not always last."[1]

On May 25, following the belated truce to bury the dead and remove the wounded, Grant issued the appropriate instructions. "Corps commanders will immediately commence the work of reducing the enemy by regular approaches. It is desirable that no more loss of life shall be sustained in the reduction of Vicksburg and the capture of the garrison. Every advantage will be taken of the natural inequalities of the ground to gain positions from which to start mines, trenches or advance batteries." The massive undertaking was placed under the general supervision of Capt. Frederick E. Prime, the army's chief engineer.[2]

Grant was not the only officer whose thoughts turned to siege operations as the surest means of compelling the surrender of Vicksburg. Engineers in both armies had anticipated such a development and prepared accordingly. One man who ventured out of the Vicksburg defenses during the brief truce was Samuel Lockett. Scanning the ground in front of Stockade Redan, he looked for clues as to how the Federals might approach his earthworks. While standing on the parapet Lockett was approached by a Union orderly who informed him that Sherman wished to speak to him. Surprised, Lockett followed the orderly along Graveyard

Road toward the Union line. Sherman stepped forward and said: "I saw that you were an officer by your insignia of rank, and have asked you to meet me, to put into your hands some letters intrusted to me by Northern friends of some of your officers and men. I thought this would be a good opportunity to deliver this mail before it got too old." Lockett replied, "Yes, General, it would have been very old, indeed, if you had kept it until you brought it into Vicksburg yourself." Sherman was amused at Lockett's impertinence. "So you think, then, I am a very slow mail route." Lockett had confidence in the strength of his fortifications and responded with a slight boast, "Well, rather, when you have to travel by regular approaches, parallels, and zigzags." "Yes, that is a slow way of getting into a place," agreed Sherman, "but it is a very sure way, and I was determined to deliver those letters sooner or later."

The officers then sat and talked about things other than war. Lockett recalled that it was a "pleasant conversation" in which the time quickly passed. Finally returning to the events at hand, Sherman remarked, "You have an admirable position for defense here, and you have taken excellent advantage of the ground." "Yes, General," came Lockett's reply, "but it is equally as well adapted to offensive operations, and your engineers have not been slow to discover it." Both men were correct in their assessment. The siege of Vicksburg would be waged with pick and shovel more than with musket and bayonet. Before long the truce expired and everyone returned to their lines. "Intentionally or not," lamented Lockett of his conversation with Sherman, "his civility certainly prevented me seeing many other points in our front that I as chief engineer was very anxious to examine."[3]

An officer on a similar mission during the truce was Capt. Andrew Hickenlooper, chief engineer of McPherson's Seventeenth Corps. Hickenlooper examined the area near the Jackson Road and noticed that the Third Louisiana Redan, jutting out from the Confederate line, dominated the adjacent earthworks. He realized that if the Federals gained possession of that fort, the Confederate defenses on lower ground to either side would be untenable. Unlike Lockett, Hickenlooper was able to make a careful analysis of the terrain without being distracted. Once the truce ended he returned to his tent and prepared a map on which he plotted the best route of approach to the Rebel bastion.

The next morning Union engineers began digging thirteen approaches, or saps, toward the Confederate defenses. The work of constructing these was the focus of siege operations for the next six weeks. Such activity drew little attention from the Northern newspapermen who covered Grant's army. The reporters and their editors considered siege operations monotonous and mundane and therefore printed surprisingly little about the principal activity of the Union army at Vicksburg. Soldiers also considered shoveling dirt to be boring and left only sketchy accounts of their daily labors.

Of the thirteen saps dug by the Federals during the siege, the most successful was the one Hickenlooper pushed forward along the Jackson Road toward the Third Louisiana Redan. It was known as Logan's Approach, after Maj. Gen. John Logan, commander of the division occupying the front where the sap was located. On May 26 a force of three hundred men, working in shifts of one hundred men each, began work on the approach under Hickenlooper's direction. The sappers, as they were called, broke ground south of the Jackson Road approximately 150 feet southeast of the Shirley house and four hundred yards east of their objective.

A typical sap of the Civil War era was about seven feet deep and eight feet wide, deep enough to allow the average man of the time to stand up without exposing himself to enemy sharpshooters and wide enough to allow the passage of a column of assault troops four abreast. Because excavated dirt was piled up on either side of the approach, its effective depth often was closer to ten feet. The sappers at Vicksburg worked round the clock with picks and shovels in terrific heat and humidity, but as the Confederates had discovered the previous year, excavation of the soft loess soil was easy and thus progress was rapid. By the end of the first day, the sap extended several hundred feet westward from its starting point.

Union sappers at Vicksburg and elsewhere were protected from Confederate small-arms fire by sap rollers, large barrel-shaped bundles of cane and vine woven together and packed with dirt, cotton, or whatever would stop a bullet. A sap roller was assembled and placed on the ground just in front of the head of an approach. As the excavation progressed the sappers used poles to push the roller forward. In the case of Logan's Approach, however, the initial sap roller was a railroad flatcar fitted with wooden wheels and stacked high with twenty cotton bales. The flatcar also served as a mobile firing platform, for the cotton barricade was complete with headlogs and loopholes for riflemen. Hickenlooper's sappers essentially had their own fire support. In this fashion the Federals drove the approach forward toward the Third Louisiana Redan with little fear of Confederate sharpshooters.

On the morning of May 27, Hickenlooper turned the approach south to avoid a ravine and followed a low ridge back to the Jackson Road. The sap reached the road two days later, at which point Hickenlooper again turned west toward his objective, now only two hundred yards away. Pleased with the progress achieved thus far, Hickenlooper reduced the number of sappers by one-third, though the digging continued round the clock. "Every man in the investing line became an army engineer day and night," recalled one veteran of the siege. "The soldiers got so they bored like gophers and beavers, with a spade in one hand and a gun in the other."[4]

By June 3, despite increased Confederate fire, Logan's Approach reached a commanding knoll only 130 yards east of the Third Louisiana Redan. Digging to left and right along the crest of the knoll, the Federals established an advanced artillery position, designated Battery Hickenlooper. Two 24-pound howitzers and one 6-pound gun were rolled forward along the sap, then manhandled into place atop the knoll. The breaching battery, as it was called, roared into action on June 6. Two weeks later two powerful 30-pound Parrott rifled guns were added. The Parrotts soon created a breach in the earthen parapet of the redan.

Although the Confederates attempted to repair the Third Louisiana Redan under cover of darkness, it was a futile effort. Federal artillery opposite the position, and nearly everywhere else along the siege lines, dug holes in the soft earthworks faster than the defenders could fill them in. By the end of the siege, the Union army had 220 guns of all types pounding away at the Vicksburg defenses. That number was augmented by 13 heavy guns from Porter's fleet. The huge naval weapons were hauled up the bluffs and placed in batteries overlooking the Mississippi River. In addition, gunboats and mortar boats blasted away without letup. Pemberton could do little to counter the barrage of artillery fire that slowly pulverized his defenses and crashed into the town from all directions. Following the heavy loss of artillery pieces during the inland campaign, especially at Champion Hill, he had only 128 guns left to place in the landward defenses, and these were mostly light field pieces. As the siege dragged on the Confederate earthworks were slowly reduced to shapeless lumps of earth.

By June 8 Logan's Approach was within seventy-five yards of the battered Third Louisiana Redan, so close that the Confederates could shoot down into the approaching trench from atop their earthworks. The Federals countered by creating an even higher position. Lt. Henry C. Foster of the Twenty-third Indiana Infantry, known as "Coonskin" for the fur cap he persisted in wearing despite the enervating heat, was considered a crack shot. Foster and his fellow Hoosiers under cover of darkness erected a tower of railroad ties in the Jackson Road just behind Battery Hickenlooper. "Coonskin's Tower," as the edifice came to be called, gave the Federals the high ground on this portion of the siege lines. From their perch Foster and his fellow sharpshooters could see over the parapets of all the Confederate earthworks in the vicinity, including the redan. Their deadly fire forced opposing marksmen to keep their heads down and permitted Hickenlooper's sappers to get back to work. Rebel artillery attempted to wreck the tower, which was a rather ramshackle affair that probably could not have withstood more than a few hits. But whenever the muzzle of a Confederate gun appeared, it was smothered by a barrage of fire from the far more numerous and generally heavier Union guns on either side of the Jackson Road, including the guns of Battery Hickenlooper.

Coonskin's Tower stood for the duration of the siege, a monument to individual initiative and industrial superiority. And it became a popular attraction. After being rotated off the firing line, many bored and curious Federals made their way to the Jackson Road and asked to climb to the top, so many, in fact, that Foster began charging an admission fee of twenty-five cents, a hefty sum in 1863. Among the frequent visitors to Coonskin's Tower was no less a personage than Ulysses Grant. He developed the habit of riding along the Union lines in the uniform of a common private, his only insignia of rank were two stars on his shoulders, so as not to draw the attention of Confederate marksmen. One day late in June Grant was atop the tower examining the Confederate lines through his binoculars. He foolishly leaned too far forward and was noticed by a Confederate soldier, who advised him in very strong language to get his head down or get it shot off. Grant heeded the warning.

Desperate to halt the progress of Logan's Approach toward their bastion, Brig. Gen. Louis Hébert and the men of the Third Louisiana resorted to chemical warfare of sorts. They wrapped bullets with tow soaked in turpentine and fired them into the cotton bales on the sap roller. The bales smoldered, then burst into flames. The railroad car was soon ablaze. This Confederate triumph, however, had little effect on Hickenlooper's operation. The Federals quickly assembled a more conventional roller, and the sappers resumed their work. By June 16 the head of Logan's Approach was within twenty-five yards of the Third Louisiana Redan. Concerned about the possibility of a surprise Confederate raid, Hickenlooper discontinued night shifts and constructed two lines of rifle pits on either side of the sap to provide additional protection. The approach finally reached the battered apex of the redan on June 22.

On June 23 Hickenlooper commenced mining operations. Prior to this stage of the project, the sap was a trench running crookedly along the surface of the ground. Now it became a shaft that descended below ground. Working in shifts in stifling conditions, thirty-five experienced coal and lead miners, all volunteers, tunneled under the apex of the redan and excavated a chamber, called a gallery. The mining operation was audible to the Confederates inside the fort, who sank a countermine—a shaft of their own—in the hope of locating the Union mine before the inevitable explosion. As the Rebels frantically tunneled into the earth, they could hear the sound of digging somewhere close by and even make out snatches of conversation, but they were never able to tell where the noises were coming from.

On the morning of June 25 the ground beneath the Third Louisiana Redan became ominously silent as the Union miners completed their task and withdrew. Ordnance personnel packed the gallery with twenty-two hundred pounds of black powder while thousands of infantrymen massed in the winding sap. Grant joined McPherson at Battery Hickenlooper to observe the explosion, scheduled to take place at three o'clock in the afternoon. Once all was in readiness, the fuse was lit.

Hébert was an engineer in the prewar army and knew what was coming. He withdrew his men from the apex of the redan, the most likely place of danger. Pemberton also realized that an explosion, very likely followed by an assault, was imminent. He moved troops into position behind the redan to support Hébert and check a possible Union breakthrough. Tension ran high among the soldiers of both armies as three o'clock came and went without an explosion. Nervous Federals at the head of the assault column wondered if "volunteers" would be ordered into the tunnel to investigate the cause of the delay. The clock reached 3:15, 3:20, then 3:25, and still all was quiet.

At 3:28 there was a muffled thud and the ground began to swell beneath the redan. Then came a terrific crash and a huge mass of dirt and flames erupted into the air. Chaplain Nathan M. Baker of the 116th Illinois likened the explosion to an "immense fountain of finely pulverized earth" and noted that the column of dirt was "mingled with flashes of fire and clouds of smoke, through which could occasionally be caught glimpses of dark objects—men, gun carriages, shelters, and so on." The blast blew away the forward part of the redan and tore a hole in the earth thirty feet across and fifteen feet deep.[5]

Moments after the blast Hickenlooper and a party of pioneer troops stumbled forward through a heavy rain of dirt to try to clear a path across the crater for the infantrymen following close behind. While these men frantically shoveled debris out of the way, wildly shouting soldiers of the Forty-fifth Illinois led by Lt. Col. Melancthon Smith surged forward through the sap four abreast and disappeared into a dense cloud of dust and smoke. Plunging straight ahead Color Sgt. Henry H. Taylor scrambled up the pulverized wall of the redan and planted the Stars and Stripes on the highest spot he could find, an action that earned him a Medal of Honor.

As Union soldiers poured through the smoking breach at the front of the redan, stunned Confederate troops entered the open rear of the fort in a desperate attempt to drive them back. The ensuing battle raged for hours with horrific intensity. Men fought with clubbed muskets, bayonets, and fists. As the sun sank in the western sky, fleeing from the scene of carnage, the crater slowly filled with the bodies of the dead and wounded, both blue and gray. Reinforcements poured in from both directions and attackers and defenders were still locked in bitter combat as darkness enveloped the field. Union and Confederate soldiers hammered away at one another all night in a grim struggle for possession of the ruined redan. More and more fresh troops entered the fray. Incredibly, fighting continued without respite as the sun rose on June 26. But as the morning wore on, Grant finally concluded that success had eluded him once again. He ordered McPherson to recall his men from the crater and dig in along the ravaged exterior slope of the fort.

The struggle inside the Third Louisiana Redan lasted more than twenty hours. Miraculously casualties on both sides were minimized by the relatively small size of the position, which allowed only a fraction of the troops committed to the battle to be engaged at any one time. The Federals lost 34 men killed and 209 wounded in the melee; the Confederates, 21 killed and 73 wounded. Among the Rebel dead was Col. Eugene Erwin of the Sixth Missouri.

Hickenlooper began construction of another shaft on June 26. The Confederates sank another countermine, dug by eight slaves, but again failed to locate the Union mine. At three o'clock on the afternoon of July 1, the second mine—a charge of eighteen hundred pounds of powder—was detonated. More of the redan was demolished, but the explosion was not followed by an infantry assault. The blast was intended to give Hickenlooper's men a sense of satisfaction and impress upon the Confederates the hopelessness of their situation. The second blast killed seven of the slaves in the countermine, but the eighth, a remarkably fortunate man named Abraham, was blown into the air and landed behind Federal lines. A Union soldier described how "one Negro was thrown a 150 feet, lighting on his head and shoulders, scarcely hurting him. He attempted to run back, but a half dozen leveled muskets brought him back." The Northerners dusted off the lucky man and asked, "How high did you go?" to which he responded, "Dunno, massa, but t'ink about t'ree mile." Abraham was an instant celebrity. During the remainder of the siege, enterprising soldiers placed him in a tent and charged their comrades ten cents to see America's first aeronaut.[6]

Union engineers and fatigue parties dug thirteen approaches toward the Confederate defenses during the six-week siege. Saps and mines were dangerous and dramatic affairs, but they were only a part of the extensive engineering efforts at Vicksburg. The Federals created a mirror image of Lockett's landward defenses. The Interior Line, as it came to be known, was a system of trenches called parallels that roughly conformed to the Rebel earthworks. At first a hodgepodge of disconnected diggings, it grew into a complex maze of approaches, battery positions, covered ways, and other features anchored on the Mississippi River both above and below the town. Altogether it included more than sixty thousand linear feet of excavations.

The Interior Line served several purposes. It prevented the Confederates from breaking out or obtaining supplies. It also permitted the Federals to move men and material about with impunity. Finally, the constant construction gave the great mass of Yankees something to do while waiting for Pemberton to give up. This web of trenches sealed the doom of Vicksburg. During the siege "spades were trump," and Grant held all the cards.

On June 30 Grant was informed that all of the saps would reach Confederate lines within a few days. When that happened up to thirteen mines could be detonated simultaneously. This was the goal the general and his soldiers had been working toward throughout the siege. The unsuccessful affair at the Third Louisiana Redan was studied and appropriate lessons were drawn. Sappers widened their approaches to permit the rapid passage of larger masses of infantry and artillery to the front, and planks and sandbags were readied to fill in craters and ditches. The final assault was tentatively scheduled for July 6. The curtain was about to open on the final act in the great Vicksburg drama.

# CHAPTER THIRTEEN

# Too Weak to Save Vicksburg

As the noose around Vicksburg tightened, citizens and soldiers alike found themselves trapped in a quest for survival. For many in the beleaguered city, life under siege soon translated into life underground. Those who could fled to caves dug deep into the hills to escape the constant bombardment of Union guns and mortars that rained iron down upon the city. "The caves were plainly becoming a necessity, as some persons had been killed on the streets by fragments of shell," recorded Mary Loughborough. "Caves were the fashion—the rage—over besieged Vicksburg," remarked another resident. "Negroes, who understood their business, hired themselves out to dig them, at from thirty to fifty dollars, according to size." A woman observed that "so great was the demand for cave workmen, that a new branch of industry sprang up and became popular." Yet another remarked that the hills were so "honeycombed with caves that the streets look like avenues in a cemetery."[1]

Despite subterranean living many of the townspeople remained defiant. Among them was Emma Balfour, who entered in her diary on May 30: "The general impression is that they fire at this city, in that way thinking that they will wear out the women and children and sick, and Gen. Pemberton will be impatient to surrender the place on that account, but they little know the spirit of the Vicksburg women and children if they expect this." A woman whose remarkable strength would be taxed to the limit, she declared, "Rather than let them know that they are causing us any suffering, I would be content to suffer martyrdom!"[2]

Balfour's sentiments were shared by many in the early days of siege, but as the bombardment continued day after weary day, week after week, even the most resolute began to weaken and waver. During one of the more intense periods of shelling, Dr. William Lord, rector of Christ Church, and his family crouched in the basement of their house of worship. His wife, Margaret, tried to comfort their daughter, Lida, who was terrified by the shells that exploded nearby. "Don't cry my darling," she soothed the child, "God will protect us." The little girl sobbed uncontrollably, "But, momma, I'm so afraid that God's killed too."[3]

The shelling and constant fear of death or dismemberment wore as heavily on the soldiers in the trenches as it did on the citizenry of the town. The June 9 entry in Lieutenant Drennan's diary reads: "Another day like the past twenty-one as one day could be like another. Monotony does not convey all the sameness of these days imposes on one." Two days later Drennan wrote of the specter that overshadowed the monotony of the siege: "The mortality here at this time is very great; hardly a day passes but I see dozens of men carried to their last homes. They are buried in a trench with a blanket for their shroud. Coffins can not be had for all of them. Graves are dug today for use tomorrow."[4]

Everyone began to fear the worst as the siege continued into the summer. The besieging Union army slowly strangled the life out of Vicksburg. Rations for military personnel dwindled and declined in quality. Food supplies for townspeople became scarce as well, and prices for all commodities grew exorbitant. By the end of June one could walk through the marketplaces along Washington Street and see "skinned rats" hanging for sale. The *Daily Citizen,* Vicksburg's leading newspaper, resorted to publishing on wallpaper. Yet even amid the hardships, most people had reason for hope. They reasoned that the authorities in Richmond would not forsake so important a place as Vicksburg. Knowing that Gen. Joseph Johnston had been sent to Mississippi to rescue the Hill City and its besieged garrison, relief was on their minds, and their constant prayer was for deliverance.

The relief of Vicksburg was indeed the focus of attention in Richmond. The gas chandeliers at the Confederate Executive Mansion burned late into the warming nights throughout May and June 1863. President Davis directed that troops from as far away as the Atlantic coast be rushed to Johnston. He and Secretary of War James A. Seddon even contemplated detaching troops from the Army of Northern Virginia, including Gen. Robert E. Lee, and sending them fifteen hundred miles westward in a desperate attempt to relieve the city. Lee, however, envisioned other plans to ease pressure on Vicksburg by taking the war in the East northward into Maryland and Pennsylvania.

In desperation Davis looked to Confederate forces west of the Mississippi River as a possible source of relief for the besieged garrison. He urged Edmund Kirby Smith, recently appointed to command the Trans-Mississippi Department, to do whatever he could to aid Pemberton. Smith did not think his tiny forces could accomplish much but directed both Richard Taylor in Louisiana and Theophilus Holmes in Arkansas to strike at Federal outposts on the west side of the Mississippi. Such attacks, if successful, might compel Grant to weaken his forces around Vicksburg and thereby provide Johnston with an opportunity to relieve Pemberton.

Taylor's objective was the string of Union camps at Milliken's Bend, Young's Point, and Lake Providence. A few months earlier these staging areas were crowded with thousands of Union soldiers and tons of supplies, but by early June the war had passed them by, and they were little more than camps of instruction for new black regiments. Transports carrying supplies and reinforcements for the Army of the Tennessee now proceeded up the Yazoo River to the bluffs north of Vicksburg. The west bank of the Mississippi River opposite the Hill City had become a backwater. Taylor suspected as much. He did not believe that attacks on outposts such as Milliken's Bend would deter or distract Grant in the slightest. He wanted to return to south-central Louisiana and threaten Union-occupied New Orleans. But Taylor did as instructed and led his small command into northeast Louisiana. "Remonstrances were to no avail," he later wrote. "I was informed that all the Confederate authorities in the east were urgent for some effort on our part in behalf of Vicksburg, and that public opinion would condemn us if we did not *try to do something.*"[5]

Anxious to strike immediately and be done with it, Taylor decided to send Maj. Gen. John G. Walker's Texas division against Milliken's Bend and Young's Point, while Col. Frank Bartlett's Thirteenth Louisiana Cavalry Battalion struck at Lake Providence. According to recent intelligence the Union camps were occupied by small numbers of white soldiers and large numbers of recently recruited black troops. Taylor did not anticipate much resistance.

The Confederates left Richmond, Louisiana, on the evening of June 6 with the intent of arriving at the Union camps by sunrise. One Texan recorded of the night march: "In sections four abreast, and close order, the troops took up the line of march, in anticipation of meeting almost certain death, but with undaunted, unquailing spirits. In breathless silence, with the high glittering stars looking down upon them, through dark and deep defiles marched the dense array of men, moving steadily forward; not a whisper was heard—no sound of clanking saber, or rattle of canteen and cup." At Oak Grove plantation the road forked. Walker sent Brig. Gen. Henry E. McCulloch's brigade toward Milliken's Bend and Brig. Gen. James M. Hawes's brigade toward Young's Point a few miles downstream. Walker remained at Oak Grove with one brigade in reserve.[6]

Col. Hermann Lieb was in charge at Milliken's Bend. His command consisted of the Twenty-third Iowa and several Louisiana colored regiments in various stages of training. At dawn on June 7 McCulloch deployed his troops into line of battle and advanced across the level countryside, quickly driving the outnumbered Federals behind a levee topped with a barricade of cotton bales. Shouting, "No quarter for the officers, kill the damned abolitionists, spare the niggers," the Texans stormed the levee. A withering volley from the Iowans and the colored regiments stunned the Confederates, but many of the inexperienced black soldiers were unable to reload their weapons before the Texans were upon them. McCulloch reported, "The line was formed under a heavy fire from the enemy, and the troops charged the breastworks, carrying it instantly, killing and wounding many of the enemy by their deadly fire, as well as the bayonet." The intensely partisan McCulloch noted, "This charge was resisted by the negro portion of the enemy's force with considerable obstinacy, while the white or true Yankee portion ran like whipped curs almost as soon as the charge was ordered."[7]

A vicious melee erupted as the Texans surged over the levee and into the Union encampment. Joseph P. Blessington of the Sixteenth Texas recalled: "The enemy gave away and stampeded pell-mell over the levee, in great terror and confusion. Our troops followed after them, bayoneting them by hundreds." Surviving Federals fled in disorder to a second levee nearer the river. McCulloch's men approached but were halted by artillery fire from the ironclad *Choctaw,* which Porter had stationed near Milliken's Bend for just this sort of emergency. McCulloch sent an urgent request to Walker for reinforcements, but before help arrived another gunboat, the *Lexington,* steamed into sight. Realizing that his troops were no match for the Union navy, McCulloch withdrew to Oak Grove.[8]

The Texans lost 185 men (44 killed, 131 wounded, and 10 missing) but inflicted 652 casualties on the unprepared Union force (101 killed, 285 wounded, and 266 missing). Many of the missing Federals were black soldiers carried off by the withdrawing Confederates as recovered runaway slaves. From the Rebel perspective Milliken's Bend was a tactical victory but a strategic failure. The encounters at Young's Point and Lake Providence were of even less significance. By the beginning of June events on the west bank of the Mississippi River had no effect whatsoever on the siege of Vicksburg. Smith acknowledged as much by permitting Taylor to hurry south and attempt to throw a fright into the Union occupation force at New Orleans. It remained to be seen whether Taylor would reach the Crescent City in time to make a difference.

According to some highly imaginative accounts that received widespread publicity, Lieb's black recruits acquitted themselves well at Milliken's Bend. One witness noted, with considerable exaggeration, that after initially giving way, the colored regiments "rallied with great fury and routed the enemy." Brig. Gen. Elias Dennis was not present, but that did not stop him from declaring, "It is impossible for men to show greater gallantry than the Negro troops in that fight." Far more important than the outcome of the battle, or even the actual performance of the black troops, which was about what could be expected from inexperienced men taken by surprise in their first clash, was the widespread belief that former slaves would and could fight. As Charles Dana observed: "The bravery of the blacks in the battle of Milliken's Bend completely revolutionized the sentiment of the army with regard to the employment of Negro troops. I heard prominent officers, who formerly in private had sneered at the idea of Negroes fighting, express themselves after that as heartily in favor of it." The presence of black men in Union blue on the banks of the Mississippi River was a harbinger of things to come.[9]

Farther north in Little Rock Holmes had long contemplated an attack against the Union enclave of Helena on the west bank of the Mississippi River. Located on a rare stretch of high rolling ground in eastern Arkansas, the town was an important supply depot and a center for recruiting colored soldiers. It was fortified and garrisoned by approximately four thousand Federals under Maj. Gen. Benjamin M. Prentiss of Shiloh fame. Helena would be a great challenge, but it was an important Union possession, and a Confederate success there might cause Grant to divert men and resources away from Vicksburg in order to recapture the place.

Confederate plans for the assault against Helena matured very slowly. Rather than make the proposed movement in conjunction with Taylor's strike in northeast Louisiana, Holmes did not get underway until June 22. After the calamities of Prairie Grove and Arkansas Post six months earlier,

Holmes was desperately short of manpower, but he threw everything he had into the Helena operation. In late June the Confederates began moving eastward from Little Rock and Jacksonport with a force of over seventy-six hundred men. On July 3 the converging columns were only five miles from Helena. Holmes intended to attack with the rising sun on the Fourth of July.

In Helena Prentiss grew alarmed by the increased Confederate activity around his perimeter. He put soldiers and freedmen to work strengthening the town's defenses, which consisted of a large redoubt known as Fort Curtis immediately west of town and four smaller outlying redoubts on commanding hills and simply labeled from north to south as Batteries A, B, C, and D. A semicircular line of rifle pits connected these five positions. The Federals felled hundreds of trees in front of their works and across all of the roads leading into town. Prentiss was reasonably confident that he could deal with whatever Holmes had in mind.

The Confederate commander was anxious to strike. "This is my fight," he declared to his subordinates. "If I succeed, I want the glory; and if I fail, I am willing to bear the odium." His enthusiasm was shared by the men in the ranks, who began to move forward around midnight. Darkness slowed the advance and, within a mile of Helena, it was stopped altogether by massive tangles of felled trees. The Rebels had no pioneer troops to clear a path; the men broke ranks and crawled through the timber barricades, but they had to leave their artillery behind.[10]

The Confederate onslaught began at dawn. On the left Brig. Gen. John S. Marmaduke's brigade approached Battery A on Rightor Hill, while Brig. Gen. James F. Fagan's brigade advanced against Battery D atop Hindman Hill on the right. The principal attack came in the center, where Sterling Price's three-thousand-man division surged up Graveyard Hill against Battery C, "yelling like so many fiends let loose from a bottomless pit," in the words of Edward N. Waldon of the Twenty-eighth Wisconsin. Price's men advanced through a deadly crossfire and overran Battery C only to discover that the Federals had spiked one gun and rendered the other useless by carrying away the friction primers. Graveyard Hill commanded Fort Curtis, the principal defensive feature. Artillery fire from that eminence probably would have forced the Federals to flee or surrender, but Holmes's own guns were far to the rear, beyond the timber barricades, and could not be brought up in time.[11]

Prentiss formed a new defensive line and brought all available Union artillery, including the heavy guns aboard the gunboat *Tyler*, to bear on

Graveyard Hill. The hail of projectiles took a fearful toll and spread confusion in the Confederate ranks. "The air was full of shells and we could see the rebels lines open and see them falling in all directions," noted Minos Miller of the Second Arkansas (U.S.). After repulsing a feeble assault against Fort Curtis, Prentiss ordered a counterattack and recovered Battery C. The Confederates fell back in great disorder to Little Rock, leaving the slopes around Helena strewn with their dead and wounded.[12]

The bitter Independence Day engagement at Helena is little known today, but it was one of the most intense battles of the war and a resounding Confederate defeat. Holmes lost 21 percent of his command, 1,636 of the 7,646 troops he committed to battle. Despite being outnumbered nearly two to one, Federal casualties were remarkably light. Prentiss lost only 239 men: 57 killed, 146 wounded, and 36 missing. Helena was the only occasion during the Vicksburg campaign in which the Confederates assaulted fixed fortifications, and the results were sadly predictable.

Could Confederate operations in Louisiana and Arkansas have been successful? Historian Edwin C. Bearss believes so, writing, "If undertaken at an earlier date, in late April or early May, a slashing Southern onslaught against one or more of General Grant's Louisiana enclaves . . . might have jeopardized the Union campaign." He goes on to state, "It was only after Pemberton's army was under siege, and the situation had become desperate that the Trans-Mississippi soldiers were committed. And when they were, it was too little, too late." Even had Holmes succeeded in overwhelming the defenders at Helena, it would have been a hollow victory. At the height of the Confederate assault against Graveyard Hill on the morning of July 4, white flags fluttered in the breeze above the Vicksburg defenses.[13]

Back in Mississippi Johnston's swelling force represented the only real hope of saving Vicksburg. Johnston, however, was far less resolute than his counterparts in Louisiana and Arkansas. After evacuating Jackson on May 14, he established himself at Canton and began to assemble what he called the "Army of Relief." Davis and Seddon did their part. They hurried soldiers and equipment toward Canton from all parts of the eastern Confederacy except Virginia. By early June they had provided Johnston with thirty-two thousand troops, a truly remarkable achievement given the paucity of Confederate resources and the precarious condition of the Southern transportation system. When Pemberton's thirty-thousand-man garrison in Vicksburg is taken into account, the Rebels enjoyed a substantial numerical advantage over Grant. Although this advantage did not last long, Johnston was presented with a window of opportunity to save Vicksburg. But he failed to act, paralyzed by his own defeatism.

Such a lack of temerity on Johnston's part was inconceivable to Pemberton's soldiers. Weeks into the siege they remained confident that the renowned Joe Johnston was moving heaven and earth to relieve them and that the boom of his guns would be heard any day. On June 1 Lieutenant Drennen confided to his diary: "I have every reason to believe that ten days will bring relief in the person of General Johnson and 50,000 men. God send him quickly." The belief—or hope—expressed by the young lieutenant and shared by many of his comrades slowly faded. Ten days later Drennen's optimism had dimmed, and he lamented, "I had fixed on the 10th of the month for General Johnson to come to our relief. But that day has come and gone and no relief in hearing as yet. I do not despair, by any means, yet I confess that I feel disheartened."[14]

Pemberton too began to have his doubts about Johnston. "I think your movement should be made as soon as possible," he urged on June 15, nearly a month into the siege. But by that time Pemberton probably harbored little confidence that Johnston would move quickly or decisively. When Pemberton finally asked his superior, "What aid am I to expect from you?" Johnston replied, "I am too weak to save Vicksburg." It was an echo of his infamous message to Richmond four weeks earlier on May 13 ("I am too late."). Its effect on Pemberton can be imagined.[15]

Davis and members of his cabinet urged Johnston to move quickly, none more forcefully than Secretary of War Seddon, who admonished the general: "Vicksburg must not be lost without a desperate struggle. The interest and honor of the Confederacy forbid it." Johnston remained unmoved and immobile. Having convinced himself that nothing could be done, he did nothing.[16]

Despite prodding from his superiors in Richmond, pleas from Vicksburg, and a rising clamor for action in the press, the general on whom the hopes of the Confederacy rested would not act. As the weeks slipped by, Johnston complained of his lack of men, horses, wagons, artillery, and supplies, offering an array of creative reasons for his inactivity. In truth, as historian Michael B. Ballard asserts: "Johnston never had any intention of trying to save Vicksburg or its defenders. As usual when a bold, offensive maneuver was necessary, Johnston found every excuse not to move."[17]

Aware that Johnston was massing troops, Grant requested reinforcements of his own. The Lincoln administration responded with alacrity and ordered troops to Vicksburg from nearly every corner of the Union. In mid-June, for example, Maj. Gen. John G. Parke's Ninth Corps, veterans of Antietam and Fredericksburg who had only recently been detached from the Army of the Potomac, arrived from Kentucky. In contrast to the Confederates the Union high command did not hesitate to call upon forces in the trans-Mississippi. Following the battle of Prairie Grove, Maj. Gen. Francis J. Herron's Third Division of the Army of the Frontier marched across the Ozark Plateau from northwest Arkansas and made its way to Mississippi.

Grant used Herron's men to complete the investment of Vicksburg by placing them on the extreme left of the Union Interior Line near the Mississippi River south of town. But he used the bulk of the new arrivals to establish what became known as the Exterior Line. This new ring of earthworks paralleled the Union trenches that encircled Vicksburg, but it faced outward. The fortifications ran east from Haynes' Bluff, overlooking the Yazoo River north of Vicksburg, to Oak Ridge and then south to the railroad bridge across the Big Black River east of town, the scene of the battle on May 17. The line did not extend south of the railroad bridge because Grant did not believe Johnston could cross the lower Big Black.

The Exterior Line was less than half the length of the Interior Line, but it was ultimately manned by thirty-four thousand troops supported by seventy-two guns, all under Sherman's personal command. The sole purpose of the bristling array of redoubts and rifle pits was to keep Johnston at bay should he attempt to relieve Pemberton. In retrospect, construction of the Exterior Line was unnecessary, for Grant greatly overestimated Johnston's inclination for bold offensive movements. When the Confederate finally ordered his troops out of Canton on July 1, he made no attempt to test the Union fortifications. Cautiously approaching the Big Black River two days later, Johnston immediately concluded that he could not force a crossing in the face of such impressive defenses and prepared to return to Canton.

But by then whatever Johnston did was immaterial. As the misnamed Army of Relief hovered east of the Big Black, officers and men noticed that the distant boom of artillery had stopped. An ominous silence settled over the region, indicating that time had expired for the defenders of Vicksburg.

# CHAPTER FOURTEEN

# The Glorious Fourth

As June faded into July, the siege of Vicksburg entered its seventh week. Pemberton and his soldiers despaired of rescue, and a feeling of gloom hung over the army much as a thick shroud. Union saps had reached the outer ditch at several points along the eight-mile line of crumbling earthworks. In some places the Confederates could hear the ominous sound of mining operations beneath their feet. In others they could extend their arms over the top of the battered parapet and touch Union soldiers on the other side—the only thing separating the two armies was the parapet itself. Here and there enterprising Federals even gouged holes in the parapet with their bayonets and fired point-blank into the faces of Confederates on the other side. By July 3 all knew that time was about to expire for the fortress city and its defenders.

For the citizens and soldiers who had endured so much for so long, the events of May 17 must have seemed like a distant memory. On that day, when the Confederates poured into the city following the debacle at Big Black River Bridge, Alex S. Abrams, a news correspondent from Georgia, observed, "A feeling of despondence could be observed among the troops, and curses, loud and deep, were hurled at Lieutenant General Pemberton for his mismanagement of the army—many of the troops declaring their willingness to desert rather than serve under him again."[1]

Pemberton was cognizant of the widespread criticism of his leadership, but he did not comprehend the depth of discontent within the army. The seriousness of the situation was finally impressed upon him by a letter from General Bowen, who warned that the "wildest and most absurd rumors of surrender are in existence, not only among the men, but the officers of the command." The note informed Pemberton that

Union prisoners were spreading the word that he and Grant had an understanding and that Vicksburg would be theirs before May 20. Bowen urged his commander to proclaim his determination to hold the city.[2]

Alarmed by the possibility of a mutiny, Pemberton followed Bowen's advice and issued a proclamation that read in part: "You have heard that I was incompetent, and a traitor, and that it was my intention to sell Vicksburg. Follow me, and you will see the cost at which I will sell Vicksburg. When the last pound of beef, bacon, and flour, the last grain of corn, the last cow and hog and horse and dog shall have been consumed, and the last man shall have perished in the trenches, then, and only then will I sell Vicksburg." It was not exactly an inspirational pronouncement, but it served its purpose, and talk of mutiny faded away. Morale improved noticeably following the repulse of the Union assaults on May 19 and 22. "They judged their general wrong," Lt. Col. Robert Bevier of Missouri wrote of those who thought ill of Pemberton. "He was incapable of harboring a thought of treason; he may not have been an able commander, but he was brave and they soon found that he would surrender to nothing but starvation."[3]

Pemberton was true to his word. On May 21, looking to conserve the precious supply of food and forage on hand to meet the exigencies of a protracted siege, he directed that most of the army's horses and mules be driven beyond the lines for pasturage. Although these animals fell into enemy hands, at least the Confederates no longer had to feed them. Rations were reduced again and again until, by the end of the siege, each soldier subsisted on only a handful of peas and rice per day. Water also was rationed, eventually at the rate of only one cup per day, barely enough to maintain bodily functions. The streams that supplied Vicksburg originated east of town, behind Union lines. To make life as miserable as possible for the garrison, the Federals threw animal carcasses into the streams to render the water unfit for drinking. Union batteries on De Soto Point fired on soldiers and civilians who attempted to draw muddy water from the Mississippi. The shortage of water was exacerbated by the terrible heat of a Southern summer.

Disease added to the suffering caused by the scarcity of food and water. Dysentery, diarrhea, malaria, and a host of other infections ran rampant through the ranks. As was always the case in the Civil War, more men died from disease than from gunfire. Thousands of Confederates ended up in the hospitals as the siege went on, and the line of defenders was spread dangerously thin. Those who remained in the trenches bore mute testimony to the rigors of the siege, with their glazed eyes and emaciated forms. Civilians were better off at first, but as the weeks passed, they too suffered from the hard hand of war.

At the beginning of July Pemberton began to lose hope. Joe Johnston would not or could not relieve the beleaguered garrison. There were but two alternatives left: surrender or attempt to cut through the encircling Union lines. With a view to the latter, in June Pemberton had ordered hundreds of skiffs constructed and concealed in warehouses along the waterfront. The idea of crossing the Mississippi River to Louisiana, however, was soon abandoned, for it would be suicidal to make such an attempt in the presence of Porter's gunboats. Pemberton also had considered breaking out at South Fort, the southernmost point of his landward defenses, where the Warrenton Road ran south along the edge of the bluffs overlooking the Mississippi. Grant was slow to close off that avenue of escape because of a lack of manpower, but by the time Pemberton seriously began to consider getting out of Vicksburg, it was too late. Union reinforcements had arrived in substantial numbers, and Grant had extended the Interior Line all the way to the banks of the Mississippi. The Confederates were trapped.

On July 1 Pemberton issued a circular to his division commanders. "Unless the siege of Vicksburg is raised or supplies are thrown in, it will become necessary very shortly to evacuate the place," he informed his subordinates, most of whom already had come to the same conclusion. With candor he expressed his own thoughts, "I see no prospect of the former, and there are many great, if not insuperable, obstacles in the way of the letter." As time was of the essence, he urged that they report "with as little delay as possible as to the condition of your troops, and their ability to make the marches and undergo the fatigues necessary to accomplish a successful evacuation." As usual when faced with a difficult decision, Pemberton attempted to achieve a consensus as to the proper course of action.[4]

The response from his subordinates was almost unanimous. For a breakout attempt to succeed, they reasoned, the Army of Vicksburg would have to place the Big Black River between itself and the enemy in a single day's march, otherwise it would be gobbled up by Grant's larger and more mobile force. The army would have to abandon its artillery and wagons (there were no draft animals available), which meant that the men would have to carry a substantial load of food and ammunition. In their gravely weakened state they would not long hold up under the strain. The generals declared that the soldiers had suffered enough and recommended that "an immediate proposition be made to capitulate."[5]

Years later Samuel Lockett recalled that Pemberton was so distraught he flirted with the idea of leading a suicidal attempt to break through Union lines. He quoted the general as saying that such a desperate act was the "only hope of saving myself from shame and disgrace." According to Lockett Pemberton eventually submitted to a higher sense of honor and acknowledged that a more noble course of action would be to bear the opprobrium of surrender, that is, "to sacrifice myself to save the army which has so nobly done its duty to defend Vicksburg." It seems unlikely that the prosaic Pemberton ever used such flowery words, but he may well have expressed sentiments along those lines.[6]

The soldiers of the Army of Vicksburg expressed themselves in much plainer language. Despite all manner of deprivations and hardships, they still maintained a certain dark humor right up to the end, as when they warned the Federals to "look out as we have a new general . . . General Starvation," but they too realized that the game was up. A remarkable letter from the ranks made its way to Pemberton and confirmed his decision to surrender. Entitled "Appeal for help," the letter urged the general to bring matters to a close. "If you can't feed us, you had better surrender us, horrible as the idea is, than suffer this noble army to disgrace themselves by desertion." The document was signed "MANY SOLDIERS."[7]

Pemberton informed his officers that he would offer to surrender the Army of Vicksburg on the Fourth of July. He explained that he likely would be able to obtain more favorable terms on Independence Day. "I know my people [that is, Northerners]," he said. "To gratify their national vanity they would yield then what could not be extorted from them at any other time." With this in mind Pemberton opened communications with Grant.[8]

As the sun rose on July 3, soldiers and citizens were puzzled by the unusual quiet of the morning. The quiet was due to the presence of white flags fluttering above the earthworks near the center of the Confederate line. Bowen and Lt. Col. Louis Montgomery of Pemberton's staff rode out of the besieged city around midmorning and made their way to the Union lines. They delivered a letter from Pemberton to Grant requesting that an armistice be granted in order to arrange terms for the capitulation of Vicksburg. Grant's answer was typically blunt. "The useless effusion of blood you propose stopping by this course can be ended at any time you may choose, by an unconditional surrender of the city and garrison."

Grant recognized that he was the master of the situation. He had fought too long and hard to demand anything less than unconditional surrender. These terms he believed he owed to himself and his army. The Confederate officers returned to Pemberton's headquarters with the terse reply.[9]

In the company of his generals at army headquarters on Crawford Street, Pemberton reviewed Grant's response. He had hoped for more favorable terms and was disappointed. In the discussion that followed Bowen stated that Grant seemed to desire an informal interview with Pemberton to discuss the matter of surrender. Encouraged by this additional information, which apparently was colored by Bowen's desire to bring matters to a conclusion, Pemberton informed Grant that he would like to meet him on the Jackson Road that afternoon.

Shortly before three o'clock flags of truce again appeared atop the Confederate earthworks and firing sputtered to a halt. Grant appeared on the Jackson Road accompanied by James McPherson and Andrew Smith, among others. He was in good spirits. "It was a glorious sight to officers and soldiers on the line where these white flags were visible," wrote Grant, "and the news soon spread to all parts of the command." He continued, "The troops felt that their long and weary marches, hard fighting, ceaseless watching by day and night, in a hot climate, exposure to all sorts of weather, to disease, and, worst of all, to the gibes of many Northern papers that came to them saying all their suffering was in vain, that Vicksburg would never be taken, were at last at an end and the Union sure to be saved."[10]

A far more solemn group of horsemen dressed in gray emerged from the besieged fortifications. The Confederates exchanged few words during the ride from headquarters in Vicksburg, but at one point Pemberton said, perhaps more to himself than to Bowen and Montgomery, "I feel a confidence that I shall stand justified to my government, if not to the Southern people." He added, "the consolation of having done the only thing which in my opinion could give security to Vicksburg and the surrounding country . . . will be reward enough." As he probably expected, the consolation of which he spoke was to be his only reward.[11]

The two groups of officers met in a swale between the lines, dismounted, and shook hands. Grant recalled, "Pemberton and I had served in the same division during part of the Mexican War. I knew him very well, therefore, and greeted him as an old acquaintance." Pemberton, however, was ill at ease and responded stiffly to his opponent's greeting. To Grant his counterpart seemed "much excited."[12]

An awkward silence ensued as both commanders waited for the other to begin discussing the matter at hand. Pemberton finally announced that it was his understanding that Grant had requested the interview. He was taken aback when the general replied in the negative. He turned to Bowen and remarked, "Then there is a misunderstanding; I certainly understood differently." Red faced, Bowen admitted that the interview had been his idea. Pemberton then inquired of Grant, "In your letter of this morning you state that you have no other terms than an unconditional surrender." Grant nodded, "I have no others." "Then, sir," rejoined Pemberton, "it is unnecessary that you and I should hold any further conversation; we will go to fighting again at once." Apparently feeling a need to end the abortive conference on a defiant note, he declared, "I can assure you, sir, that you will bury many more of your men before you will enter Vicksburg," adding that the garrison had sufficient stores to hold out for weeks. Grant knew that such talk was largely bravado. The nightly trickle of hungry deserters had recently turned into a flood, proof that the Confederate larder was almost empty.[13]

In the hope that a surrender could be consummated then and there, Grant abandoned his demand for an unconditional surrender. He proposed that the two commanders step aside while McPherson, Bowen, Smith, and Montgomery discussed terms. Sensing that Grant was making an effort to meet him halfway, Pemberton agreed. The two men then walked a short distance and, in the shade of a stunted and splintered oak, one of the few trees still standing between the lines, they sat and reminisced about their days in Mexico. Meanwhile the other four officers hammered out a list of mutually acceptable terms of surrender. (It was Bowen's final contribution to the Confederacy. He already was ill with the dysentery that would claim his life on July 13.) When Grant heard the proposed terms, he rejected them as too lenient but informed Pemberton that he would submit alternate conditions that evening. After agreeing to continue the truce until the next day, the two groups of officers mounted their horses and rode their separate ways. Pemberton undoubtedly took some satisfaction from the fact that he had gotten Grant to agree to a negotiated surrender, while Grant must have been pleased that victory was only a few hours away.

Rumors spread like wildfire among the soldiers of both armies. It was commonly believed that the end of the struggle was at hand. Capt. George H. Hynds of the Thirty-first Tennessee Infantry wrote, "I believe we have been sold and Pemberton is now giving the bill of sale for us and receiving his reward." He added ruefully, "It is hard to be sold and not get part of the purchase money." The thought of surrender had little appeal for diarist William Drennan. "Oh! It is heart-sickening, for should Vicksburg be surrendered and we be taken prisoners, I have no idea that we shall see outside prison walls for months—perhaps not during the war. A prison has no charms for me and I still hope that they parole."[14]

The afternoon of July 3 was oppressively hot. Despite the truce occasional shots were fired. Around five o'clock the last gun was fired in the defense of Vicksburg, and a strange silence ensued. After weeks of unceasing combat, soldiers of both armies found the quiet unnatural. To Lt. Richard L. Howard of the 124th Illinois: "The silence began to be fearfully oppressive. For so many long days and nights it had been a continuous battle. Not a minute but the crack of the rifle or the boom of the cannon had been in our ears. And much of the time it had been deafening. Now it was still, absolutely still. . . . It was leaden. We could not bear it; it settled down so close; it hugged us with its hollow, unseen arms till we could scarcely breathe." On the other side of the fortifications, Chaplain William L. Foster of the 35th Mississippi recalled: "I heard the shrill note of the artillery-man's bugle. It was the first time I heard the blast of the bugle during the siege. In a moment our canon ceased firing. The enemy beyond the river also ceased and stillness again rested upon the peaceful bosom of the father of waters." Although an end to bloodshed and suffering appeared to be at hand, the cleric added that a "painful silence, foreboding evil, reigns over the doomed city."[15]

Upon returning to his headquarters Grant informed Admiral Porter of what was happening and asked that the navy honor the ceasefire. Then he sent for the corps and division commanders holding the Interior Line, the only time in the campaign that Grant held something that might be described as a council of war. (Sherman and the other generals stationed on the Exterior Line were watching Johnston's Army of Relief on the far side of the Big Black River and did not attend.) Grant told everyone of his meeting with Pemberton. He said that while he still favored an unconditional surrender or something close to it, he was willing to make a few concessions in order to bring matters to a close. Grant then asked for suggestions as to terms for surrender.

To Grant's surprise his subordinates urged him to make Pemberton an offer of parole. They argued that transporting twenty or thirty thousand prisoners up the Mississippi River to camps in the Midwest and feeding them along the way would tie up an immense amount of shipping and consume a mountain of resources. Parole meant that the Confederates would promise not to take up arms against the U.S. government until properly exchanged, but they would be free to leave Vicksburg. Afterward the hard-pressed Confederacy would have the responsibility of transporting, feeding, and looking after Pemberton's defeated and demoralized army of noncombatants. Parole was a major concession indeed, but after some reflection Grant anticipated that it would be welcomed by Pemberton's weary soldiers. He ordered "some discreet men" placed on picket duty that night "to communicate to the enemy's pickets the fact that Gen. Grant has offered, in case Pemberton surrenders, to parole all the officers and men, and permit them to go home from here." Grant believed that many dispirited Confederates would be quick to accept this generous offer and would make their feelings known to their superiors. He also believed, or at least hoped, that many would leave for home—that is, desert—after the capitulation.[16]

As promised Grant sent in his amended terms of surrender to Confederate headquarters that night. Pemberton submitted them without comment to his division and brigade commanders. The assembled generals thought the conditions were "as good as we can expect" and urged Pemberton to accept them. Only two officers, one of them Stephen Lee, urged their commander to hold out a little longer. Pemberton took pen in hand and informed Grant, "in the main your terms are accepted," by which he meant the offer of parole, but then he attempted to reopen negotiations. Pemberton proposed to consummate the surrender the next morning "by marching out with my colors and arms, stacking them in front of my present lines, after which you will take possession." By this he meant that the Confederate army would simply march away from Vicksburg after giving up their flags and arms. He assured Grant that this would "perfect the agreement between us."[17]

By now it was after midnight on Independence Day, and Grant was tired of Pemberton's delaying tactics. He agreed to a limited surrender ceremony, an important point of military honor in the nineteenth century, but insisted that the Confederates return to their camps in order to be properly paroled, a process that involved a good deal of paperwork. Determined to bring matters to a close, he warned Pemberton that if he did not receive a conclusive response to his terms by nine o'clock in the morning, "I shall regard them as having been rejected, and shall act accordingly." Pemberton knew the game was up. Enough blood had been shed in defense of Vicksburg. He informed Grant, "[the] terms proposed by you are accepted."[18]

On the morning of July 4, 1863, white flags appeared along the entire length of the Vicksburg fortifications. Around ten o'clock those Confederates still on their feet marched out from their works, furled their flags, stacked their arms, turned over their accouterments, and returned to their camps. Jubilant soldiers of the Army of the Tennessee then marched past the empty defensive fortifications and took possession of the Gibraltar on the Mississippi that had resisted them for so long.

The capture of Vicksburg and its garrison was a strategic victory of almost incalculable proportions, the single greatest feat of arms achieved by either side during the entire Civil War. In addition to receiving the surrender of a garrison of 29,500 men (the largest surrender of American troops in the nation's history), the Federals seized a huge amount of military stores: 172 pieces of artillery, 38,000 artillery projectiles, 58,000 pounds of black powder, 50,000 firearms, and 600,000 rounds of ammunition—resources in men and material that the Confederacy could ill afford to lose.

Grant rode into Vicksburg on the Jackson Road past the ruins of the Third Louisiana Redan. He stopped at the Warren County Courthouse and watched as the Stars and Stripes were unfurled atop the building. Then he rode down to the waterfront, where he congratulated Porter and thanked him for the invaluable assistance rendered by the navy during the long and costly campaign. Almost as an afterthought he sent the ram *General Price* racing down the Mississippi River to inform Banks at Port Hudson that Vicksburg was in Union hands. A similar message went upstream aboard the fast steamer *V. F. Wilson* to Cairo, Illinois. From there the electrifying news was telegraphed to the War Department in Washington and rushed to the Executive Mansion. "I cannot, in words, tell you my joy over this result," cried President Lincoln. "It is great!"[19]

When coupled with reports of Union victories at Gettysburg and Helena, the news from Mississippi was positively glorious. Within days there would be even more good news for Lincoln to celebrate.

# CHAPTER FIFTEEN

# No Longer a Point of Danger

"Glory hallelujah!" declared William Sherman when he learned that John Pemberton had agreed to surrender. "The best Fourth of July since 1776." Both Grant and Sherman desired to press the advantage and immediately turned their attention toward Joseph Johnston, whose so-called Army of Relief was slowly approaching the Big Black River north of the Southern Railroad. "I want Johnston broken up as effectually as possible, and roads destroyed," directed Grant. Eager to take the field, Sherman replied, "telegraph me the moment you have Vicksburg in possession, and I will secure all the crossings of [Big] Black River, and move on Jackson or Canton, as you may advise."[1]

Twenty miles east of Vicksburg the Confederates were puzzled by the ominous silence. Johnston, however, knew or at least suspected what it meant. In the last communication from the besieged garrison, dated June 23, Pemberton had made it clear that the end was near. "I will strain every nerve to hold out, if there is hope of our ultimate relief, for fifteen days longer." At the end of that time the garrison would be compelled to capitulate. Pemberton had suggested that if relief was not possible, Johnston should contact Grant as soon as possible and negotiate the best possible surrender terms. But the general did not want to have anything to do with the surrender of Vicksburg. "Negotiations with Grant for the relief of the garrison, should they become necessary, must be made by you," he informed Pemberton on June 27. "It would be a confession of weakness on my part, which I ought not to make, to propose them. When it becomes necessary to make terms, they may be considered as made under my authority." Although only twelve days rather than fifteen had passed since Pemberton penned the dire warning of imminent catastrophe, Johnston was all but certain that the silence meant that the defenders of Vicksburg had reached the limits of human endurance and had capitulated.[2]

Incredibly Johnston had not scouted the approaches to Vicksburg. He spent much of July 3 and 4 examining reconnaissance reports of roads, fords, and enemy positions between Jackson and the Hill City. These revealed that Grant's Exterior Line was considerably stronger than anticipated. This should not have been a surprise since Johnston's six weeks of inactivity at Canton had allowed the Federals to dig miles of outward-facing earthworks without interference. The general concluded that it would be futile to attempt to force a crossing of the Big Black River north of the Southern Railroad in the face of an entrenched enemy. He reasoned that there might be a soft spot in the Union defenses somewhere south of the tracks. Johnston therefore decided to move down the east side of the Big Black. In truth he was searching for any reason to avoid actually having to make an attack. But before his troops could take up the line of march on July 5, the fears of all were confirmed with the news of Vicksburg's surrender.

Correctly fearing that Grant would now turn on him, Johnston headed east. Morale within the Confederate ranks sank as the gray columns trudged toward Jackson through merciless heat and choking dust. It did not go unnoticed that the pace of Johnston's withdrawal was considerably faster than his advance. Even so it required two dismal days for the Confederates to reach the Mississippi capital. On the evening of July 7, Confederate troops filed into the defenses located on the west side of Jackson. Johnston was dissatisfied as usual. "These intrenchments were very badly located and constructed," he noted, "and offered very slight obstacle to a vigorous assault." The following morning he set large fatigue parties to work strengthening the fortifications. Under a blazing sun soldiers toiled alongside impressed slaves and extended the line to the north and south so that it was anchored on the Pearl River above and below Jackson.[3]

These preparations were completed not a moment too soon, for reports arrived announcing the approach of several Union columns. To inspire his men for the coming struggle, Johnston issued an address on July 9: "An insolent foe, flushed with hope by his recent successes at Vicksburg, confronts you, threatening the people, whose homes and liberties you are here to protect, with plunder and conquest. Their guns may even now be heard at intervals as they advance. This enemy it is at once the mission and duty of you brave men to chastise and expel from the soil of Mississippi.

The commanding general confidently relies on you to sustain this pledge he makes in advance, and will be with you in your good work unto the end." In closing Johnston admonished his soldiers to act responsibly. "The country expects in this, the great crisis of its destiny, that every man will do his duty." The irony of that statement probably escaped him.[4]

The Union expeditionary force closing on Jackson consisted of forty-six thousand men in thirteen divisions from the Ninth, Thirteenth, and Fifteenth Corps. In this operation Sherman commanded roughly two-thirds of Grant's heavily reinforced army, more men than had taken part in the earlier inland campaign prior to the siege. His columns crossed the Big Black River at three locations, and by July 7 the Federals were loosely concentrated near Bolton, fewer than twenty miles west of Jackson.

Sherman's troops also suffered from the heat and dust as they marched along under the blistering Mississippi sun. Their plight was worsened by a shortage of water. The retreating Confederates had poisoned the wells and streams along the route. Thus the Federals had to haul their drinking water from the Big Black River on mules. To make matters worse most of the men had been inactive for weeks and were in poor shape for hard marching. Sherman limited marching to the morning and the late afternoon and early evening. Because the pace of the Union advance on Jackson was unavoidably slow, Johnston had plenty of time to prepare.

The Federals arrived at Jackson on July 10. Sherman rode to the front to personally reconnoiter the city's defenses. What he saw convinced him that Johnston had indeed taken refuge in the city and that he seemed inclined to stand his ground. He informed Grant "that everything betokens a strong resistance." Not wishing to commit his men to another hopeless assault against earthworks, Sherman issued orders for his commanders to spread out to left and right and "form lines of circumvallation about 1,500 yards from the enemy's parapet, with skirmishers close up, and their supports within 500 yards." Once that was accomplished everyone was to break out axes and shovels and dig trenches and battery positions. The siege of Jackson had begun.[5]

Throughout July 11 the Federals moved into position around the capital and extended their lines to the Pearl River on both flanks. On the Union right, or south, astride the Raymond Road was Maj. Gen. E. O. C. Ord's Thirteenth Corps. To the north the Union left was manned by Maj. Gen. John Parke's Ninth Corps, while Sherman's own Fifteenth Corps occupied the center on either side of the Clinton Road. With Sherman in command of the entire expeditionary force, Maj. Gen. Frederick Steele was acting corps commander. Federal infantrymen threw up earthworks while artillerymen manhandled their weapons into position on such commanding ground as could be found. By day's end Sherman was satisfied with the way the digging was progressing and ordered his guns to begin a general bombardment of the Confederate fortifications at seven o'clock the next morning.

But an unexpected problem developed. In setting out after Johnston Sherman had anticipated a battle or a running fight, anything but another prolonged siege. His artillery batteries carried only a limited amount of ammunition, far too little to maintain a continuous bombardment for days on end. Staff officers dashed westward with instructions for the reserve ordnance train to cross the Big Black River and hasten toward Jackson. Until the wagons arrived it would be necessary for the Federals to conserve artillery ammunition without appearing to do so.

Union guns opened a lavish bombardment on the morning of July 12, but it lasted less than one hour. Sherman's orders on the subject were precise. "Each gun will fire not to exceed thirty rounds, solid shot and shell in proper proportions," read the order. "The shots will be directed against any groups of the enemy's troops, or in direction of the town of Jackson." Despite these limitations Federal gunners fired more than three thousand projectiles and greatly depleted the available supply of shot and shell.[6]

Once the guns fell silent, skirmishing erupted all along the lines as the Federals resumed strengthening and in a few places rearranging their earthworks. On the far right of the Union line, a costly and unnecessary fight flared up when Ord directed Brig. Gen. Alvin P. Hovey to move his division closer to the enemy lines and entrench. Hovey notified Brig. Gen. Jacob Lauman, whose division was on Hovey's right, of his intentions. Lauman advanced accordingly but did not realize that he was only supposed to move closer to the Confederate lines, having the mistaken impression that he was to attack any Confederate force in his front. This breakdown in communications would lead to the needless death of many Union soldiers.

Hovey advanced northward on the west side of the New Orleans, Jackson, and Great Northern Railroad. In accordance with Ord's instructions he halted his division about five hundred yards south of the Confederate line and ordered his men to dig in. Lauman's division on the east side of the railroad continued forward. The lead brigade commanded by Col. Isaac Pugh moved ahead loosely in conjunction with Hovey's division.

But when it halted, Pugh continued to advance through a thick stand of timber. Steadily closing on the Confederate works, Pugh's soldiers emerged from the woods into a wide cornfield; a line of earthworks was at the opposite end. Reluctant to go any farther, Pugh halted his men and requested that Lauman come to the front. After surveying the field Lauman ordered Pugh to resume the advance. "As soon as the line had crossed the field," reported Pugh, "the enemy opened a murderous fire on my whole line." The unsupported brigade closed to within eighty yards of the Confederate position before the hail of bullets and canister brought the Federals to a halt. Pugh reported that "what officers and men were left fell back." Not all, however, raced to the rear through the gauntlet of fire. Scores of men fastened handkerchiefs to their ramrods and waved them as a sign of surrender.[7]

In this ill-fated action Pugh lost more than half of his brigade: 465 men killed, wounded, and missing, the latter mostly captured, to no purpose. Confederate casualties were 2 killed and 5 wounded. Lauman was relieved of command for this costly debacle.

Fighting flared at various other points along the semicircular lines, but there were no more assaults, intended or otherwise. Sherman bided his time while waiting for the ammunition train to arrive. With his batteries knee deep in ammunition, Sherman planned to open up on Johnston with every gun he had and "make the town too hot to hold him."[8]

Johnston agreed with Sherman that a crossfire of shot and shell from the Union guns would make Jackson untenable. A bombardment from three directions—north, west, and south—would enfilade Confederate lines and reach every corner of the town. On July 11 Johnston informed the War Department of his situation: "If the position and works were not bad, want of stores (which could not be collected) would make it impossible to stand a siege. If the enemy will not attack, we must, or at the last moment withdraw. We cannot attack seriously without risking the army." This was a remarkable statement. Jackson was besieged but not surrounded. Three functioning railroads from north, east, and west came to within a few miles of the city and fed men and material to Johnston right up to the end. Moreover Sherman's men had little difficulty locating food in the vicinity. Four days later Johnston telegraphed President Davis in a similar defeatist vein: "The enemy is evidently making a siege which we cannot resist." In an echo of earlier messages ("I am too late"; "I am too weak to save Vicksburg") Johnston added, "It would be madness to attack him."[9]

On July 14 Johnston learned that a large Union supply train—Sherman's ammunition train—had crossed the Big Black River and was moving east. He summoned the commander of his cavalry division, Brig. Gen. William H. Jackson, to his headquarters and directed him to locate and capture or destroy the wagons. Jackson had commanded a brigade in Earl Van Dorn's Holly Springs raid in 1862, so presumably he knew what was expected of him.

As the sun faded in the western sky on July 14, Jackson got underway. His horsemen rode north and west around the left flank of Sherman's force, then turned south toward Clinton, where Jackson planned to strike the Union train. A Confederate deserter told the Federals of Jackson's mission, however, and Sherman directed a brigade stationed near the Champion Hill battleground midway between Vicksburg and Clinton to escort the train to Clinton. He then dispatched another brigade from his own force to hurry to Clinton and await the arrival of the train. At daybreak on July 16, as the unsuspecting Confederates approached Clinton, they encountered a substantial force of Union infantry and artillery. After an hour of skirmishing Jackson withdrew and scoured the countryside for the elusive wagons. A small force of Rebels finally discovered the train but took note of the heavy escort and decided not to press their luck. The train rumbled eastward without incident and reached Sherman's expeditionary force late that evening.

Johnston's sole offensive effort of the campaign, if Jackson's raid can be characterized as such, had gone awry. The Confederate general decided not to wait for the Union artillery to resume the bombardment and ordered his Army of Relief to evacuate Jackson at once. After dark on July 16, Confederate artillery and infantry filed out of their works as quietly as possible and crossed the Pearl River. Once on the east side they fired the bridges. For the second time in eight weeks, Johnston had abandoned Mississippi's capital city to the enemy.

The dispirited Confederates marched eastward through the night in order to put as much distance as possible between themselves and the Federals. The rising sun on July 17 found the gray column still in motion. The Confederates finally halted near Brandon, a dozen miles east of Jackson. The following morning the retreat resumed. Thundershowers settled the dust and provided relief from the drought, but the rain made the road difficult for the passage of wagons and artillery. On July 20

Johnston's men reached Morton, forty miles from Jackson, and there they finally halted. The siege of Jackson and its aftermath were an inglorious end to the Army of Relief.

Union soldiers spotted the glow from the burning bridges over the Pearl River on the night of July 16. Many of them were convinced that the Confederates were evacuating the city, but Sherman somehow concluded that Johnston was strengthening his position. It was not until the morning of July 17 that he finally suspected the truth. Skirmishers advanced at various points along the line. On the Canton Road they spotted a jubilant black man waving a white flag. He informed the Federals that the Rebels were gone. Sherman notified Grant: "I have just made the circuit of Jackson. We are in full possession, and Johnston is retreating east, with 30,000 men, who will perish by heat, thirst, and disappointment." The Stars and Stripes again floated in victory atop the Mississippi State Capitol. Sherman sent a small force across the Pearl River to scout around, but because of the "intense heat, dust, and fatigue of the men," he did not attempt a pursuit.[10]

Flushed with victory, Sherman established his headquarters in the vacant governor's mansion and invited his generals to dinner. He had every reason to celebrate. In addition to nudging Johnston out of Jackson, his expeditionary force seized three guns, 1,396 firearms, and 23,245 rounds of artillery ammunition and burned three thousand bales of cotton used by the Confederates in the construction of their fortifications. All this had been achieved with the loss of approximately one thousand men, half in the fiasco on the Federal right.

The Federals thought they had neutralized Jackson during their brief visit two months earlier, but obviously they had been mistaken. Sherman was determined to do a better job the second time around. "I will perfect the work of destruction," he informed Grant. "I propose to break railroad 10 miles, south, east, and north, and out for 40 and 60 miles in spots." Union soldiers set about the task of destruction with a vengeance. Those shops, stores, hotels, factories, and warehouses that had escaped destruction in May were burned, and the railroads that radiated from Jackson were wrecked beyond any hope of repair. Eugene Beauge of the Forty-fifth Pennsylvania Infantry described the work of railroad destruction. "A good way to dispose of the ties and rails at the same time, after tearing up the track, was to pile up the ties, set them afire, then lay the rails crosswise on top; the rails in this way, when red hot, ending and warping themselves out of shape while the ties went up in smoke." Beauge noted that another method "was to take a rail, red hot in the middle, and bend it around a tree." Rails thus destroyed were referred to as "Sherman's neckties."[11]

The Federals kept busy until July 23. Sherman boasted to Grant that "Jackson will no longer be a point of danger." Much of the city was a smoldering ruin, and for years thereafter the state capital was known as "Chimneyville." Though little damage was done to residential neighborhoods, the complete destruction of commercial, manufacturing, and transportation facilities was another sign that the war was taking a new turn. Despite his postwar reputation for ruthlessness, Sherman did not leave the citizens of Jackson destitute. When the mayor appealed for help in feeding the several hundred residents who had not fled, Sherman provided two hundred barrels of flour and one hundred barrels of salt pork.[12]

On July 20, with the work of destruction well underway, elements of Sherman's expeditionary force began the return march. Three days later the rest of the Federals left Jackson. Despite straggling caused by the heat and humidity, the last of Sherman's men crossed the Big Black River and reached Vicksburg on July 25. They had been in the field for nearly two weeks. For the remainder of the summer, the Federals enjoyed some much needed rest after an unduly long and wearing season of campaigning.

In summing up the Jackson campaign, Sherman wrote: "It seems to me a fit supplement to the reconquest of the Mississippi River itself, and makes that perfect which otherwise would have been imperfect." The campaign for Vicksburg was over. But the struggle for control of the Mississippi River was still in progress. Port Hudson remained defiant.[13]

# CHAPTER SIXTEEN

# The Mississippi Is Opened

While the struggle for Vicksburg was taking place, an equally intense contest was underway one hundred miles to the south at Port Hudson. On May 7, 1863, Nathaniel Banks and two divisions of the Army of the Gulf marched into Alexandria after a whirlwind offensive through south-central Louisiana that sent Richard Taylor and Edmund Kirby Smith packing. Banks expected to link up with James McPherson's corps of the Army of the Tennessee, which he believed was making its way from Lake Providence to the Red River through a maze of smaller waterways west of the Mississippi River. He believed McPherson would bring not only reinforcements but also much needed transportation; unlike Grant, Banks was essentially land bound because of a scarcity of steamboats and barges. Once McPherson arrived Banks intended to move down the Red and overwhelm Port Hudson, then proceed up the Mississippi and join Grant at Vicksburg.

Waiting in Alexandria for Banks instead was a flotilla of gunboats from the Mississippi Squadron. Following the fight at Grand Gulf and the ferrying operation at Bruinsburg, Adm. David Porter had steamed down the Mississippi and joined David Farragut at the mouth of the Red. He then made his way up the Red and reached Alexandria a few hours before the Army of the Gulf tramped into town. Porter informed Banks that McPherson was not coming. Grant had crossed the Mississippi River a week earlier and was driving inland with his entire army. Banks was stunned by this unexpected change in plans. He generated a blizzard of letters imploring Grant to turn south and join him or at least send a substantial force in his direction. But it was too late. The Army of the Tennessee was on its way to Jackson and ultimately Vicksburg. "Banks was greatly cast down," recalled a member of his staff, "and his plans underwent many changes and perturbations."[1]

Banks was in a quandary over what to do next. He had to move, but in what direction and to what purpose? He could turn up the Red River and continue on to Shreveport, driving the Rebels before him, but another "wild goose chase" into the trans-Mississippi would undoubtedly cause an explosion in Washington. He could retrace his steps to Brashear City and thence to New Orleans, but friend and foe alike would interpret such a withdrawal as a retreat. Even worse it would put him back where he started with nothing to show for his efforts. After considering these unappealing options for several days, Banks decided that if Grant would not come to him, he would go to Grant. With the help of Farragut's warships, Porter's gunboats, and his own tiny flotilla of transports, he would transfer his command to Grand Gulf and from there inland to wherever Grant was located.

For this bold move to succeed, Banks would have to travel light. During the march north from Brashear City, the Army of the Gulf had accumulated an immense train of commandeered vehicles filled with food, forage, and plunder. Banks sent the train back to Brashear City with a strong escort. It was trailed by thousands of refugee freedmen and large herds of horses and cattle. Lt. Col. Richard B. Irwin later wrote of this unwieldy caravan, "With the possible exception of the herd that set out to follow Sherman's march through Georgia, this was perhaps the most curious column ever put in motion since that which defiled after Noah into the ark." Train, escort, refugees, and herds reached Brashear City safely.[2]

Between May 14 and 17, while Grant captured Jackson and then clashed with Pemberton at Champion Hill and Big Black River Bridge, the Army of the Gulf evacuated Alexandria and marched in an easterly direction down the south side of the Red River. But by the time the blue column reached Simmesport at the head of the Atchafalaya River, Banks had developed second thoughts about the wisdom of joining Grant in Mississippi. More worrying than his lack of transportation was the precarious situation of the isolated Union garrison in New Orleans. In the event of a popular uprising or a Confederate attack, the Army of the Gulf would be too far away to help. Banks reluctantly but correctly concluded that he could not hazard the loss of the Crescent City. The political and diplomatic ramifications of such a disaster were beyond calculation. Despite high hopes and a promising beginning, Banks realized that circumstances would not permit him join forces with Grant. "It is out of human power to do this," he concluded, "and I am left to move against Port Hudson alone."[3]

About this time it dawned on Henry Halleck in Washington that Grant and Banks, instead of drawing closer, were on opposite sides of the Mississippi River and seemed to be moving in different directions. "If these eccentric movements . . . do not lead to some serious disaster," he informed Banks, "it will be because the enemy does not take full advantage of his opportunity. I assure you the Government is exceedingly disappointed that you and General Grant are not acting in conjunction." The rebuke was unfair to Banks, who tried his best to link up with Grant, but it vividly illustrated the anxiety in the capital at this crucial moment in the struggle for the Mississippi River.[4]

Finally committed to a campaign against Port Hudson, Banks made use of all the resources at his disposal. Casualties, expirations of service, and detachments had whittled his army in the field down to about ten thousand soldiers. More manpower was needed. On May 16 Banks boarded a transport and returned to New Orleans via the Atchafalaya River. He traveled in the wake of Admiral Farragut, who had departed for the Crescent City a few days earlier. Cmdr. James S. Palmer remained behind with *Hartford* and her consorts to continue the Union navy's dual mission of blockading the Red River and supporting the army.

Upon reaching New Orleans Banks was encouraged by reports that the Confederate force at Port Hudson was much reduced. This information was substantially correct. When Pemberton realized that Grant was striking inland, he ordered Maj. Gen. Franklin Gardner to take five thousand men from Port Hudson and proceed to Jackson. Gardner and two brigades marched eastward sixty miles to Osyka on the New Orleans, Jackson, and Great Northern Railroad. There they waited for the next available northbound train.

Monitoring developments from Richmond, President Davis directed Pemberton to keep his grip on the Mississippi River at each end of the vital corridor, even providing an elementary geography lesson to make his point. "To hold both Vicksburg and Port Hudson is necessary to a connection with [the] Trans-Mississippi," Davis explained helpfully. Pemberton told Gardner to send the two brigades at Osyka on to Jackson, then return to Port Hudson "and hold it to the last" with his now smaller garrison. To give this order a little more weight, Pemberton added that the "President says both places must be held." The muddled nature of the Confederate command situation in the West became painfully evident when Joseph Johnston entered the fray and ordered Gardner to "evacuate Port Hudson forthwith." Gardner reasonably enough chose not to disobey both his immediate superior and his commander in chief. He ignored the order to evacuate, stayed at his post, and even asked Johnston for reinforcements.[5]

The end result of this telegraphic contest of wills was a dramatic reduction in the size of the Port Hudson garrison. When Grant crossed the Mississippi at the end of April, Gardner had about 11,500 men under his immediate command. By the time Banks crossed the river three weeks later, Gardner had fewer than 5,800 men.

While the Confederates burned up the telegraph wires, Banks hurried back to Simmesport and set his forces in motion. On May 19, the day Grant launched his first unsuccessful assault against Vicksburg, Cuvier Grover's division crossed the Atchafalaya River and marched twenty-two miles to Morganza, a landing on the west bank of the Mississippi. Six miles below Morganza on the east bank is Bayou Sara. Godfrey Weitzel's provisional division, composed of orphaned brigades from several different commands, crowded aboard the handful of transports at Simmesport and steamed directly down the Red and the Mississippi to Bayou Sara.

The second Union crossing of the Mississippi River began shortly after midnight on May 22, the day Grant carried out his second and final assault against Vicksburg. Steamboats packed with men, animals, and equipment shuttled back and forth between Morganza and Bayou Sara under the guns of *Hartford, Albatross, Pittsburg,* and a half dozen other warships and gunboats. There was no Confederate opposition. By this stage of the campaign, Banks and his lieutenants were familiar with amphibious operations and everything went smoothly. The Federals trudged up the bluffs from Bayou Sara to St. Francisville, then turned south toward Port Hudson, only twelve miles away.

Gardner was taken completely by surprise. It never occurred to him that Banks, having once threatened Port Hudson from the south, then having bypassed the place far to the west, would complete an enormous circle and approach from the north. Like his predecessors Gardner had assumed that a Federal attack would come from the direction of Baton Rouge. He had not bothered to fortify the defensive perimeter north of Port Hudson. The Confederate earthworks began on the bluffs overlooking the Mississippi River south of town but did not extend all the way

Banks concentrates against Port Hudson

around to the river north of town. The heavily wooded area along Big and Little Sandy Creeks between St. Francisville and Port Hudson was wide open. If Banks moved quickly enough he could simply walk in and take the place. When word reached Port Hudson that the Federals were pouring ashore at Bayou Sara, Gardner put every available man to work felling trees and piling up dirt in a desperate attempt to plug the mile-long gap in his lines. Banks did not know that the Confederate fortifications were unfinished, and his steady but unhurried movement from Bayou Sara gave Gardner just enough time to construct an intermittent line of earthworks overlooking Big and Little Sandy Creeks.

Banks reached the Port Hudson vicinity late on May 22, about the time Grant's soldiers were falling back from the Vicksburg defenses. Over the next four days his troops sorted themselves out and closed in on the Confederate works. Weitzel's and Grover's divisions arrived from Bayou Sara and formed the right wing of the reunited Army of the Gulf. Maj. Gen. Christopher Augur's division and Brig. Gen. Thomas Sherman's divisions arrived from Baton Rouge and New Orleans respectively and formed the left wing. Port Hudson was encircled. (Sherman's participation left Brig. Gen. William Emory with only a handful of regiments to hold New Orleans. It was a calculated gamble based on Banks's belief that the Confederate bastion could be captured quickly.) The simultaneous convergence at Port Hudson of three separate forces moving by land and water from Alexandria, Baton Rouge, and New Orleans reflected a high degree of administrative skill on the part of Banks and his staff. Unfortunately for the Union cause the Army of the Gulf never again achieved such an impressive level of efficiency.

Gardner recognized that his situation was hopeless, but he remained defiant. He told a group of his soldiers, "The enemy are coming, but mark you, many a one will get to hell before he gets to Port Hudson." Gardner had 5,765 men under his immediate command. Fourteen heavy guns overlooked the Mississippi River, and forty lighter guns supported the landward defenses. About 1,300 Confederate cavalry roamed the countryside to the east under the command of Col. John L. Logan, an aggressive officer who frequently raided the Union rear. But Logan's force was too small to affect the outcome of the siege.[6]

Banks probably had between twenty-five and thirty thousand troops at Port Hudson at this stage of the campaign, a numerical advantage of better than four to one. (The precise number of Federals has been in dispute since 1863.) But the heavy Union superiority in men was offset not only by the tumbled terrain and the stout Confederate defenses but also by the personal and professional failings of the Union commander and several of his principal subordinates. For reasons that are difficult to fathom at this distance in time, Banks was unable to get his division and brigade commanders to function as a team at Port Hudson. This breakdown is particularly puzzling because during the recent campaign Banks and the general officers under his immediate command had performed well. Perhaps four divisions were too much for Banks to handle, or perhaps the different mix of personalities at Port Hudson, where most of the senior officers were thrown together for the first time, was the root of the problem.

One officer with whom Banks continued to have an effective working relationship was Admiral Farragut. The commander of the West Gulf Blockading Squadron was supposed to be at sea supervising operations in the Gulf of Mexico, but he had a particular interest in the reduction of Port Hudson. After dealing with administrative matters in New Orleans, Farragut returned to the fray. He did not rejoin *Hartford,* however, but steamed directly up the Mississippi to Port Hudson and hoisted his flag aboard *Monongahela.* Throughout the siege he and Banks cooperated closely. Union warships, gunboats, and mortar boats bombarded Rebel positions from above and below Port Hudson.

Banks wanted to avoid a lengthy siege. Although Joe Johnston was not hovering in his rear, he had plenty of other things to worry about. The approach of the sickly season, the impending departure of the nine-month regiments (which made up half of his army), and the vulnerability of New Orleans all weighed heavily on his mind. A siege might drag on into the dreadful Louisiana summer, with the Union army and navy becoming weaker by the day and occupied Louisiana growing increasingly unstable. Better to end the standoff with a single blow.

On May 26 Banks held a council of war. He proposed that the army make an immediate assault all along the line and overwhelm the defenders by sheer force of numbers. A heated discussion followed, but the commanding general got his way. "Port Hudson must be taken tomorrow" was his final word on the subject. Whether because of fatigue, aggravation, or other reasons, Banks failed to coordinate the attacks in his planning. When the council of war ended, all that had been decided was that each of the division commanders would advance in the morning. When, where, and how they chose to attack was up to each of them. It was a recipe for disaster.[7]

Gardner suspected that a Union assault was coming. His infantry force was divided into three small brigades. On the Confederate left, facing north and northwest, Col. Isaiah G. W. Steedman commanded about 2,100 Alabama, Arkansas, and Mississippi troops. Holding the center of the Confederate position, facing northeast and east, was Brig. Gen. William N. R. Beall and 2,300 soldiers, nearly all of them Arkansans. On the right, facing southeast, was Col. William R. Miles with 1,150 Louisiana troops. The remainder of the garrison manned the heavy artillery along the river. The line of defenders was so thin a Union assault along the entire perimeter would likely be successful, which is exactly what Banks was counting on.

Of particular concern to Gardner was the vulnerable northern section of the line held by Steedman's brigade. The Confederate left was not actually a continuous line at all but a series of hastily constructed redoubts separated by steep gullies and ravines draining into Big and Little Sandy Creeks. None of the redoubts had formal names, but as the struggle raged, they became known to soldiers on both sides as the Bull Pen, the Priest's Cap, and Fort Desperate. Gardner was right to be worried. As luck would have it this section of the Confederate works would receive the heaviest blow.

The attack began on the morning of May 27 when Weitzel sent four brigades of New York and New England troops toward Steedman's position on the left of the Confederate line. Six thousand Federals plunged into the jumbled terrain eroded by Big and Little Sandy Creeks. "One is unable to comprehend the lay of the land even after having traveled through it," wrote Banks. "Ravines, woods, and obstructions of every sort disconcert the movement of troops and break up lines." It was, he concluded, a "perfect labyrinth." Within an hour the assault lost forward momentum as officers and men floundered around under a hail of Rebel fire. Instead of retreating, however, the Federals discovered that the maze of ridges and ravines provided them with natural parapets and trenches only a stone's throw away from the Rebel earthworks. Entrenching with bayonets and bare hands, the Federals established a strong advanced position known as Fort Babcock, after Lt. Col. Willoughby Babcock of the Seventy-fifth New York.[8]

As Weitzel's assault petered out Grover launched a weaker attack against the left center of the Confederate line. Pushing blindly ahead, seven New England regiments approached an isolated redoubt, known forever after as Fort Desperate, held by Col. Benjamin W. Johnson and about two hundred men of the Fifteenth Arkansas. The ragged line of New Englanders overlapped the redoubt, which stood on a plateau north of a bend in Little Sandy Creek. The Twelfth Maine and Thirty-eighth Massachusetts reached the ditch and tried several times to scale the walls, but the attack ultimately failed. Falling back to the nearest ridge, the Federals dug in.

While this was taking place the First and Third Louisiana Native Guards of the Corps d'Afrique struck the extreme left of the Confederate fortifications. All the line officers and troops of the First Louisiana Native Guards were members of New Orleans's large free-black and mulatto community. The Third Louisiana Native Guards was composed of white officers and black troops, nearly all of the latter newly liberated slaves. The two regiments ran into a torrent of fire and were driven back in short order. The ill-advised attack was the first major test of black troops in the Civil War. It was a tactical failure but a public relations triumph. As was the case with the fight at Milliken's Bend, still ten days in the future, exaggerated accounts of the success of the assault filled Northern newspapers and convinced an uncertain populace that black men would fight for their freedom and the Union cause. (It is worth noting that this episode at Port Hudson took place seven weeks *before* the more celebrated but equally unsuccessful attack of the black Fifty-fourth Massachusetts and four white regiments at Battery Wagner, South Carolina.)

As the morning wore on, Banks realized that only the right wing of his army was in action. Mystified and not a little annoyed, the commander rode south until he reached Thomas Sherman's division on the far left of the Union line. There he found Sherman having an early lunch in his tent. Sherman was convinced that an attack would fail and so had decided not to attack at all. A furious Banks relieved the general of his command, but Sherman (who may have been intoxicated) defiantly mounted his horse and led his division of New York, New England, and Michigan troops toward the right center of the Confederate line. The Federals advanced across a level expanse of farmland with the ominous name of Slaughter's Field.

Beall, commanding the Confederate defenses opposite Sherman, was in a fix. He had sent half of his strength to support Steedman, and those troops had not returned. His remaining men watched the long blue lines approach in perfect order. "It was a magnificent sight, but the great odds against us looked appalling as our line was weak, averaging about one man to every five feet, and no reserve force," remembered Lt. Joseph M.

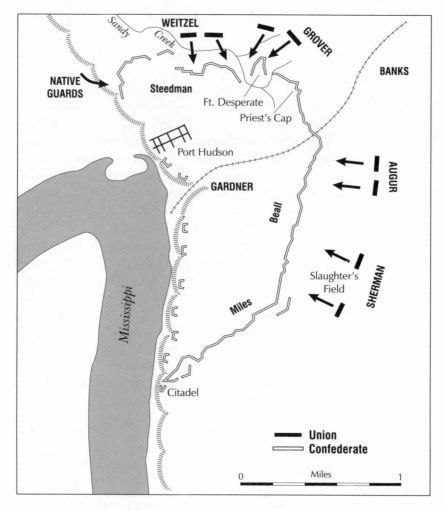

Port Hudson: May 27 attack

Bailey of the Sixteenth Arkansas. "Every company officer, as far as I could see, stood in line with his men, musket in hand. To facilitate rapid firing, most if not all of the men, placed their cartridges on the works in their front. Varied were the expressions on the faces of the men. Some were serious and silent. Others joked, danced, or sang short snatches of song, but there was an intense earnestness about it all." Holding the far right of the Confederate line, Miles saw Beall's plight and shifted his small force of Louisiana troops as far to the left as possible.[9]

When the Federals came within range, the Confederates swept Slaughter's Field with a storm of artillery and rifle fire. Several hundred Union soldiers reached the ditch in front of the thinly held Confederate earthworks, but all were killed or driven back. The attack was a dismal failure as Sherman had predicted. Sherman himself suffered a severe wound and was sent to New Orleans to convalesce. That should have been the end of it, but Augur belatedly sent a brigade forward in a hopeless attack against the Confederate center. The Federals struggled through what had recently been a forest, the tangle of felled trees disrupting formations and slowing the advance to a crawl. Beall's Arkansans shifted their fire to this new assault with devastating results. A handful of Union soldiers reached the abatis but got no farther.

Colonel Irwin of Banks's staff summed up the events of May 27 in five words: "The day was miserably lost." The uncoordinated Union assaults were all that the hard-pressed Confederates could have hoped for. The Army of the Gulf suffered at least 1,995 casualties: 293 killed, 1,545 wounded, and 157 missing. Contemporaries (and some historians) have accused Banks of doctoring the figures to minimize the cost of the assault, but there is no evidence that he did so. In fact Banks informed Grant the next day, "The fight was very bitter and our losses severe." Because the difficult terrain north of Port Hudson hid as well as hindered the attackers, Weitzel's and Grover's divisions experienced losses of about 8 percent. Sherman's and Augur's divisions advanced for half a mile across open ground east of Port Hudson and suffered a casualty rate of 20 percent. The Confederates lost between 300 and 350 soldiers, most of them in Steedman's hard-pressed brigade.[10]

The Army of the Gulf never fully recovered from the events of May 27. Morale plummeted and confidence in Banks and other officers was badly shaken. Conversely Gardner's Confederates were greatly encouraged by their victory and for a time even dared hope that the demoralized Yankees would give up and go away.

Banks was dismayed by the failure of the May 27 assault, but he was not about to admit defeat. He brought in picks and shovels and put soldiers and freedmen to work digging their way into Port Hudson. Trenches and artillery redoubts soon appeared on the Union side of the battleground. Banks also sought out every idle infantry regiment and artillery battery in the Department of the Gulf and brought them to Port Hudson. By mid-June over 130 guns of every size and type were banging away at the Confederate defenses. Farragut's vessels in the Mississippi added another 50 heavy guns and mortars to the total. Shot and shell rained on Port Hudson around the clock.

To save ammunition the embattled Confederates rarely fired back. Instead working parties labored day and night to improve or repair the earthworks. When not wielding shovels there was little for the defenders to do except endure the shelling and stand ready to repel another assault. There was no relief from the scorching heat except during the occasional summer thunderstorms that flooded the trenches and created a miasma of humidity. The storms stayed away toward the end of the siege and water ran short. During one dry spell Union artillery set a storehouse on fire and destroyed tons of food. The supply of fresh beef and salted pork eventually ran out, and the garrison turned to horses, mules, and even rats. Diseases and malnourishment struck down hundreds of men. The Confederates hung on week after week without much hope of relief. Desertions increased as the situation became more desperate. Some nights as many as two dozen Rebels scrambled into Federal lines.

Banks realized that Port Hudson was doomed, but he remained anxious to bring the matter to a close. Early predictions that Gardner would give up within a week or two had proved far too optimistic. The Federals had plenty of food and ammunition, but they suffered from heat, drought, and disease as much as the Confederates. And there was also the departure of the nine-month regiments and the safety of New Orleans to worry about. Three weeks into the siege Banks lost patience and decided to try another assault. Unfortunately he all but announced his intentions when he sent Gardner a futile demand for surrender.

Banks met with his senior officers on the evening of June 13 and drew up a detailed plan of attack. This time there would be no attempt at a general assault. Instead the army would concentrate on two potentially vulnerable points on the Confederate line. The primary target was an oddly shaped salient called the Priest's Cap, located on the left center of the line a few hundred yards southeast of Fort Desperate. The secondary target was the Citadel, an angular redoubt on the extreme right of the Confederate line where the landward defenses met the river batteries. The Union plan of attack was sound, but Banks again fumbled the matter of timing. The attack was scheduled to begin early on June 14, only a few hours after the council of war ended. Officers and men had little time to prepare.

In the predawn darkness Brig. Gen. Halbert E. Paine personally led the three brigades of his newly created division toward the east side of the Priest's Cap. "Men, I want you to follow me right into those works" was his final command. The position was defended by the First Mississippi and the Forty-ninth Alabama. The Confederates huddled in their "gopher holes" (the Civil War equivalent of foxholes) during the fierce pre-assault bombardment, then mounted the parapets and sent a storm of fire into the Union ranks. The leading Union regiments suffered horrendous casualties and Paine was severely wounded, but his gallant performance inspired soldiers from the Fourth Wisconsin, Eighth New Hampshire, and Twenty-fifth Connecticut to fight their way into the Confederate works. All who managed to get over the parapet were killed or captured, however, and the attack failed. It was a sign of the demoralization in the Army of the Gulf that half or more of Paine's troops refused to go forward; many were members of nine-month regiments whose enlistments had expired or were about to do so.[11]

Grover was supposed to launch a simultaneous strike against the opposite, or north, side of the Priest's Cap, but his attack was late, leaderless, and mismanaged. Three brigades filed through a narrow sap in a column of twos toward the Confederate position. The sap provided protection from enemy fire, but it was congested and ended more than one hundred yards short of the Priest's Cap. When the Federals emerged from the trench it was daylight and they found themselves entangled in an abatis. Paine's attack on the east side had ended an hour earlier, and the weary soldiers of the First Mississippi and Forty-ninth Alabama moved to the north side of the Priest's Cap and rained bullets and canister down on this new mass of targets. Grover's attack was a dismal failure and accomplished nothing except to increase the list of Union casualties.

Three miles to the south Brig. Gen. William Dwight, now in command of Sherman's division, launched an equally ineffectual attack against the Citadel. This bungled effort resulted in the only Union accomplishment of the day: the occupation of a plateau a few hundred yards south of the Citadel known as Mount Pleasant. This eminence became the site

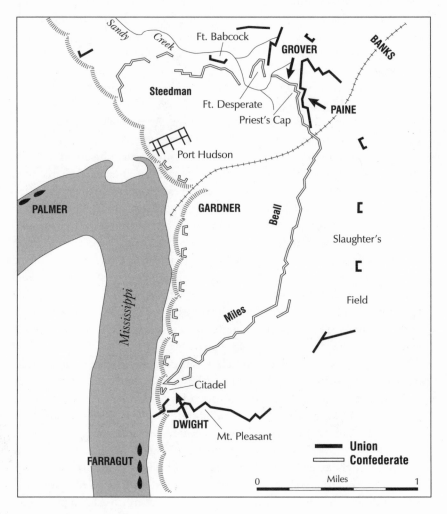

Port Hudson: June 14 attack

of a massive artillery battery that gradually pounded the Confederate strongpoint into a shapeless mass of dirt.

The June 14 assault was a disaster. The Army of the Gulf suffered at least 1,805 casualties: 216 killed, 1,401 wounded, and 188 missing. These figures do not tell the whole story, however, because so many of the 8,000 troops in the assault force sat out the fight. Losses were concentrated in the handful of regiments that actually engaged the enemy. The Fourth Wisconsin, for example, followed Paine right up to the parapet of the Priest's Cap and suffered an incredible 64 percent casualty rate. Confederate losses are not known for certain but probably amounted to less than one-fourth of the Union total. Sound planning was undone by failures in leadership, resolution, and execution on one side and stout defenses and determined defenders on the other. The June 14 assault left Banks deeply depressed and his officers and men demoralized as never before. Discipline eroded and alarming instances of insubordinate, even mutinous, behavior took place. The Rebels, as might be expected, felt great satisfaction at having once again held off the Yankee hordes.

It now was evident that the Army of the Gulf was not going to take Port Hudson by storm and that victory would be won with the shovel, not the bayonet. Regular siege operations were intensified under the direction of Capt. John C. Palfrey, the army's new chief engineer. The web of Union parallels and saps steadily drew closer to the Confederate lines. All of this activity, however onerous and even dangerous in the intense heat, kept the troops busy and gave them a sense of purpose. Morale gradually revived.

For the next three weeks the siege dragged on. Deserters trickled out of Port Hudson in ever larger numbers and reported the garrison to be in desperate straits. It was obvious that a Confederate surrender was only a matter of time, but Banks once again grew impatient. He concluded that a third assault, if done properly, could succeed. Palfrey's engineers and pioneers dug a parallel to within twenty yards of the Priest's Cap, then tunneled beneath the Confederate earthworks. They excavated two galleries and filled them with hundreds of pounds of gunpowder. While those preparations went forward Banks created an all-volunteer assault force to exploit the chaos and devastation caused by the planned blast. After the mine was detonated the assault force would rush into the smoldering ruins of the Priest's Cap, overwhelm the dazed survivors, and clear a path for a column of infantry. In late June the assault force began intensive training. The destruction of the Priest's Cap was tentatively scheduled for early July.

At the beginning of May Richard Taylor and his tiny Confederate army were encamped in the vicinity of Natchitoches, well up the Red River. After Banks evacuated Alexandria and besieged Port Hudson, Taylor wanted to return to south-central Louisiana and threaten New Orleans. He believed that Banks would relax his grip on Port Hudson in order to protect the Crescent City. But Edmund Kirby Smith insisted that Taylor first move against Grant's supposed rear in northeast Louisiana. When that operation came to naught after the meaningless fight at Milliken's Bend on June 7, Taylor finally received permission to carry out his plan to relieve Port Hudson.

The Louisianan moved down Bayou Teche with a force of about three thousand men divided into two brigades commanded by Brig. Gen. Alfred Mouton (Gardner's brother-in-law) and Brig. Gen. Thomas Green. Because Banks had concentrated every available Federal soldier at Port Hudson, most of Union-occupied Louisiana was hardly occupied at all. Brashear City, for example, was defended by only about seven hundred Yankees, half of whom were convalescents. On June 23 the Confederates crossed the Atchafalaya River and captured the entire Union garrison along with tons of stores and supplies. Then they pushed east along the Opelousas and Great Western Railroad and captured another four hundred Federals the next day. The operation to relieve Port Hudson was proceeding more rapidly than Taylor could have imagined.

At Thibodaux Taylor continued east toward New Orleans with Mouton's brigade, while Green and his brigade of 1,800 men turned north along Bayou Lafourche to strike at Donaldsonville on the west bank of the Mississippi below Baton Rouge. On June 28 Green reached Donaldsonville and rashly attacked Fort Butler, a stout position occupied by 180 Federals. Here the Confederates discovered the futility of charging earthworks held by determined defenders. Green lost over 300 men; the Federals fewer than two dozen. Before the Rebels could make another assault upon the fort, Union reinforcements arrived in the form of warships and gunboats and drove them away.

Meanwhile the approach of Taylor's small column generated great excitement and consternation in New Orleans. Pro-Confederate residents dreamed of liberation, while pro-Union residents and Federal soldiers fretted about a Confederate attack. On July 4 General Emory, the Union commander, lost his head and informed Banks, "you can only save this city by sending me reinforcements immediately and at any cost. It is a choice between Port Hudson and New Orleans." Emory apparently forgot that the Crescent City lay on the east bank of the Mississippi River, which was patrolled by Union warships, and that Taylor's small force was approaching from the west side. Banks knew that Taylor had no realistic chance of reaching New Orleans, which was protected by the widest moat in North America. But he was concerned about the possibility of an uprising within the city, so he hurried preparations for the final assault on Port Hudson.[12]

Taylor had no illusions about his ability to walk on water. He turned north and placed artillery atop the levee on the west bank of the Mississippi River above New Orleans. On July 4, the day Vicksburg surrendered, Confederate gunners opened fire on Union transports shuttling up and down the river. For several days Taylor effectively shut down Federal logistical activities between New Orleans and Port Hudson. Farragut decided to deal with the pesky Rebels himself. He led *Monongahela, Kineo,* the ironclad *Essex,* and other vessels down the river and drove the Confederates away. As soon as Farragut departed, however, Taylor's artillerymen moved to other locations and resumed taking potshots at passing transports.

This cat-and-mouse game might have gone on for some time, but everything changed on July 7, when the ram *General Price,* captured so long ago at Memphis, nosed into the bank above Port Hudson. The vessel carried a most welcome message from Grant: Vicksburg had surrendered. The news spread like wildfire along the Union lines and made its way inside the Confederate defenses. Gardner asked Banks if the information was accurate. Banks assured him that it was. Gardner conferred with his senior officers, who agreed that there was nothing to be gained by prolonging the inevitable for a few more days. Port Hudson surrendered on July 9. After nearly seven weeks of intense struggle, the longest siege in American history was over. "The Mississippi is opened," Banks informed Grant.[13]

Gardner had 5,765 soldiers under his immediate command when the siege began. He surrendered 5,001 officers and men, of whom 483 were wounded. During the siege he lost 764 men: 488 killed or mortally wounded and 376 missing (nearly all deserted). Only 3,000 Confederates were well enough to take part in the surrender ceremony. A total of fifty-one guns, some in disrepair, fell into Union hands. In accordance with the terms of surrender, enlisted men were paroled, but officers were made prisoners of war. Union losses came to 4,363 men: 708 killed, 3,336 wounded, and 307 missing (nearly all killed). Approximately one out of every seven Union soldiers who served at Port Hudson became a casualty. Uncounted thousands of other soldiers and black laborers were felled by disease and heatstroke. When the siege finally ended, Banks had barely 8,000 men fit for duty. Victory had come at a heavy price.

The contest for Port Hudson was over, but there was more work to be done. Just as Grant had moved swiftly to drive Johnston away from his rear after the fall of Vicksburg, so Banks acted immediately to deal with Taylor. As soon as the brief surrender ceremony at Port Hudson was over, two Union divisions filed down the bluffs onto waiting transports and churned downstream to Donaldsonville. Taylor realized the game was up and withdrew across the Atchafalaya River to the Bayou Teche country. Union forces reoccupied Brashear City on July 25 and finally brought the Port Hudson campaign to a close. The Confederacy was severed.

Taylor accomplished more than any other Confederate commander, but like all other attempts to relieve the besieged garrisons, his was a case of too little too late. Nevertheless one can only speculate how this story might have turned out had Jefferson Davis placed the bold and resourceful Taylor rather than the weak and vacillating Johnston in charge of the relief of Vicksburg. As it was Banks emerged victorious at Port Hudson, but he had not seen the last of Taylor. The two would meet again on the Red River a year hence.

While Banks engaged in mopping-up operations between Donaldsonville and Brashear City, a momentous event occurred in New Orleans. On July 16 the steamboat *Imperial*, eight days out of St. Louis, docked in the Crescent City without fuss or fanfare. The struggle for the Mississippi River was over.

# Epilogue

The struggle for the Mississippi River was the longest and most complex campaign, or series of campaigns, of the Civil War. It was marked by an extraordinary diversity of military operations, including naval engagements, cavalry raids, amphibious landings, pitched battles, and the two longest sieges in American history. Every existing type of naval vessel, from sailing ship to armored ram, played a role, and military engineers practiced their art on a scale never before witnessed in modern warfare.

When the bitter contest finally reached its climax at Vicksburg and Port Hudson in July 1863, the Confederacy suffered a blow from which it would not, could not, recover. The hard-won Union triumph did not mean that the end of the war was at hand, but without the trans-Mississippi there was little realistic hope of an independent Southern nation. Loss of access to the resource-rich states west of the Mississippi was an economic as well as a military disaster for the Confederacy. Compounding this was the defeat of Gen. Robert E. Lee's Army of Northern Virginia at Gettysburg the same week that Vicksburg and Port Hudson went under. Reflecting on the calamitous series of events, Col. Josiah Gorgas, chief of the Confederate Ordnance Bureau, lamented: "Yesterday we rode on the pinnacle of success—today absolute ruin seems to be our portion. The Confederacy totters to its destruction."

For those who experienced victory and defeat on scattered battlefields in Missouri, Kentucky, Tennessee, Arkansas, Louisiana, and Mississippi or on the muddy waters of the western waterways, the struggle for control of the Mississippi River was a defining experience. It may interest the reader to learn the individual destinies that awaited some of the actors in that military drama:

Nathaniel P. Banks received the thanks of Congress for the capture of Port Hudson. It was the high point of his checkered military career. In 1864 he suffered a crushing defeat in the Red River campaign in Louisiana. He served ten terms in the House of Representatives after the war and retired from public life in 1890. In recognition of his service as a soldier and statesman, Congress voted him an annual pension of twelve hundred dollars. He died at his home in 1894.

Isaac N. Brown was given command of the ironclad *Charleston* in South Carolina after the fall of Vicksburg. Following the war he farmed in Mississippi and then in Texas, where he died in 1889, having proved himself one of the most daring naval officers in the Confederacy.

Benjamin Butler went on to command the Army of the James in Virginia. Although militarily incompetent, he was politically influential and was not relieved of command until 1865. He returned to Congress and became a leading figure among the Radical Republicans. Butler was elected governor of Massachusetts in 1882 and ran unsuccessfully for president in 1884.

David G. Farragut continued in command of the West Gulf Blockading Squadron. His last and perhaps most famous action came in 1864 at Mobile Bay when, lashed to the rigging of the *Hartford,* he shouted to the helmsman, "Damn the torpedoes, full speed ahead!" He was elevated to vice admiral in 1864 and admiral in 1866. Farragut died in 1870, having spent virtually his entire life in the U.S. Navy.

Franklin Gardner, whose father had been adjutant general of the U. S. Army during the War of 1812, was a prisoner of war after his surrender of Port Hudson. Exchanged in August 1864, he served for the duration of the war in Mississippi and Alabama under Richard Taylor. He returned to Louisiana following the close of hostilities and was a planter until his death in 1873 at the age of fifty.

Joseph E. Johnston abandoned the Army of Vicksburg to its fate, but he always refused to accept any blame for the disaster in Mississippi. He succeeded Braxton Bragg as commander of the Army of Tennessee, but his failure to halt William T. Sherman's advance on Atlanta in 1864 resulted in his removal. After being restored to command the following year, Johnston surrendered what was left of his army to Sherman in North Carolina. He served briefly in the House of Representatives and was appointed commissioner of railroads by Pres. Grover Cleveland. Johnston spent the balance of his life clinging to his inflated military reputation. His self-serving *Narrative of Military Operations,* published in 1874, failed to quiet his critics. Johnston died in 1891 after attending Sherman's funeral.

Stephen D. Lee became the youngest Confederate lieutenant general and commanded a corps in the Army of Tennessee. After the war he was the first president of what is today Mississippi State University. Lee devoted the closing years of his life to honoring veterans of the Civil War. He helped establish Vicksburg National Military Park and was its first chairman— the only former Confederate to serve in such a position. He also served as commander of the United Confederate Veterans. Lee died in 1908.

Samuel Lockett was assigned a number of other Confederate engineering projects, none as challenging as designing and constructing the Vicksburg fortifications. Following the war he wrote extensively of his experiences, most notably in an essay, "The Defense of Vicksburg," that appeared in *Century Magazine.*

John A. McClernand was restored to command of the Thirteenth Corps in 1864 and took part in the ill-fated Red River campaign. He returned to the arena of politics but never regained the influence he had once held in Congress. McClernand lived until 1900, long enough to see a magnificent equestrian statue of himself erected in Vicksburg National Military Park by the state of Illinois. There is an equally impressive statue of Ulysses Grant in the park, but none of either Sherman or James B. McPherson.

James B. McPherson was praised by Grant and Sherman for his role in the Vicksburg campaign, but the caution he demonstrated at Raymond would be repeated on other fields. Although he succeeded Sherman in command of the Army of the Tennessee, he never justified the confidence his superiors placed in him. In 1864 he was killed in action outside Atlanta—the only Union army commander to die in battle.

David D. Porter led the Mississippi Squadron up the Red River in conjunction with Banks's army in 1864. His gunboats were stranded at Alexandria when the Confederates dammed the river upstream. The squadron was saved by Union army engineers who constructed wing dams and raised the water level high enough to float the gunboats to safety. Later that year Porter assumed command of the North Atlantic Blockading Squadron and helped reduce Fort Fisher in North Carolina.

Following the war he served as superintendent of the Naval Academy at Annapolis. He was promoted to vice admiral in 1866 and admiral in 1870. Porter died in 1891.

William T. Sherman succeeded Grant as commander of the Army of the Tennessee. He was promoted to lieutenant general in 1866 and general in 1869, serving as general in chief of the U.S. Army for fourteen years. His readable but not always reliable *Memoirs of General William T. Sherman* sparked considerable controversy when it appeared in 1875. He died in 1891, having been covered with honors during his postwar life. Sherman understood the totality of war to a greater degree than most of his contemporaries. Recognizing that the morale of the Southern civilian population had to be crushed in order to end the rebellion, Sherman perfected his concept of hard war—rehearsed in Mississippi in 1863— during his epic marches across Georgia and the Carolinas in 1864–65.

Edmund Kirby Smith continued in command of the Trans-Mississippi Department following the loss of Vicksburg and Port Hudson. Cut off from the rest of the Confederacy, his isolated department became known as "Kirby Smithdom." After a brief postwar sojourn in Mexico, Smith returned to the United States and devoted the remainder of his life to education, serving first as chancellor of the University of Nashville, then as mathematics instructor at the University of the South. He died in 1893 and is buried on the campus at Sewanee, Tennessee.

Richard Taylor was frustrated at every turn in 1863 but was promoted to lieutenant general in recognition of his victory over Banks in the Red River campaign the following year. He commanded the Department of East Louisiana, Mississippi, and Alabama in 1864–65 and was the last Confederate general east of the Mississippi River to surrender. In the postwar era he worked tirelessly, using his personal friendship with Presidents Andrew Johnson and Grant to promote leniency toward the Southern states. He also penned *Destruction and Reconstruction,* one of the best memoirs of the Civil War. Taylor died in 1879 at the age of fifty-three.

Earl Van Dorn did not live to see the surrender of Vicksburg and Port Hudson. Transferred to the Army of Tennessee after his victory at Holly Springs, he was killed by an outraged husband in May 1863.

Godfrey Weitzel was transferred to Virginia and served as chief engineer of the Army of the James. Promoted to major general in 1864, he commanded the all-black Twenty-fifth Corps, whose troops captured Richmond in 1865. Weitzel returned to the Corps of Engineers after the war and supervised the construction of the Sault Ste. Marie locks, one of the greatest engineering feats of the time. He died in 1884 at the age of forty-nine.

The two most prominent figures of the campaign, whose very names have become synonymous with triumph and defeat, experienced similarly divergent fates after Vicksburg:

John C. Pemberton resigned his general's commission after the surrender of Vicksburg and served as a lieutenant colonel of artillery until the war's end. He tried his hand at farming in Virginia afterward, but in this endeavor he also failed. Pemberton quietly lived out the remainder of his life in his native Philadelphia and died in 1881. His passing was largely ignored in the South. Biographer Michael Ballard writes of Pemberton's obscurity as being "the saddest fate." Perhaps, but in 1917 a statue of Pemberton was unveiled in Vicksburg National Military Park, a signal honor denied Joseph Johnston and a host of other Confederate generals.

Ulysses S. Grant was launched into national prominence after Vicksburg. Following another spectacular triumph at Chattanooga a few months later, he was elevated to lieutenant general and named general in chief of the Union army in 1864. Battling his way to the gates of Richmond and Petersburg in Virginia, he received the surrender of the last intact Confederate army at Appomattox in 1865. Grant was later promoted to general, the first American to hold that rank. Although he served two terms as president, Grant is best remembered for his military service during the Civil War. Throughout his life he remained a plain, unassuming man of impeccable honesty who was loyal to his family, country, and fellow soldiers. His character is best expressed by a photograph of him on the porch of his residence in Mount McGregor, New York. Fighting a losing battle with throat cancer, he sits in a chair with his legs crossed, wearing glasses and a stovepipe hat, a scarf wrapped around his neck, struggling to finish his memoirs in the hope of providing financial security for his family. When the manuscript was completed in May 1885, Grant wrote from the heart: "These volumes are dedicated to the American soldier and sailor." Two months later he died. *Personal Memoirs of U.S. Grant* was a tremendous critical and financial success.

And what of the fields themselves where soldiers from the North and South gave what Abraham Lincoln termed "the last full measure of devotion"? The titanic struggle for the Mississippi River took place well over a century ago, but much of the historic landscape survives today. Fort Donelson and Shiloh on the banks of the Cumberland and Tennessee Rivers are maintained by the National Park Service, as are portions of the fields where the battle and siege of Corinth took place. Although Fort Hindman disappeared into the Arkansas River decades ago, the rest of Arkansas Post is also protected by the National Park Service. Kentucky and Tennessee state parks encompass the extensive earthworks overlooking the Mississippi River at Columbus and Fort Pillow, but only a few faint traces remain of the fortifications that once ringed Helena, Arkansas. A fragment of Fort Pemberton survives as a roadside park.

Fort Jackson is a Louisiana state park on the west bank of the Mississippi River below New Orleans. Fort St. Philip survives in a ruined condition on the opposite side of the river. New Orleans contains hundreds of buildings dating from the Civil War era, some of them associated with Butler, Banks, and Farragut. The old Gothic-revival state capitol in Baton Rouge was restored after the fire and is now a museum, though the nearby Baton Rouge battlefield was overrun by the city long ago. Fort De Russy along the Red River is a state park, but Irish Bend along Bayou Teche is private property. The roads Banks followed in his campaign across southern Louisiana still exist in one form or another, and it is even possible to take a ferry across the Mississippi River and land at Bayou Sara.

A few miles downstream from the ferry crossing, Port Hudson State Historic Site, a Louisiana state park, protects the northern one-third of the Union and Confederate siege lines. Elevated boardwalks allow visitors to explore a maze of remarkably well-preserved earthworks. The eastern and southern two-thirds of the fortifications, also in excellent condition, survive in private hands, but the defenses that frustrated Farragut have long since been washed away by the Mississippi. Though nothing remains of the hamlet of Port Hudson, nearby Clinton and St. Francisville contain a wealth of wartime buildings.

One hundred miles to the north, Vicksburg National Military Park encloses the northern two-thirds of the Union and Confederate siege lines. Most of the original earthworks were demolished after the siege, but some original segments remain. Along with several reconstructed forts they provide a sense of how the miles and miles of fortifications once looked. The steeply rolling landscape is covered with over thirteen hundred tablets, markers, and monuments that provide a wealth of detail to interested visitors. A long-term project to clear away modern forest cover and restore a part of the historic viewscape is underway. The wreck of the ironclad *Cairo*, sunk by mines in the Yazoo River, is within the park's boundaries, as is the only surviving fragment of the Union canal across De Soto Point. The Chickasaw Bayou battlefield lies outside the park and is threatened by development.

The city of Vicksburg contains many sites associated with the siege, including the Balfour house, scene of the 1862 Christmas Eve party, and Pemberton's headquarters. But the Hill City's historic crown jewel is the Warren County Courthouse, now a museum, still dominating the skyline as it did a century and a half ago.

The countryside around Vicksburg is awash in historic sites. Traces of the Lake Providence and Duckport canals exist, and the circuitous route of the Union army down the west side of the Mississippi River to Disharoon plantation is largely intact and dotted with historical markers. The route (or routes) on the east side of the river from Bruinsburg to Jackson and thence to Vicksburg also survives in large part, though it is less well marked. The massive Grand Gulf fortifications are enclosed within a Mississippi state park, but only bits and pieces of the battlefields at Port Gibson, Raymond, Champion Hill, and Big Black River Bridge are protected. Nearly all of the battlefields and fortifications at Jackson have been lost to urban sprawl.

Fortunately in recent years preservation efforts have been launched throughout Mississippi to protect hallowed ground. At the time of this publication, public and private funds were being used to mark campaign routes, develop driving tours, and acquire portions of the Chickasaw Bayou, Port Gibson, Raymond, and Champion Hill battlefields.

Much can be learned from books about the long and costly struggle for the Mississippi River, but there is no substitute for standing in the places where men fought for their beliefs. In the spirit of those who fought and died in the struggle for the Mississippi River, more—much more— needs to be done to ensure that these fields will be saved so that future generations of Americans can study and contemplate the sacrifices made to forge our nation.

# Notes

## 1. THE RIVER AND THE WAR

1. John D. Milligan, *Gunboats down the Mississippi* (Annapolis: Naval Institute Press, 1965), xxii.

2. Henry Walke, "The Western Flotilla at Fort Donelson, Island Number Ten, Fort Pillow and Memphis," in *Battles and Leaders of the Civil War,* eds. Robert U. Johnson and Clarence C. Buel, 4 vols. (New York: Century, 1887–88), 1:441.

3. Charles L. Dufour, *The Night the War Was Lost* (Garden City NY: Doubleday, 1960).

4. *Official Records of the Union and Confederate Navies in the War of the Rebellion,* 30 vols. (Washington: Government Printing Office, 1894–1922), 18:155 [hereafter cited as *ORN*].

5. Letter, June 16, 1862, William H. Smith Letters, Hill Memorial Library, Louisiana State University, Baton Rouge.

6. *The War of the Rebellion: A Compilation of the Official Records of the Union and Confederate Armies,* 70 vols. in 128 parts (Washington: Government Printing Office, 1880–1901), 15:6 [hereafter cited as *OR*]; *ORN,* 18:492.

## 2. GIBRALTAR ON THE MISSISSIPPI

1. Samuel H. Lockett, "The Defense of Vicksburg," in Johnson and Buel, *Battles and Leaders,* 3:484.

2. *ORN,* 18:589.

3. *OR,* 15:1121.

4. Edward T. Eggleston Diary, July 15, 1862, Letters and Diaries, Vicksburg National Military Park (hereafter cited as VNMP).

5. Charles L. Lewis, *David Glasgow Farragut: Our First Admiral* (Annapolis: Naval Institute Press, 1943), 114.

6. *ORN,* 23:237.

7. Lewis, *Farragut,* 120.

8. Edwin C. Bearss, *Rebel Victory at Vicksburg* (Little Rock: Pioneer, 1963), 280.

9. *OR*, 15:16.

10. *OR*, 15:794, 786.

11. *OR*, 15:81.

12. *OR*, 15:555.

### 3. ON TO VICKSBURG

1. Lockett, "Defense," 3:488.

2. John Y. Simon, ed., *The Papers of Ulysses S. Grant,* 22 vols. to date (Carbondale: Southern Illinois University Press, 1967– ), 6:288.

3. Ulysses S. Grant, *Personal Memoirs of U. S. Grant* 2 vols. (New York: Charles L. Webster, 1885–86), 1:430.

4. Simon, *Grant Papers,* 7:33.

5. Simon, *Grant Papers,* 7:44.

6. Richard Lowe, ed., *A Texas Cavalry Officer's Civil War: The Diary and Letters of James C. Bates* (Baton Rouge, Louisiana State University Press, 1999), 220–21.

7. Grant, *Memoirs,* 1:435.

8. Lewis Eyman Letters, Letters and Diaries, VNMP.

9. Grant, *Memoirs,* 1:437.

### 4. THE FIRST ONSLAUGHT

1. Steven E. Woodworth, ed., *The Musick of the Mocking Birds, the Roar of the Cannon: The Civil War Diary and Letters of William Winters* (Lincoln, University of Nebraska Press, 1998), 13.

2. Herman Hattaway, *General Stephen D. Lee* (Jackson: University Press of Mississippi, 1976), 68.

3. George W. Morgan, "The Assault on Chickasaw Bluffs," in Johnson and Buel, *Battles and Leaders,* 3:467.

4. Morgan, "Assault," 3:468.

5. E. Paul Reichelm Diary, Dec. 29, 1862, Letters and Diaries, VNMP.

6. Brooks D. Simpson and Jean V. Berlin, eds., *Sherman's Civil War: Selected Correspondence of William T. Sherman, 1860–1865* (Chapel Hill: University of North Carolina Press, 1999), 349.

7. *OR*, 17(1):613.

8. Eggleston Diary, Jan. 3, 1863, VNMP.

9. *OR*, 17(1):781.

10. Mark K. Christ, ed., *Rugged and Sublime: The Civil War in Arkansas* (Fayetteville: University of Arkansas Press, 1994), 64; C. Ainsworth Diary, Jan. 11, 1863, Letters and Diaries, VNMP.

11. Christ, *Rugged and Sublime,* 64.

12. Simpson and Berlin, *Sherman's Civil War,* 358.

13. Simon, *Grant Papers,* 7:209–10.

## 5. DARK WINTER

1. Woodworth, *Musick of the Mocking Birds*, 27–28; Mildred Thorne, ed., *The Civil War Diary of Cyrus F. Boyd, Fifteenth Iowa Infantry, 1861–1863* (Baton Rouge: Louisiana State University Press, 1998), 114.

2. Eggleston Diary, Jan. 25, 1863, VNMP.

3. *OR*, 24(3):38.

4. Chester G. Hearn, *Ellet's Brigade: The Strangest Outfit of All* (Baton Rouge: Louisiana State University Press, 2000), 96.

5. *ORN*, 24:376.

6. *ORN*, 24:382.

7. *OR*, 24(1):373.

8. Edwin C. Bearss, *The Campaign for Vicksburg*, 3 vols. (Dayton OH: Morningside, 1985–86), 1:537; Gregory J. W. Urwin and Cathy K. Urwin, eds., *History of the 33d Iowa Infantry Regiment, 1863–6, by A. F. Sperry* (Fayetteville: University of Arkansas Press, 1999), 24.

9. Urwin and Urwin, *History of the 33d Iowa*, 26.

10. Urwin and Urwin, *History of the 33d Iowa*, 26.

11. *ORN*, 24:477.


## 6. DETOUR IN LOUISIANA

1. *OR*, 15:590–91.

2. Alfred T. Mahan, *Admiral Farragut* (New York: Appleton, 1892), 213.

3. Lawrence L. Hewitt, *Port Hudson, Confederate Bastion on the Mississippi* (Baton Rouge: Louisiana State University Press, 1987), 79.

4. *ORN*, 19:769.

5. Hewitt, *Port Hudson*, 91–92.

6. *ORN*, 20:11.

7. *OR*, 15:671, 690.

8. *ORN*, 20:42.

9. James G. Hollandsworth, *Pretense of Glory: The Life of General Nathaniel P. Banks* (Baton Rouge: Louisiana State University Press, 1998), 117.

10. *OR*, 15:725–26.


## 7. RIVER OF NO RETURN

1. Otto F. Bond, ed., *Under the Flag of the Nation: Diaries and Letters of a Yankee Volunteer in the Civil War* (Columbus: Ohio State University Press, 1961), 51.

2. *OR*, 24(3):157.

3. *OR*, 24(3):220.

4. Simon, *Grant Papers*, 8:49.

5. *OR*, 24(3):730, 733.

6. *OR*, 24(3):733.

7. *OR*, 24(3):730.

8. *ORN*, 24:518.

9. Simon, *Grant Papers*, 8:3–4.

10. *ORN*, 24:682.

11. William E. Strong, "The Campaign against Vicksburg," *Military Essays and Recollections: Papers Read before the Commandery of the State of Illinois, Military Order of the Loyal Legion of the United States* (Chicago, A. C. McClurg, 1894), 2:324.

12. *OR*, 24(3):765.

13. *OR*, 24(3):797.

14. *ORN*, 24:627.

15. *OR*, 24(3):804.

16. *ORN*, 24:610.

## 8. THE ODDS ARE OVERPOWERING

1. *History of the Forty-sixth Indiana Volunteer Infantry, September 1861–September 1865* (Logansport IN, 1888), 56.

2. Grant, *Memoirs*, 1:480–81.

3. Charles B. Johnson, *Muskets and Medicine; or Army Life in the Sixties* (Iowa City, 1907), 29.

4. Samuel C. Jones, *Reminiscences of the Twenty-second Iowa Volunteer Infantry* (Iowa City, 1907), 29.

5. Charles A. Hobbs Diary, April 30, 1863, Regimental Files (99th Illinois), VNMP.

6. George Crooke, *The Twenty-first Regiment of Iowa Volunteer Infantry* (Milwaukee, 1891), 55.

7. *OR*, 24(3):797.

8. Bearss, *Campaign for Vicksburg*, 2:357.

9. *Pine Bluff Commercial*, Dec. 17, 1904.

10. *OR*, 24(1):626.

11. *OR*, 24(1):627.

12. Bearss, *Campaign for Vicksburg*, 2:393 n.

13. *OR*, 24(1):664; Robert S. Bevier, *The Confederate First and Second Missouri Brigades* (St. Louis, 1879), 180.

14. Francis Obenchain to William T. Rigby, July 4, 1903, Regimental Files (Botetourt Artillery), VNMP.

15. Frederick D. Grant, "A Boy's Experience at Vicksburg," *Personal Recollections of the War of the Rebellion: Addresses Delivered before the Commandery of the State of New York*, MOLLUS, 4 vols. (New York: Little, 1907), 3:89–90.

16. *OR*, 24(1):659.

17. *OR*, 24(3):807.

## 9. THE SHRIEK OF AN EAGLE

1. Unidentified source, Miscellaneous Files (XV Corps), VNMP.

2. *The Story of the Fifty-fifth Illinois Volunteer Infantry in the Civil War, 1861–1865* (Clinton IL, 1887), 231.

3. *OR*, 24(3):285.

4. *OR*, 24(1):36.

5. W. B. Halsey Diary, May 11, 1863, Letters and Diaries, VNMP.

6. Osborn Oldroyd, *A Soldier's Story of the Siege of Vicksburg* (Springfield IL, 1885), 16–17.

7. *OR*, 24(1):215.

8. Jefferson Brumback to wife, May 20, 1863, Regimental Files (95th Ohio), VNMP.

## 10. INDECISION, INDECISION, INDECISION

1. Bearss, *Campaign for Vicksburg*, 2:482.

2. *OR*, 24(3):877.

3. *OR*, 24(2):125.

4. *OR*, 24(3):882.

5. *OR*, 24(2):75.

6. Bevier, *First and Second Missouri Brigades,* 186; William A. Drennan to wife, May 30, 1863, William A. Drennan Letters, Mississippi Department of Archives and History, Jackson (hereafter cited as MDAH).

7. Drennen to wife, May 30, 1863.

8. Alfred Cumming to Stephen D. Lee, Nov. 3, 1899, Folder 15, Vol. 12, Record Group 12, MDAH; Ulysses S. Grant, "The Vicksburg Campaign," in Johnson and Buel, *Battles and Leaders*, 3:511.

9. Ephraim M. Anderson, *Memoirs: Historical and Personal; including the Campaigns of the First Missouri Confederate Brigade,* ed. Edwin C. Bearss (Dayton OH: Morningside, 1972), 311.

10. Anderson, *Memoirs,* 312, 313; Bearss, *Campaign for Vicksburg*, 2:637.

11. Bearss, *Campaign for Vicksburg*, 2:637.

12. The authors have silently corrected a misspelled word ("Indedecision") in the phrase. John A. Leavy Diary, May 16, 1863, Letters and Diaries, VNMP; Mary Loughborough, *My Cave Life in Vicksburg* (Spartanburg SC: Reprint Company, 1976), 43.

13. Lockett, "Defense," 3:488.

## 11. A GRAND AND APPALLING SIGHT

1. Emma Balfour Diary, May 17, 1863, Letters and Diaries, VNMP; Loughborough, *My Cave Life,* 41–42.

2. Loughborough, *My Cave Life,* 42.

3. Balfour Diary, May 17, 1863.

4. Balfour Diary, May 17, 1863.

5. William T. Sherman, *Memoirs of General William T. Sherman,* 2 vols. (New York: 1875), 1:352.

6. Lloyd Lewis, *Sherman: Fighting Prophet* (New York, Harcourt, Brace, 1932), 277.

7. William L. Foster, *Vicksburg: Southern City under Siege* (New Orleans: Historic New Orleans Collection, 1982), 6.

8. Thomas J. Higgins to C. A. Dobbs, Dec. 7, 1878, Regimental Files (99th Illinois), VNMP.

9. J. D. Pearson to Stephen D. Lee, May 17, 1902, Regimental Files (30th Alabama), VNMP.

10. *OR,* 24(1):172.

11. *OR,* 24(1):276–77.

12. Oldroyd, *Soldier's Story,* 35.

## 12. OUTCAMP THE ENEMY

1. Grant, *Memoirs,* 1:446.

2. *OR,* 24(3):348.

3. Lockett, "Defense," 3:488.

4. Unidentified source, Miscellaneous Files (XV Corps), VNMP.

5. Nathan M. Baker Diary, June 25, 1863, Regimental Files (116th Illinois), VNMP.

6. Seth J. Wells, *The Siege of Vicksburg from the Diary of Seth J. Wells, Including Weeks of Preparation and of Occupation after the Surrender* (Detroit, 1915), 85.

## 13. TOO WEAK TO SAVE VICKSBURG

1. Loughborough, *My Cave Life,* 56, 72.

2. Balfour Diary, May 30, 1863, VNMP.

3. William W. Lord, "A Child at the Siege of Vicksburg," *Harpers Monthly Magazine* 118 (Dec. 1908): 44.

4. William A. Drennan Diary, June 9, 11, 1863, Letters and Diaries, VNMP.

5. Richard Taylor, *Destruction and Reconstruction* (New York, 1879), 138.

6. Joseph P. Blessington, *The Campaigns of Walker's Texas Division* (Austin: Pemberton, 1968), 94.

7. Bearss, *Campaign for Vicksburg,* 3:1180; , 24(2):467.

8. Blessington, *Walker's Texas Division,* 96.

9. *OR,* 24(1):95; Charles A. Dana, *Recollections of the Civil War* (New York: Appleton, 1898), 86–87.

10. Albert Castel, *General Sterling Price and the War in the West* (Baton Rouge: Louisiana State University Press, 1968), 146.

11. Christ, *Rugged and Sublime,* 82.

12. Christ, *Rugged and Sublime,* 82.

13. Bearss, *Campaign for Vicksburg,* 3:1153, 1203.

14. Drennan Diary, June 1, 11, 1863, VNMP.

15. *OR*, 24(3):964, 965, 967.

16. *OR*, 24(1):226.

17. Michael B. Ballard, *Pemberton: A Biography* (Jackson: University Press of Mississippi, 1991), 175.

## 14. THE GLORIOUS FOURTH

1. Alexander S. Abrams, *A Full and Detailed History of the Siege of Vicksburg* (Atlanta, 1863), 29.

2. *OR*, 24(3):890.

3. John S. C. Abbott, *The History of the Civil War in America* (New York, 1873), 2:292; Bevier, *First and Second Missouri Brigades,* 199–200.

4. *OR*, 24(1):281.

5. *OR*, 24(1):283.

6. Lockett, "Defense," 3:492.

7. *OR*, 24(3):982–83.

8. Lockett, "Defense," 3:492; , 24(1):285.

9. *OR*, 24(1):283–84.

10. Grant, *Memoirs,* 1:466.

11. John C. Pemberton, *Pemberton: Defender of Vicksburg* (Chapel Hill: University of North Carolina Press, 1942), 228.

12. Grant, *Memoirs,* 1:467.

13. John C. Pemberton, "The Terms of Surrender," in Johnson and Buel, *Battles and Leaders,* 3:544.

14. George Hynds Diary, July 3, 1863, Regimental Files (31st Tennessee), VNMP; Drennan Diary, July 3, 1863, VNMP.

15. Richard L. Howard, *History of the 124th Illinois Infantry Volunteers* (Springfield, 1880), [130]; Foster, *Vicksburg,* 57.

16. *OR*, 24(3):460.

17. Lockett, "Defense," 3:492; , 24(1):284.

18. *OR*, 24(1):285.

19. Richard S. West Jr., *Lincoln's Navy* (New York, 1957), 223.

## 15. NO LONGER A POINT OF DANGER

1. *OR*, 24(3):460–61; Sherman, *Memoirs,* 1:358.

2. *OR*, 24(3):974, 980.

3. Joseph E. Johnston, *Narrative of Military Operations during the Late War between the States* (New York, 1874), 205.

4. *OR*, 24(3):994–95.

5. *OR*, 24(2):522, 525.

6. *OR*, 24(3):502–503.

7. *OR*, 24(2):604.

8. *OR*, 24(2):524.

9. Johnston, *Narrative*, 207.

10. *OR*, 24(2):528.

11. *OR*, 24(2):528; Eugene Beauge, "The Forty-fifth in Kentucky and Mississippi," in *History of the Forty-fifth Regiment of Pennsylvania Veteran Volunteer Infantry, 1861–1865*, ed. Allen D. Albert (Williamsport, 1912), 75.

12. *OR*, 24(2):529.

13. *OR*, 24(2):537.


## 16. THE MISSISSIPPI IS OPENED

1. Richard B. Irwin, *History of the Nineteenth Army Corps* (New York: Putnam, 1892), 149.

2. Irwin, *Nineteenth Army Corps*, 156–57.

3. *OR*, 15:731.

4. *OR*, 26(1):500.

5. *OR*, 15:1059, 1071, 1080–81.

6. David C. Edmonds, *The Guns of Port Hudson*, 2 vols. (Lafayette LA: Acadiana, 1983–84), 2:5.

7. *OR*, 26(1):509.

8. *ORN*, 20:213.

9. Hewitt, *Port Hudson*, 158.

10. Irwin, *Nineteenth Army Corps*, 181; , 26(1):520.

11. Edmonds, *Guns of Port Hudson*, 2:202.

12. *OR*, 26(1):51.

13. *OR*, 26(1):624.

# Bibliographical Essay

Excellent histories of the early stages of the campaign on land and water include Benjamin F. Cooling, *Forts Henry and Donelson: The Key to the Confederate Heartland* (Knoxville: University of Tennessee Press, 1987); and Chester G. Hearn, *The Capture of New Orleans, 1862* (Baton Rouge: Louisiana State University Press, 1995). Larry J. Daniel, *Shiloh: The Battle that Changed the Civil War* (New York: Simon and Schuster, 1997), is the best brief account of that dreadful affair; and Peter Cozzens, *The Darkest Days of the War: The Battles of Iuka and Corinth* (Chapel Hill: University of North Carolina Press, 1997), covers those closely related engagements. Also see Larry J. Daniel and Lynn N. Bock, *Island No 10: Struggle for the Mississippi Valley* (Tuscaloosa: University of Alabama Press, 1996). Edwin C. Bearss, *Hardluck Ironclad: The Sinking and Salvage of the Cairo* (Baton Rouge: Louisiana State University Press, 1980), contains much information about the Union navy. Also by Edwin C. Bearss is *Rebel Victory at Vicksburg* (Little Rock: Pioneer, 1963; reprint, Wilmington NC: Broadfoot, 1989), the most detailed account of the naval siege of Vicksburg and the saga of the CSS *Arkansas*.

The best introduction to the siege of Port Hudson is Lawrence L. Hewitt, *Port Hudson, Confederate Bastion on the Mississippi* (Baton Rouge: Louisiana State University Press, 1987), but the book ends after the first Union assault. Edward Cunningham, *The Port Hudson Campaign, 1862–1863* (Baton Rouge: Louisiana State University Press, 1963), is a brief overview, now somewhat dated. A detailed though rather quirky account is David C. Edmonds, *The Guns of Port Hudson* (2 vols.; Lafayette LA: Acadiana, 1983–84). An authoritative history of the costly struggle for Port Hudson is sorely needed.

Such a history already exists for the mammoth operations that led to the Union capture of Vicksburg: Edwin C. Bearss, *The Vicksburg Campaign* (3 vols.; Dayton OH: Morningside, 1985–86). No other account compares with Bearss's detailed and comprehensive work, though Warren E. Grabau, *Ninety-Eight Days: A Geographer's View of the Vicksburg Campaign* (Knoxville: University of Tennessee Press, 2000), provides a fresh and illuminating approach. Solid one-volume overviews are Samuel Carter III, *The Final Fortress: The Campaign for Vicksburg, 1862–1863* (New York: St. Martin's, 1980); and, old but still worthwhile, Francis V. Greene, *The Mississippi* (1882; Wilmington, NC: Broadfoot, 1989). The best study of engineering at Vicksburg is David F. Bastian, *Grant's Canal: The Union's Attempt to Bypass Vicksburg* (Shippensburg PA: White Mane, 1995).

There are no detailed histories of the clashes at Port Gibson, Raymond, and Big Black River or of Grant's inland campaign generally. The only accounts of individual actions are Edwin C. Bearss, *The Battle of Jackson/The Siege of Jackson* (Baltimore: Gateway, 1981); and Dee Alexander Brown, *Grierson's Raid* (Urbana: University of Illinois Press, 1954). The lack of a book about Champion Hill, one of the most dramatic and decisive battles of the Civil War, is simply inexplicable.

Good biographies abound. Among the best are T. Michael Parrish, *Richard Taylor: Soldier Prince of Dixie* (Chapel Hill: University of North Carolina Press, 1992); and Brooks D. Simpson, *Ulysses S. Grant: Triumph over Adversity, 1822–1865* (Boston: Houghton Mifflin, 2000). Solid treatments include John F. Marszalek, *Sherman: A Soldier's Passion for Order* (New York: Free Press, 1993); and Richard L. Kiper, *Major General John Alexander McClernand: Politician in Uniform* (Kent OH: Kent State University Press, 1999). Brief but worthwhile biographies include Michael B. Ballard, *Pemberton: A Biography* (Jackson: University of Mississippi Press, 1991); James G. Hollandsworth, *Pretense of Glory: The Life of General Nathaniel P. Banks* (Baton Rouge: Louisiana State University Press, 1998); Chester G. Hearn, *Admiral David Glasgow Farragut: The Civil War Years* (Annapolis: Naval Institute Press, 1998); and Hearn, *Admiral David Dixon Porter: The Civil War Years* (Annapolis: Naval Institute Press, 1996). Craig L. Symonds, *Joseph E. Johnston: A Civil War Biography* (New York: Norton, 1992), is biased in favor of its subject.

Peter F. Walker, *Vicksburg: A People at War, 1860–1865* (Chapel Hill: University of North Carolina Press, 1960), is a good introduction to the civilian side of the conflict. On a more personal level see Mary Loughborough, *My Cave Life in Vicksburg* (Spartanburg SC: Reprint Company, 1976). Dozens of soldier accounts of Vicksburg and Port Hudson are available. Among the best are William L. Foster, *Vicksburg: Southern City under Siege* (New Orleans: Historic New Orleans Collection, 1980); Osborn Oldroyd, *A Soldier's Story of the Siege of Vicksburg* (Springfield IL, 1885); William P. Chambers, *Blood and Sacrifice: The Civil War Journal of a Confederate Soldier* (Huntington WV: Blue Acorn, 1994); and John W. DeForest, *A Volunteer's Adventures: A Union Captain's Record of the Civil War* (New Haven: Yale University Press, 1946).

# Index

Abrams, Alex S., 170
Adams, Col. Wirt, 132
*Albatross*, 81, 82, 83, 88, 190
Alden, Cmdr. James, 81
Alexandria LA, 18, 79, 87, 88, 187–88
Algiers LA, 84
Anaconda Plan, 1
Anderson, Ephraim, 135
*Anglo-Saxon*, 99
*Arizona*, 88
*Arkansas*, 12, 23, 24–27, 30–31
Arkansas Post (Post of Arkansas), 56–58, 59, 210
Arkansas River, 50, 56, 57, 58–59
Army of Relief, 167, 179, 184–85
Army of the Gulf (Nineteenth Corps), 77, 84, 87, 88, 187, 188, 192, 197, 199, 201
Army of the Mississippi, 55, 59
Army of the Tennessee (Thirteenth Corps, Fifteenth Corps, Sixteenth Corps, Seventeenth Corps), 35, 36, 38, 41, 43, 45, 47, 60, 62, 91, 102, 106, 117–24, 129, 151
Army of Vicksburg, 127, 129, 130, 137, 138, 172
Atchafalaya River (Atchafalaya

Swamp), 84, 85, 88, 188, 189, 190, 202, 204
Augur, Maj. Gen. Christopher C., 77, 197
Autrey, Lt. Col. James L., 16

Babcock, Lt. Col. Willoughby, 194
Bailey, Lt. Joseph M., 195–97
Baker, Nathan M., 158
Bakers Creek, 130, 133–37
Baldwin, Brig. Gen. William E., 112
Balfour, William T., 47
Balfour, Emma, 140–41, 161
Ballard, Michael B., 168,
Banks, Maj. Gen. Nathaniel P., xii, 190–93, 206; in Louisiana, 76–78, 80, 84; moves to Alexandria, 84–89; concentrates against Port Hudson, 187, 188, 189; besieges and captures Port Hudson, 194–204
*Baron de Kalb*, 57, 69
Bartlett, Col. Frank, 163
Bates, Capt. James C., 44
Baton Rouge LA, 2, 15, 27, 29, 29–30, 77, 80, 210
Bayou Baxter, 63
Bayou Lafourche, 84, 202

Bayou Macon, 63

Bayou Pierre, 108, 114, 115

Bayou Sara, 83, 190–92, 210

Bayou Teche, 84, 85, 202, 204, 210

Bayou Vidal, 101

Beall, Brig. Gen. William N. R., 79, 194, 195–97

Bearss, Edwin C., 110, 167

Beauge, Eugene, 185

Beauregard, Gen. Pierre G. T., 11

Bell, Lt. John S., 111

Belmont MO, 6

*Benton*, 96, 98, 103, 105, 106

Benton, Brig. Gen. William P., 150

Bevier, Lt. Col. Robert, 171

Big Black River, 102, 116, 117–18, 120, 124, 137, 138–39, 140, 142, 143, 169, 172, 179, 180, 181, 182, 184, 186, 211

Big Sandy Creek (Little Sandy Creek), 192, 194, 195

Big Sunflower River, 72

Black Bayou, 72–73

*Black Hawk*, 57

Black River, 63

Blair, Brig. Gen. Frank P., 53, 131, 146

Blessington, Joseph P., 164

Blood, Lt. Col. James H., 53

Bolivar TN, 44

Bolton MS, 121, 131, 181

Bovina MS, 128

Bowen, Brig. Gen. John S., 95, 101, 102–4, 109–10, 112–15, 116, 130–31, 135–36, 142, 170–71, 173–75

Bowling Green KY, 6, 8

Boyd, Cyrus F., 60

Bragg, Gen. Braxton, 34, 35, 44, 93, 94

Brandon MS, 184

Brashear City (Morgan City) LA, 83, 84, 85, 87, 202, 204

Breckinridge, Maj. Gen. John C., 21, 29–30, 31

Brent, Maj. Joseph L., 67–68

Bridgeport MS, 142

Brierfield, 48

Brown, Lt. Cmdr. George, 65–68

Brown, Lt. Isaac L., 24–25, 26, 70, 71, 206

Bruinsburg MS, 104, 105, 106, 108, 110, 116, 119, 211

Buchanan, Capt. Robert, 149

Buell, Maj. Gen. Don C., 8, 11, 34, 35

Burbridge, Brig. Gen. Stephen G., 150

Butler, Maj. Gen. Benjamin F., 14, 16, 23, 29, 31, 76, 206

Butte-a-la-Rose (Butte la Rose) LA, 88

*Cairo*, 47, 211

Cairo IL, 2, 6, 178

Camp Moore LA, 29

Canton MS, 125, 128, 167, 169

*Carondelet*, 24, 96, 103

Carr, Brig. Gen. Eugene A., 111, 131

Champion Hill MS, 130, 133–37, 184, 211

Chickasaw Bayou, 47, 48, 52, 53–55, 57, 59, 72, 143, 211

*Chillicothe*, 69, 71

*Choctaw*, 164

Churchill, Brig. Gen. Thomas J., 56–58

*Cincinnati*, 57

Clinton LA, 78, 184, 210

Clinton MS, 124, 128, 129, 131, 132

Cockrell, Col. Francis M., 95, 112, 135

Coffee Point, 103–4

Coldwater River, 68, 70, 73

Columbus KY, 2, 5–6, 8, 11, 33, 35, 210

Cooke, Lt. Cmdr. Augustus P., 88

Corinth MS, 10, 11, 21, 33, 34–35, 45, 69, 210

Corps d'Afrique, 77, 195

Covell, Capt. George W., 114

Crocker, Brig. Gen. Marcellus M., 131

Cumberland River, 6, 7, 12, 95, 210

Curtis, Maj. Gen. Samuel R., 7, 21, 28, 33, 56, 63

Dana, Charles A., 61

Daniel, L. L., 47

Davis Bend, 48, 67

Davis, Flag Officer Charles H., 10, 11, 12, 15, 16, 20, 21, 22, 24–26, 27–28

Davis, Jefferson, 5, 12, 13, 15, 20, 29, 36, 48–52, 100, 124–25, 162, 167–68, 189, 204

Davis, Joseph, 67

De Courcey, Col. John F., 53, 55

Deer Creek, 72, 73, 74

Dennis, Brig. Gen. Elias, 165

Department of Mississippi and East Louisiana, 20, 34, 36

Department of the Gulf, 35, 76, 77, 78, 89, 198

Department of the Missouri, 33, 35, 46, 56

Department of the Tennessee, 35, 41, 69

Department of the West, 48

De Soto Point (Grant's Canal), 18, 21, 22, 25, 26, 28, 47, 48, 60, 62, 63, 64, 65, 67, 68, 75, 82, 94, 98, 99–100, 171, 211

Dewey, Lt. George, 81

*Diana*, 85

Disharoon, 104–5, 106, 119, 211

District of West Tennessee, 33

Donaldsonville LA, 84, 202, 204

Drennan, Lt. William, 132, 162, 168, 176

Drumgould's Bluff, 38

Duckport LA, 91, 118, 211

Dufour, Charles L., 15

Dwight, Brig. Gen. William, 199

*Eastport*, 7

Edwards Station MS, 121, 128, 130, 131, 136, 138

Eggleston, Sgt. Edward T., 61–62

Ellet, Lt. Col. Alfred W., 11, 21, 23, 24, 26, 54, 82

Ellet, Col. Charles, Jr., 11, 64

Ellet, Col. Charles R., 64–65, 68

Ellison, Sarah, 130–31

Emory, Brig. Gen. William H., 77, 192

*Empire City*, 99

Enterprise MS, 125

Erwin, Col. Eugene, 115, 159

*Essex*, 26, 27, 31, 80, 203

*Estrella*, 88

Eyman, Capt. Lewis, 45

Fagan, Brig. Gen. James F., 166

Fall, Philip H., 47–48

Farragut, Flag Officer David G., 13–15, 16, 18, 20; passes Vicksburg, 21–22; 23, 24; engages *Arkansas*, 25–27, 30, 31; passes Port Hudson, 80–82, 83, 87, 88, 96, 102, 187, 189, 193, 203, 206

Featherston, Brig. Gen. Winfield S., 73–74, 132

Ferguson, Lt. Col. Samuel W., 73–74

Fifteenth Corps (Army of the Tennessee), 43, 57, 59, 101, 118–19, 121, 124, 125, 146–47, 152, 181

Foote, Flag Officer Andrew H., 7, 8, 9, 10

*Forest Queen*, 99

Forney, Maj. Gen. John H., 142

Forrest, Brig. Gen. Nathan B., 44, 93

Fort Bisland, 85, 89

Fort Burton, 88

Fort Butler, 202

Fort De Russey. *See* Fort Taylor

Fort Donelson, 6, 7–8, 9, 11, 18, 39, 210

Fort Henry, 6, 7, 11

Fort Jackson, 13–14, 20, 27, 210

Fort Pemberton, 70–71, 72, 73, 127, 210

Fort Pillow, 9, 10, 11, 15, 18, 21, 35, 210

Fort St. Phillip, 13–14, 27, 210

Fort Taylor (Fort De Russey), 65, 87, 210

Foster, Lt. Henry C., 156–57

Foster, William L., 143, 176

Franklin LA, 85

Friar's Point, 38

Fuller, J. F. C., 137

Gardner, Maj. Gen. Franklin, 79, 80, 85, 189, 190–91, 192, 194, 206; in siege of Port Hudson, 198–203

Garrott, Col. Isham W., 115

*General Price*, 96, 178, 203

*Genesee*, 81

Gettysburg PA, xii, 178, 205

*Glide*, 57

Gorgas, Col. Josiah, 205

Grand Gulf MS, 2, 38, 88, 90, 95, 101, 102, 103–4, 105, 109, 110, 112, 115, 116, 118, 188, 211

Grand Lake, 85, 88, 89

Grant, Fred, 115

Grant, Maj. Gen. Ulysses S., xii, 6, 7, 8, 9, 11, 33, 34, 35, 36, 38, 39, 41, 42, 43, 44, 47, 51, 55, 59, 61, 62, 63, 64, 69, 72, 73, 75, 78, 83, 88, 89, 179, 180, 185, 186, 189, 203, 209; moves down west side of Mississippi, 90–105; 106, 109;

at Port Gibson, 112–16; moves inland, 117–24; 126, 127, 128, 129, 131, 132; at Champion Hill, 133–37; 142, 143; assaults Vicksburg, 146–51; besieges Vicksburg, 152–78

Grant's Canal. *See* De Soto Point

Green, Brig. Gen. Martin E., 110–16

Green, Brig. Gen. Thomas, 202

Greenville MS (Greenville expedition), 91–92, 94

Greenwood MS, 70

Gregg, Brig. Gen. John, 121, 123–24, 125–26

Grenada MS, 38, 39, 41, 44, 45, 48, 50, 51, 52, 55, 69, 70, 71, 127

Grierson, Col. Benjamin H. (Grierson's raid), 93, 101, 104–5, 118, 138

Griffith, Lt. Col. John S., 43

Griffith, Sgt. Joseph, 151

Grover, Brig. Gen. Cuvier, 77, 85, 194, 199

Gulf of Mexico, 1, 2, 12, 28, 39, 77, 83–84, 88, 193

Halleck, Maj. Gen. Henry W., 6, 8, 9, 10, 11, 23, 33, 35, 39, 41, 43, 55, 59, 61, 63, 76, 77, 78, 84, 89, 92, 95, 119, 189

Hankinson's Ferry, 121

Hard Times LA, 102–4, 105, 118, 119

*Hartford*, 80, 81, 82, 83, 88, 189, 190, 193

Hatchie River, 35

Hawes, Brig. Gen. James M., 164

Haynes' Bluff, 38, 41, 42, 45, 47, 48, 51, 52, 54, 69, 72, 73, 96, 102, 141, 142, 169

Hebert, Brig. Gen. Louis, 157–58

Helena AR, 7, 28, 38, 41, 46, 50, 56, 68, 165–67, 178, 210

Helm, Brig. Gen. Benjamin, 150

*Henry Clay*, 99

Herron, Maj. Gen. Francis J., 169

Hickenlooper, Capt. Andrew, 154–60

Higgins, Cpl. Thomas, 150

Hobbs, Sgt. Charles A., 109

Holly Springs MS, 43–44, 45, 47, 51, 184

Holmes, Lt. Gen. Theophilus H., 50, 56–57, 58, 79, 163, 165–67

Hopkins, Owen J., 91

*Horizon*, 99

Hovey, Brig. Gen. Alvin P., 38–39, 43, 111, 131, 182

Howard, Lt. Richard L., 176

Howe, Orion P., 146–47

Huntsman, Henry C., 70

Hurlbut, Maj. Gen. Stephen A., 43, 93

Hynds, Capt. George H., 175

*Imperial*, 204

*Indianola*, 65–68, 80

Irish Bend, 85, 88, 210

Irwin, Lt. Col. Richard B., 188, 197

Island No. 10, 8, 9, 10, 20

Iuka MS, 34, 35

Jackson, Brig. Gen. William H., 184

Jackson, Maj. Gen. Thomas J., 85

Jackson MS, 18, 23, 29, 35, 36, 41, 52, 94, 116, 121, 124, 127, 131, 132, 137, 150, 167, 187, 188, 189, 211; battle of, 125–26; siege of, 181–85

Jacksonport AR, 166

Johnson, Charles B., 108

Johnson, Col. Benjamin W., 194

Johnston, Gen. Albert S., 5, 6, 8, 10, 11, 48

Johnston, Gen. Joseph E., 48, 50, 51, 94, 124–25, 128, 129, 132, 133, 162, 163, 172, 190, 193, 204, 206–7; fails to relieve Vicksburg, 167–69; falls back to Jackson, 179–81; in siege of Jackson, 181–85

Jones, Lt. Samuel C., 108

*J. W. Cheesman*, 99

*Kineo*, 81, 82, 203

*Lafayette*, 96, 99, 103

Lafayette (Vermillionville) LA, 87

La Grange TN, 93

Lake Providence LA, 47, 60, 63, 83, 89, 101, 117, 163, 165, 187, 211

Lake St. Joseph, 102, 118

*Lancaster*, 82, 96

Landram, Col. William J., 150

Lauman, Brig. Gen. Jacob, 182–83

Lawler, Brig. Gen. Michael, 150

Leavy, John A., 137

Lee, Robert L., xii, 162

Lee, Stephen D., 52, 55, 92, 133, 177, 207

*Lexington*, 57, 164

Lieb, Col. Hermann, 164

Lincoln, Abraham, xii, 1, 33, 39, 41, 61, 63, 76, 77, 90, 150, 178, 210

Lindsey, Col. Daniel W., 53

*Lioness*, 54

Little Rock, 56, 58, 59, 79, 165, 166, 167

Little Sandy Creek. *See* Big Sandy Creek

Lockett, Maj. Samuel H., 37–38, 137, 138, 173, 207

Logan, Col. John L., 192

Logan, Maj. Gen. John A., 121–23, 131, 135, 153–54, 155

Lord, William, 162

Loring, Maj. Gen. William W., 70–71, 72, 129, 132, 135–38

Loughborough, Mary, 140, 161

*Louisiana*, 13

*Louisville*, 57, 96, 103

Lovell, Maj. Gen. Mansfield, 12, 14, 15, 16, 20, 37

Mallory, Stephen R., 12, 13, 15
*Manassas*, 13, 14, 23
Marmaduke, Brig. Gen. John S., 166
McClellan, Maj. Gen. George B., 27
McClernand, Maj. Gen. John A., xii, 39, 41, 43, 55, 56, 59, 61, 76, 108–9, 110, 120, 121, 131, 136, 138; at Arkansas Post, 57–58; moves down west side of Mississippi, 90–105; at Port Gibson, 111–16; in May 22 assault against Vicksburg, 150–52, 207
McCulloch, Brig. Gen. Henry E., 164
McPherson, James B., 43, 59, 83, 90, 96, 112, 120–21, 131, 152, 158–59, 174–75, 187, 207; at Raymond, 121–24; at Jackson, 125
Memphis TN, 2, 4, 9, 11, 12, 17, 18, 21, 23, 24, 33, 35, 41, 42, 45, 46, 55, 56, 62, 64, 68, 69, 203
Messenger, Sgt. Nicholas, 151
Miles, William R., 194, 197
Miller, Minos, 167
Milliken's Bend, 55, 60, 90, 91, 92, 95, 101, 102, 118, 163, 164–65, 195, 202
*Mississippi*, 13, 81–82
Mississippi Central Railroad, 35, 36, 38, 42, 43, 47, 69
Mississippi River (Mississippi Valley), 1, 6, 7, 8, 9, 12, 13, 15, 16, 17, 18, 20, 21, 22, 23, 24, 25, 27, 28, 30, 31, 38, 39, 41, 43, 45, 46, 47, 48, 50, 54, 55, 56, 58, 59, 62, 63, 64–68, 69, 73, 75, 77, 78, 81, 83, 88, 89, 90, 94, 95, 99, 100, 101, 102, 103, 105, 106, 116, 117, 119, 156, 172, 176, 178, 187, 189, 190, 193, 198, 202, 203, 204, 205, 210; topography of, 2–3; defense of, 4–5
Mississippi Springs MS, 124
Mississippi Squadron (Western Flotilla), 7, 9, 10, 11, 12, 15, 16, 18, 20, 21, 22, 23, 26, 28, 46, 62, 64, 74, 75, 82, 88, 96, 98, 187
Mississippi Valley. *See* Mississippi River
Mobile and Ohio Railroad, 45
*Moderator*, 99
*Monarch*, 57
*Monongahela*, 81, 82, 193, 203
Monroe LA, 18, 22, 48
Montgomery, Capt. James E., 10, 11
Montgomery, Lt. Col. Louis, 173, 175
Moon Lake, 68
Morgan, Brig. Gen. George W., 53, 55, 57
Morgan City. *See* Brashear City
Morganza LA, 190
Morton MS, 185
*Mound City*, 21, 96, 103
Mouton, Alexandre, 79
Mouton, Brig. Gen. Alfred, 79, 202
Murphy, Col. Robert C., 43

Nashville TN, 8, 11, 35
Natchez MS, 2, 64
Natchitoches LA, 202
New Carthage LA, 90, 91, 92, 94, 95, 96, 99, 100, 101, 102, 105
New Madrid MO, 8, 9
New Orleans, Jackson, and Great Northern Railroad, 78, 126, 182, 189
New Orleans LA, 2, 5, 10, 12, 14–15, 18, 20, 21, 23, 24, 27, 28, 29, 30, 31, 35, 77, 80, 81, 83, 87, 96, 150, 163, 165, 188, 189, 192, 193, 197, 198, 202–3, 204, 210
Newton Station MS, 93

Nineteenth Corps. *See* Army of the Gulf

Ninth Corps (Army of the Potomac), 169, 181

Oak Grove LA, 164
Oak Ridge MS, 169
Obenchain, Sgt. Francis, 115
Ohio River, 7, 35, 95
Old Auburn MS, 121
Opelousas and Great Western Railroad, 84, 202
Opelousas LA, 77, 84, 87, 89
Ord, Maj. Gen. Edward O. C., 34, 152, 182
Osceola AR, 9
Osterhaus, Brig. Gen. Peter J., 111, 131
Osyka MS, 189
Ouachita River, 18
Oxford MS, 43

Paducah, 33
Paine, Brig. Gen. Halbert E., 199, 201
Palfrey, Capt. John C., 201
Palmer, Cmdr. James S., 189
Parke, Maj. Gen. John G., 169
Parker's Cross Roads TN, 44
Pattersonville (Patterson) LA, 85
Pea Ridge, 7, 20, 21, 36, 50
Pearl River, 180, 181, 184, 185
Pearson, Lt. J. M., 150–51
Pemberton, Lt. Gen. John C., 36, 37, 38, 39, 43, 44, 45, 47, 48, 51, 52, 55, 61, 62, 63, 69, 70, 73, 79, 91, 92, 93, 94, 95, 100, 101, 102, 104, 105, 109, 116, 117, 118, 121, 124, 138–39, 141, 151, 179, 188, 189, 209; moves against Grant, 127–32; at Champion Hill, 133–37; in siege of Vicksburg, 156–73; negotiates surrender, 173–78

Pettus, John J., 125
*Pittsburg*, 96, 103, 190
Pittsburg Landing. *See* Shiloh
Plum Point (Plum Run), 10, 11, 67
Polk, Maj. Gen. Leonidas, 5
Pope, Brig. Gen. John, 9, 11
Porter, Cmdr. David D., xii, 13, 14, 20, 26, 27, 46, 47, 54, 56, 57, 63, 64, 65, 67–68, 82, 88, 95, 101, 105, 106, 116, 164, 176, 178, 187, 207–8; in Steele's Bayou expedition, 72–75; runs past Vicksburg, 96–99; at Grand Gulf, 103–4
Porter, Cmdr. William D., 26, 27, 30–31
Port Gibson MS, 20, 104, 109, 110, 111–16, 117, 121, 186, 211
Port Hudson, xii, 2, 31, 32, 64, 65, 83, 84, 88, 89, 90, 117, 178, 187, 189, 190, 192, 205, 210; description of, 78–80; Farragut runs past, 80–82; May 27 attack against, 193–97; June 14 attack against, 198–201; siege and surrender of, 198–204
Port Hudson State Historic Site, 210
Prairie Grove, 50, 165, 169
Prentiss, Maj. Gen. Benjamin M., 165–67
Price, Maj. Gen. Sterling, 34, 79, 166
Prime, Capt. Frederick E., 153
Pugh, Col. Isaac, 182–83

*Queen of the West*, 24, 26, 64–67, 80, 88

*Rattler*, 57
Raymond MS, 121, 121–24, 127, 129, 131, 211
Rector, Henry M., 51
Red River, 18, 22, 28, 29, 31, 63, 64, 65, 67, 68, 79, 80, 82, 83–84, 87, 88, 89, 96, 101, 117, 187, 188, 189, 190, 202, 204, 210

Reichelm, Sgt. Paul, 54
*Richmond*, 81
Richmond LA, 163
River Defense Fleet, 5, 10, 11, 13, 14, 15
Rodney MS, 105, 110
Rolling Fork, 72, 73, 74
Rosecrans, Maj. Gen. William S., 34, 35, 50, 92–93, 94, 95
Ross, Brig. Gen. Leonard F., 69
Ruggles, Brig. Gen. Daniel, 79

Scott, Lt. Gen. Winfield, 1
Seddon, James, 94, 162, 167, 168
Seventeenth Corps (Army of the Tennessee), 43, 59, 108, 112, 121, 123, 124, 152, 154
Sheldon, Col. Lionel A., 53
Shenandoah Valley, 85, 87
Sherman, Brig. Gen. Thomas W., 77, 195–96
Sherman, Maj. Gen. William T., 41, 42, 43, 45, 46, 47, 48, 50, 56, 59, 61, 63, 77, 96, 98, 102, 103, 120, 121, 124, 131, 142, 143, 152, 153–54, 176, 179, 208; at Chickasaw Bayou 51–55; at Arkansas Post, 57–58; on Steele's Bayou expedition, 73–75; moves down west side of Mississippi, 118–19; at Jackson, 125–26; in May 19 and 22 assaults against Vicksburg, 146–51; in siege of Jackson, 181–86
Shiloh (Pittsburg Landing), 10–11, 33, 39, 48, 165, 210
Shreveport LA, 18, 22, 28, 87, 188
*Silver Wave*, 99
Simmesport LA, 188, 190
Sixteenth Corps (Army of the Tennessee), 43, 69, 93, 101
Smith, Brig. Gen. Andrew J., 48, 54, 57, 111, 131, 174–75

Smith, Brig. Gen. Martin L., 16, 18, 37–38, 48, 51, 52, 55, 142
Smith, Brig. Gen. Morgan L., 48
Smith, Col. Giles A., 53, 74
Smith, Lt. Cmdr. Watson, 69–71, 72
Smith, Lt. Col. Melancthon, 159
Smith, Lt. Gen. Edmund Kirby, 79, 87, 89, 163, 187, 202, 208
Smith, Maj. Gen. John E., 149
Smith, William H., 15
Snyder's Bluff, 38
Somerset, 101, 102, 105
Southern Railroad of Mississippi, 18, 28, 35, 37, 41, 93, 118, 121, 124, 128, 131, 138, 149, 179, 180
Sperry, Andrew F., 70, 72
Stanton, Edwin, 41, 61, 90
*Star of the West*, 71
Sprague, Capt. Homer B., 82
St. Charles AR, 21
Steedman, Col. Isiah G. W., 194, 195
Steele, Brig. Gen. Frederick, 57, 91–92, 181
Steele's Bayou (Steele's Bayou expedition), 72–75, 82, 83, 94
Stevens, Lt. Henry K., 30–31
Stevenson, Brig. Gen. John D., 149
Stevenson, Maj. Gen. Carter L., 50, 142
Streight, Col. Abel D., 93
St. Francisville LA, 190, 192, 210
St. Louis MO, 6, 7, 56, 204
Strong, William E., 100
Sullivan, Brig. Gen. Jeremiah, 44
*Sumter*, 25, 27, 31
*Switzerland*, 82, 83, 88, 96

Tallahatchie River, 36, 38, 39, 68, 70, 71, 73
Taylor, Maj. Gen. Richard L., 51, 65, 68, 89, 163, 187; fails to halt Banks,

85–88; threatens New Orleans, 202–4, 208

Taylor, Sgt. Henry H., 159

*Tennessee*, 12

Tennessee River, 5, 7, 8, 10, 12, 35, 95, 210

Tensas River, 63

Thayer, Brig. Gen. John M., 53

Thibodaux LA, 84, 202

Thirteenth Corps (Army of the Tennessee), 43, 57, 59, 90, 101, 108, 120, 138, 152, 181

Thomas, Brig. Gen. Lorenzo, 92

Thompson Point, 78, 81, 82

*Tigress*, 99, 100

Tilghman, Brig. Gen., 132, 137

Todd, Capt. David, 150

Tracy, Brig. Gen. Edward D., 110, 114–15

Trans-Mississippi Department, 51, 79, 163

Tupelo MS, 34

*Tuscumbia*, 96, 103–4

*Tyler*, 24, 25, 166

Utica MS, 121

Van Dorn, Maj. Gen. Earl, 20, 21, 24, 25, 26, 27, 28, 29, 30, 31, 34, 36, 43–44, 47, 50, 51, 208

Vaughan, Brig. Gen. John, 138

Vermillionville (Lafayette) LA, 87

*V. F. Wilson*, 178

Vicksburg, xii, 2, 16, 19, 20, 22, 23, 24, 25, 26, 27, 28, 29, 32, 34, 35, 36, 38, 39, 41, 45, 47, 48, 50, 51, 52, 55, 56, 58, 59, 60, 61, 62, 63, 64, 65, 67, 68, 69, 70, 71, 75, 76, 78, 82, 90, 91, 92, 93, 94, 95, 101, 102, 103, 108, 110, 112, 116, 117, 118, 120, 121, 125, 126, 127, 128, 129, 130, 131, 133, 138, 140, 141,

142, 186, 192, 203, 204, 205, 211; description of, 17–18; landward defenses of, 37; Porter runs past, 96–99; transports run past, 99–100; May 19 attack against, 146–47; May 22 attack against, 147–51; siege and surrender of, 152–78

Vicksburg National Military Park, 210

Vicksburg, Shreveport, and Texas Railroad, 18, 22, 48

Wade, Col. William, 104

Waldon, Edward N., 166

Walke, Capt. Henry, 24, 47

Walker, Maj. Gen. John G., 163–64

Walnut Bayou, 91, 95, 101, 102

Walnut Hills, 48, 51, 52, 56, 96, 102, 141, 143

Warren County Courthouse (Vicksburg), 17, 25, 100, 178, 211

Warrenton MS, 38, 141

Washington, Capt. Edward, 146–47

Weitzel, Brig. Gen. Godfrey, 83–84, 194, 208–9

Welles, Gideon, 15, 23, 68, 75, 96, 105

Western and Atlantic Railroad, 93

Western Flotilla. *See* Mississippi Squadron

West Gulf Blockading Squadron, 13, 22, 23, 26, 31, 84, 88, 96, 193

White River, 21, 59

*William H. Webb*, 64–67

Williams, Brig. Gen. Thomas, 15, 22, 27, 29, 30

Williamson, Col. James A., 53

Willow Springs MS, 118, 120–21

Wilson, Lt. Col. James H., 69

*Winona*, 15

Winters, William, 46, 60

Yalobusha River, 36, 38, 39, 42, 43, 69, 70

Yates, Richard, 112
Yazoo City MS, 12, 23, 24, 38, 70, 71
Yazoo Pass (Yazoo Pass expedition),
    68–72, 73, 75, 83, 94

Yazoo River, 23, 24, 28, 38, 41, 47, 48,
    51, 52, 54, 55, 68, 70, 71, 72, 73, 96,
    102, 163, 169, 211
Young's Point, 60, 91, 95, 102, 108,
    118, 163, 164, 165

In the Great Campaigns of the Civil War series

*Six Armies in Tennessee*
*The Chickamauga and Chattanooga Campaigns*
By Steven E. Woodworth

*Fredericksburg and Chancellorsville*
*The Dare Mark Campaign*
By Daniel E. Sutherland

*Banners to the Breeze*
*The Kentucky Campaign, Corinth, and Stones River*
By Earl J. Hess

*The Chessboard of War*
*Sherman and Hood in the Autumn Campaigns of 1864*
By Anne J. Bailey

*Atlanta 1864*
*Last Chance for the Confederacy*
By Richard M. McMurry

*Struggle for the Heartland*
*The Campaigns from Fort Henry to Corinth*
Stephen D. Engle

*And Keep Moving On*
*The Virginia Campaign, May–June 1864*
Mark Grimsley

*Vicksburg Is the Key*
*The Struggle for the Mississippi River*
William L. Shea and Terrence J. Winschel